Reluctant Prophets and Clueless Disciples

Introducing the Bible by Telling Its Stories

Robert Darden

Abingdon Press / Nashville

RELUCTANT PROPHETS AND CLUELESS DISCIPLES
INTRODUCING THE BIBLE BY TELLING ITS STORIES

This book is printed on acid-free paper.

Library of Congress Cataloging-in-Publication Data

Darden, Bob, 1954-
    Reluctant prophets and clueless disciples : introducing the Bible by telling its stories / Robert Darden.
        p. cm.
    Includes bibliographical references (p. 302).
    ISBN 0-687-49395-1 (binding: pbk., adhesive: alk. paper)
    1. Bible stories, English. I. Title.
    BS550.3.D37 2006
    220.6'1—dc22

                                                                2005032383

06 07 08 09 10 11 12 13 14 15—10 9 8 7 6 5 4 3 2 1
MANUFACTURED IN THE UNITED STATES OF AMERICA

➤ TO MY PARENTS:

Col. Robert Fulton Darden Jr. (USAF Ret.)

and Jo Ann Owens Darden

who knew the importance of the stories of the Bible

and taught them to me at an early age.

➤ SPECIAL THANKS TO:

The Rev. Raymond Bailey

Dr. Rosalie Beck

Dr. Dale Bruner

Dr. John Jonsson

Dr. Naymond Keathley

Dr. James Kennedy

The Rev. Mike Massar

Dr. Lai Ling Ngan

The Rev. Raymond Parker

Dr. Lynn Tatum

Dr. John Wood

Mike Yaconelli (1942-2003)

The members of the Roundtable Sunday school class
at 7th & James Baptist Church, Waco, TX
. . . and Mary

Contents

Contents

Preface

Some of you may have only seen Bibles in motel rooms. Others of you probably have one lying around the house somewhere, gathering dust on a shelf. And some of you have six different translations, including the one with the red letters for the words of Jesus, which you keep next to your bed on the nightstand.

For those of you who haven't used a lot of Bibles, *Reluctant Prophets and Clueless Disciples* may be a little intimidating. We use *lots* of citations from the Bible and, for the uninitiated, this may be a little confusing. We're here to help.

Most Bibles are divided into two sections, commonly called the Old Testament and the New Testament. The Old Testament is the stuff that happened before the time of Jesus Christ. The New Testament begins with the life of Christ.

Each of the Testaments is divided into smaller books. There are 39 in the Old Testament and 27 in the New Testament.

OK, so far, so good.

Now, each book is divided into chapters, and each chapter is divided into verses. Some of these chapter/verse divisions today seem kind of arbitrary, but they were done hundreds and hundreds of years after the fact.

So, if you see something like "Jonah 3:1-4," all that means is that the part we're discussing in this particular section is the book of Jonah, third chapter, verses one through four. These references are provided to help you find the stories in the Bible.

Some more notes:

The cover illustration and line drawings throughout this book are by Dan Foote, a popular Dallas-based artist whose work has appeared in national newspapers, magazines, and advertising campaigns. He has illustrated several children's books, including: *The Cobbler, The Princess*

and the Forest, God Smiled, I Know God, and The Step-by-Step Bible.
He's also a screenwriter and the designer of a line of biblically based
bobblehead dolls. Dan's covers for The Wittenburg Door have won two
national design awards.

The single-panel cartoons that appear through Reluctant Prophets and
Clueless Disciples are by a variety of artists and appear courtesy of The
Wittenburg Door, the world's oldest and largest (and probably only) reli-
gious humor and satire magazine.

It's the style of Abingdon Press (the folks who are actually publishing
Reluctant Prophets and Clueless Disciples) to use gender-neutral pronouns wherever possible when referring to God. My goal was to use all
gender-neutral pronouns, but sometimes for the sake of readability—
instead of saying "He/She" or something—I've reluctantly had to use the
masculine pronoun. You can do me a favor here. Whenever you see "He"
when I'm writing about God or the LORD or Yahweh, mentally insert the
awkward "He/She."* Thank you. I feel better already.

Finally, there are lots of places where I've taken extreme liberty in the
text and transformed the Bible verses into modern jargon. This is not
designed to replace the original wording. My goal was to be funny or
insightful or sarcastic . . . even witty. Where I have failed, the failure is
mine completely. The folks at Abingdon probably ought to include a note
somewhere that reads: "The opinions and fake dialogue expressed in
Reluctant Prophets and Clueless Disciples do not necessarily reflect the
opinions or beliefs of the publishers."** In any case, if you were offended
or mystified by one of my goofy re-interpretations, I abjectly apologize.
I believe in the sanctity and sacredness of the Bible. These little
re-envisionings of the dialogue were only done to illustrate a point. I feel
blessed to have such a supportive and courageous publisher.

—Robert Darden, November 2005

*Or, if that doesn't work for you, try: Hem = him or her; Hes = he or she
**Editor's Note: Thanks, Robert. Now we feel better, too.

One

PACKING FOR THE JOURNEY

It is a foolish thing to make a long prologue, and to be short in the story itself.
—2 Maccabees 2:32 (KJV)

Myths and stories make order out of chaos. They explain things. Sometimes they are based in actual—at least as we would understand it—fact: accounts of real kings and real battles, real people in real places.

Other stories appear on the surface to be nothing more than fanciful fairy tales—wild stories of giants and monsters and superheroes. But just because it's a tale of a dreaded creature with a bull's head on a human body (or vice versa!), doesn't mean that the story itself can't be "true"—or at least have elements of truth. The principal elements of the story—dragons, ogres, and neurotic clown fish—may be the product of someone's vivid imagination, but the human emotions, the understanding of the human condition, may be absolutely dead on.

The best animated films—*Bambi, Beauty and the Beast, Spirited Away, Toy Story, Finding Nemo, Shrek*—are about crazy creatures who express very human sentiments and feelings in an honest, revealing way. Once you get past the fact that Shrek is a green ogre, he's like a *lot* of people you know! The stories of Moses, King Saul, King David, Peter, and Paul also reveal—perhaps inadvertently—the real people who are often hidden behind the theology.

How important are these stories? Or *any* stories, for that matter?

Well, for one thing, Jesus used stories almost exclusively to reveal the most difficult—often most important—truths about his ministry and the kingdom of God. We call them *parables,* but they're really mini-stories.

The Bible itself is full of stories, from the parting of the Red (or Reed) Sea to Pentecost. But the central truth of the Bible—God has a wonderful plan for your life and that plan is possible through a belief in the resurrection of Jesus Christ—is a story too.

Here's something pretty neat: *we* are God's story. How we live our lives constitutes the elements of that story.

Life is a journey; it isn't a destination, as one of my friends used to say. We're in the process of *becoming* Christians. Our story, then, is the account of that journey. Who we meet along the way. How we respond. The barriers we encounter. How we overcome them. That's the story of our lives—as kids, as teenagers, as young adults, as adults, as senior citizens—as we try to be more like Christ.

It's a pretty confusing trip. Events are complicated. People are complicated. And story is how we make sense out of confusion. Joyce Carol Oates says that our "obliqueness" to each other is made clear *only* through story (from a speech at Calvin College Festival of Faith and Writing, 2004).

Look at it another way. In Genesis, the account says that God *spoke* creation into being: "Then God said, 'Let there be light'; and there was light" (Genesis 1:3). Skip ahead to the Gospel of John, which starts: "In the beginning was the Word, and the Word was with God, and the Word was God" (John 1:1). Creation is whispered into creation by the great lion Aslan in the *Narnia* books. Creation is also sung into being in J. R. R. Tolkien's *Silmarillion*, the prequel to *The Lord of the Rings*. Words are at the center of *all* this. And it is with words that storytellers tell the weird, wonderful, amazing, goofy, incredible, and sometimes downright unpleasant stories of our lives.

That's where we come in. It's not enough just to write the words— you've got to *be* the words! You *are* the words! Your life is a story that someone (or Someone) will read someday.

For me, that's always been a scary thought. I'm not sure what *I'm* doing—much less what everybody *else* should be doing. (My father worked at the gigantic headquarters of all U.S. military forces in the world—the Pentagon—in Washington, D.C. He said the best description of the Pentagon he ever heard was to imagine a flood. In the middle of that raging flood is a single battered log. Clinging desperately to that log are thousands of ants. And each ant thinks *he's* driving the log.) Reading the experiences and adventures of other people helps me. It helps to know that I'm not alone in what I'm doing or feeling. It helps me see different points of view. It helps me see how different people handled different problems.

Katherine Paterson has written some of the best books ever created for young adults (although they're great for all ages), including *Bridge to Terabithia* and *Jacob Have I Loved.* She says that writers write a story

2

and invite the reader to create the meaning (in a speech at the Calvin College Festival of Faith and Writing, 2004). That means that every story is different for each person who reads it.

When the Roll is Called Up Yonder and my life's story is being read by Somebody Pretty Important, I'd kind of like a little help *down here*. I'd like to know everything there is to know about the story—the journey—I'm in the middle of undertaking. I want to know what I should be looking for. I want to know *how* to read the story. I want to know what to take away from the story, how to make sense of it all. It means that—in addition to the historical facts or fantasy elements of a story—*it is important to pay attention to the story itself.* How is the story framed? What is the story-teller trying to accomplish with this story? What's to be learned from all of this? The stories of the Bible are there for a reason. The parts of the story that are included—or omitted—are done so for a reason, maybe a *lot* of reasons. Wouldn't it make sense to understand why?

Understanding the Story

One way to get a handle on that concept is to know a little about the various *types* of story forms. A storyteller uses each story form for a different set of reasons.

> There are only two or three human stories, and they go on repeating themselves as fiercely as if they had never happened before. (Willa Cather, *O Pioneers!* [New York: Oxford University Press, 1999], 67)

The oldest stories scientists can date with any certainty are the great Mesopotamian myths from the fourth to the third millennium BCE (Before the Common Era), when the first major cities were being built in what is now Iraq. These are the tales of Babylon, Nineveh, and Assyria. Next to real-life kings mentioned in the Bible, like Nebuchadnezzar, Tiglath-pileser, and Ashurbanipal, are the extraordinary stories of the heroic Gilgamesh. When most of the world cowered in caves and rude huts, the people of Mesopotamia thrilled to sophisticated stories about a flood that covered the earth, great goddesses who slew monsters to create the earth, and powerful gods who descended into hell to retrieve valued friends. These ancient stories—preserved through the centuries by being cut into soft clay and then fired in a hot oven—were created to explain the unexplainable: the creation of the universe, how all of the creatures were named, why there are four seasons.

3

A second type of story—often called a *parable*—is used to make a complex concept understandable to a general audience. Jesus, of course, was a master storyteller and the many parables of the Four Gospels contain some of his most profound teaching. In the hands of a skilled storyteller, even relatively straightforward parables, such as the parable of the Prodigal Son or the parable of the Good Samaritan, yield great riches when studied in depth by discerning eyes. And they're often more complicated, with more layers of meaning, than they appear on first reading.

A third kind of story is a relatively modern invention. When we talk today about a *three-act format* in a play or movie, we're talking about the basic ingredients of most stories:

Act I: The hero and the problem facing the hero are introduced.
Act II: The hero responds to the problem.
Act III: Through the hero's actions, the problem is resolved.

English teachers have come up with names for the various kinds of modern stories. There is the Revenge Story—which is pretty self-explanatory when you think of films such as *Rambo* or *Gladiator*. There is the Conflict Story or, as one of my teachers once called it, "Two dogs, one bone." She could have said, "Two armies, one Helen of Troy" or "Two empires, one universe" or even, "Two girls, one cute boy."

Hero's Journey

But the most famous and most common story form is that of the Hero's Journey or the Quest. This may be the oldest story of all and, according to many writers, the most satisfying. It's what unites Gilgamesh with *Gilligan's Island*. Among the first writers to identify the common elements among the great stories of the classic cultures both past and present was Joseph Campbell, who wrote *The Hero With a Thousand Faces*. Screenwriter Chris Vogler adapted that framework into *The Writer's Journey: Mythic Structure for Storytellers & Screenwriters*. Both contain fascinating insights into why some stories satisfy us more than others, why some movies endure to be watched over and over and others end up in the 99¢ bins at the video stores within a few weeks.

Using the concepts identified by Campbell and Vogler, here, in abbreviated form, are the basic elements of the Hero's Journey (and "hero" here means male or female).

4

- The Ordinary World -

This is where most great stories begin, good, old, boring, black-and-white Kansas in *The Wizard of Oz.* On the desert planet Tatooine in *Star Wars.* In the quiet, comfortable shire in *The Hobbit* and *The Lord of the Rings.* In a familiar patch of coral in *Finding Nemo.* It's a day like any other day—which is precisely the problem. Our hero is bored, or stirred by old stories, or driven by an unexplainable urge to see beyond the safe borders of home. Nothing ever seems to happen in the Ordinary World. But suddenly, as Ray Bradbury writes, "something wonderful" happens (*Let's All Kill Constance* [New York: HarperCollins, 2003], 171).

- The Call to Adventure -

On this most ordinary of days, a problem or a challenge unexpectedly arises. Outside a nondescript hobbit hole, a most extraordinary wizard in gray appears. In a cluttered garage, a battered robot beams a holograph of a beautiful princess in desperate need. A small clown fish is bagged by a fisherman as his helpless father watches in horror. And in Camelot, Arthur hears of the Holy Grail, which may heal his wounded land. *Something* has happened that may take our hero away from the familiar.

- Refusal of the Call -

Usually, the hero reluctantly refuses the challenge at first. He may be afraid. She may have other duties she thinks are more important. When

5

Gandalf sees the hobbit Bilbo Baggins for the first time, Bilbo says, "Good morning! We don't want any adventures here, thank you," and slams the door in Gandalf's face. Luke sadly returns from Obi-Wan's hideout to resume work at the family hydroponics farm. In this, we identify with the hero. We're *all* reluctant heroes. Superman and Conan the Barbarian are infinitely less interesting because they do not hesitate; they have no fear. The great filmmaker Alfred Hitchcock always selected non-heroic stars, like Jimmy Stewart, to capitalize on his *ordinary-ness*. There is an "everyman" quality about the best heroes. They're more like us. We can identify with them better.

- The Mentor -

One of two things work to change the mind of the hero. The first might be an event. When Luke returns to the farm, he finds that stormtroopers have callously murdered Aunt Beru and Uncle Owen. Dorothy is unwillingly transported by tornado to Oz. Or, in *City Slickers,* the hero's best friend's life is falling apart (as is his own) and the Billy Crystal character agrees to go on a trail drive to save the friend's sanity. The second thing that can change the hero's mind is the appearance of the mentor. In the stories of antiquity, it is usually an older, wiser man or woman. In the newer stories, it can be the crusty drill sergeant in *An Officer and a Gentleman,* Merlin in the Arthurian legends, Glenda the Good Witch in the *Wizard of Oz,* Curly in *City Slickers,* Morpheus in *The Matrix,* Dumbledore in the *Harry Potter* books, Obi-wan Kenobi in *Star Wars* or Gandalf the Grey in *The Lord of the Rings.* (Ever notice how Obi-Wan and Gandalf look and sound so much alike?) The mentor is often more powerful than our hero, and sometimes gives our hero a special weapon (a ring or a light saber), a special tool (ruby slippers or a cloak of invisibility) or piece of information (a riddle or a rhyme), but the mentor *cannot* accompany the hero the entire journey. Why? Because then it wouldn't be the Hero's Journey!

- Crossing the First Threshold -

This begins Act II, when the hero really commits to the quest or challenge. It is also where the adventure really begins. From this point on, the hero can't turn back, even if he or she wants to. Sometimes there is

6

a Threshold Guardian, a gatekeeper, but the hero quickly learns—in tales like *The Never-Ending Story* or *The Princess Bride*—the Threshold Guardian isn't always an enemy. Sometimes he or she (or it!) is just a friend you haven't made yet and conflict isn't always the best way to gain information.

– Tests, Allies, and Enemies –

In the movies, this is the longest part of the film. Our hero must slowly learn the rules of this Brave New World. This can be done in an inn (The Last Homely House in the hobbit stories) or a cantina (*Star Wars*), or by befriending those you meet along the road (*The Wizard of Oz*). It's here that the first tests or obstacles begin appearing. Our hero struggles to overcome a single *orc*, but the lessons learned from that encounter enable the hero to handle two orcs and a goblin the next time. Our hero survives—just barely—and, if he or she learns from defeats as well as victories, is now equipped to handle even more deadly challenges. In the great stories, these tests/obstacles escalate quickly. Each barrier becomes more and more difficult to overcome. And, for the tests to be truly challenging, there must be a villain worthy of our hero—Lord Voldemort, Darth Vader, the Wicked Witch of the West, the Dragon Smaug—behind the tests.

– Approach to the Inmost Cave –

We're two-thirds of the way through the story now. Ahead is the most significant test of all, the stronghold of the enemy. This is the Death Star (*Star Wars*), the Wicked Witch's fortress (*The Wizard of Oz*), the dentist's office (*Finding Nemo*), the Castle Perilous (the Arthurian legends), the madman's island hideout (*The Incredibles*). Alas, the mentor is no longer with our hero (and his or her band of boon companions). He (or she) may be dead (Obi-Wan and Curly) or away on pressing matters elsewhere (Gandalf and Glenda the Good Witch), so our hero is now left to face the gravest challenge alone, armed only with the knowledge accrued from the difficult adventures and experiences encountered along the way. Our hero's sternest test yet is entering the Inmost Cave (again, an allusion to the ancient stories of King Arthur), which constitutes crossing the second threshold.

7

- The Supreme Ordeal -

The old-time screenwriters called this *The Big Gloom*. This is when our hero is the furthest from the original goal; it's the darkness before the dawn when all seems lost. In *Star Wars*, Luke and his friends are on the Death Star, pursued by the Empire's soldiers, stuck in a trash compactor as the walls start closing in—and suddenly, Luke is pulled underwater by a monster! In *City Slickers*, our amateur cowboys must complete the cattle drive *and* save the cattle from a raging, flooded river in a thunderstorm. All hope seems lost. But the hero—who if he or she had faced this level of challenge earlier in the quest would have failed miserably—now draws on previously unknown reservoirs of strength and experience. This is often when the hero discovers what is *really* important. If the original quest had been over gold or glory, the hero sees now that the real quest is for true love, self-fulfillment, wisdom, or truth. While the choice may be hard, the true hero now makes the right choice and—for the first time—truly earns the title of "hero." Now battle-honed, more experienced, and finally fighting for the noble cause, our hero finally prevails.

- Reward -

What has been sought for so long is now made available to our hero, be it the Holy Grail, the knowledge of how to return to Kansas, or the destruction of the Death Star and the rescue of Princess Leia. On one level, the quest has been a success—the elixir that will save the villagers from the plague has been retrieved. But on a deeper, more enduring level, the greater success is the hero's acknowledgment of a more lasting treasure—true love or true wisdom. And this had been the *real* quest all along—our hero just didn't know it!

- The Road Back -

The next three elements are often missing from modern films, but Campbell and Vogler believe they are essential to the true quest story. Once the mission has been accomplished, the hero must return the way he or she came. But the people/creatures you've defeated on the way aren't always glad to see you on the way back! Hostile forces still lie in wait, particularly if our hero struck first and asked questions later. J. R. R.

8

Tolkien knew this. In both *The Hobbit* (subtitled "Or There and Back Again") and *The Lord of the Rings* trilogy, the *road back* is as important as the *road there*. While the movie version of the *Lord of the Rings* omits this section, it is many people's favorite part of the trilogy. Sam, Frodo, Merry, and Pippin return to the Shire, only to find it has fallen under Saruman's spell. Alone, without Gandalf and Strider and the Company of the Ring, our heroes must reclaim the Shire, using only what they've learned in their quest to take the Ring to Mordor.

- Resurrection -

In the old myths, the hero often has to be *reborn* before the return to the Ordinary World is possible. This section is usually combined with the Big Gloom in modern stories, but is comparable—in Christian terms—to being *born again*. One really nifty interpretation of this motif comes in *E.T., The Extra-Terrestrial*. E.T. actually dies in the operating room. He can't be reborn until the children understand that they must want what's best for E.T.—which is to return home—rather than what they selfishly want for themselves. Regardless of when the resurrection happens, the hero *must* be changed before the story can mean something to the listener. This is an important point, often missed by filmmakers. If there is no change, the entire journey has meant nothing. If you're brave, noble, and handsome before the quest and you're still brave, noble, and handsome after the quest, what is the point? Again, that's what separates movies about Superman and Sherlock Holmes from the movies that really satisfy the audience. The hero must change. Otherwise, the story has no meaning. It can be entertaining, but it won't bear up to repeated viewings.

- Return with the Elixir -

Again, this is sometimes condensed into the final minutes of modern stories. The original concept was that unless the hero changes—and brings back something that proves that change—the quest has been for nothing. The *elixir* can be knowledge or a magic potion, or a miraculous serum. It can be anything at all—*if* the bearer has changed.

All of this, of course, is just a model. There have been great stories/movies told that omit one or more elements of this framework. At the same time, it gives the listener/viewer a blueprint to help understand

9

why certain tales work better than others. The first *Matrix* film follows this format pretty closely, even to Neo's death and resurrection. But the following two installments (*Matrix: Reloaded* and *Matrix: Revolutions*) didn't follow it and didn't fare as well critically or at the box office. Likewise, *Star Wars* and *The Empire Strikes Back* (which follow the *formula*) are much beloved by fans of the George Lucas series, whereas *The Phantom Menace* and *The Attack of the Clones* (which do not) are not particularly liked by *anyone*—and let's not talk about Jar Jar Binks and say we did!

The Bible as Story

There's much more, of course, to tell about story and storytelling, but hopefully, this quick overview will provide an outline to examine the great stories of the Bible with fresh eyes. The Bible contains many elements— theology, prophecy, hymns, sermons, proverbs, even dietary rules and regulations—that are most decidedly *not* narrative history, story, *or* parable and are therefore quite beyond the scope of this book. But some of us have heard the stories of the Bible so often, their sheer power is muted if not lost. Familiarity may not breed contempt, but it can breed boredom or, at least, disinterest.

At the same time, if you're reading some of these stories for the first time, perhaps these retellings will inspire you to look to the real thing.

By looking at the great stories of the Old and New Testaments from a different vantage point, maybe we can strip away the too-familiar overlay to rediscover the power these words still contain. It's like getting some distance from a Significant Other and realizing how very special that certain someone really is, or being away from home for a long time and realizing how glad you are to be back.

Why These Stories?

One of my favorite verses in the Bible is John 21:25: "But there are also many other things that Jesus did; if every one of them were written down, I suppose that the world itself could not contain the books that would be written."

If there were many other stories, *why choose these?* They *must* be special and worthy of our time and study. The more you study them, the

10

more you realize the universality of these stories. Joyce Carol Oates has said that expressing yourself isn't the highest calling of a writer. The highest calling is "expressing what's universal with an individual voice" (in a speech at the Calvin College Festival of Faith and Writing, 2004).

Re-looking at these stories also helps us find what's universal about them. For instance, most accounts of the infamous story of Abraham and Isaac—where Abraham is about to sacrifice his beloved son, only to have his hand stayed at the last possible moment by God—emphasize Abraham's obedience, from Abraham's point of view. What about Isaac's POV? Isaac's faith is *really* tested. Or as the saying goes, "All gave some, but some gave all." Isaac was about to give *all* for his faith!

Or consider the parable of the Prodigal Son. Again, most Sunday morning sermon illustrations focus on the father's love, although some identify with the Prodigal. But there is much to be learned from re-imagining the story from the viewpoint of the Older Brother. Or how different would this story be if it had been told through the long-suffering *mother's* POV?

Barbara Brown Taylor urges us not to reduce either of the two brothers in the parable of the Prodigal Son to stereotypes. In fact, she says, "we need them both as much as they need each other" ("The Parable of the Prodigal Son," http://www.explorefaith.org/LentenHomily03.05.99.html). Each stands for a part of the Gospel.

Every character in every story, in every parable, *is a human being.* We love, laugh, mess up, hurt, cry, and sometimes lie. Every parable is *our* story. We're the younger son who gets forgiven without even having to say he's sorry. We're the older son who is angry that his younger brother blew half the family fortune, then gets a party.

That leaves, of course, the father. This is the person who prays for *both* of his sons every day. This is the guy who gets up every morning, and before he starts the backbreaking chores of farming, stands at the edge of the driveway and looks anxiously up the road for his son. This is the guy who gets to forgive everybody. This is the guy who gets to throw the great party in the end. Hmmm . . . whom does the dad sound like? We are human beings—human beings whom God loves so much that he has our pictures on his refrigerator.

The punch line is this: We are ALL of the characters in ALL of the stories and parables in the Bible. As much as we want to be Abel, we're a lot like Cain too. As much as we think we identify with the heroic, loyal Jonathan, we're really more like that sneaky, self-consumed weasel

Samuel. And the parable of the Pharisee who prayed on the street corner and the humble tax collector who prayed in his closet, we *always* get that one wrong!

Each character is in each story for a reason. The more we study the story itself, the more the meaning comes alive. Katherine Paterson again: "A story does not ask for decision . . . instead, it asks for *identification*—which is how transformation begins." At their best, she says, writers are "meaning-makers" (from a speech at the Calvin College Festival of Faith and Writing, 2004).

Why does the Hero's Journey particularly ring true? Because it is *our* story—each and every one of us. *We* live in the Ordinary World. *We* are the Reluctant Heroes. *We* live and learn from the barriers placed before us. *We*—eventually—learn what's really valuable in life.

It's important to study the stories of the Bible to help understand the themes of the Bible, to glean the multi-faceted meanings of the Great Text. And in doing so, discover (or re-discover) the truths that have been there since the first Storytellers and Bards of ancient times recited them from memory to eager listeners around a communal campfire.

Here's one last helpful story, this one from author/preacher Ben Patterson ("Heart & Soul," *Leadership*, Summer 1999). He tells the story of a missionary who took a projector to show the *Jesus* video to a primitive tribe in the deep jungle of East Asia. They'd never seen a movie before, and had never heard of Jesus. As the great story unfolded in their own language, the tribal people were horrified to see the merciful, loving Jesus beaten and held without trial. The people screamed at the men on the screen and when they wouldn't stop, turned on the missionary and threatened him!

The missionary stopped the film and explained that the story wasn't over yet. Reluctantly, they sat and watched some more.

With the horrific crucifixion sequence, the same thing happened again. Overcome by rage and grief, the tribe members moved dangerously toward the missionary and demanded that the offending video be stopped. Again the missionary told them to wait—there was still more to the story.

But with the resurrection, just the opposite happened. The tribespeople erupted in joy, dancing, and celebrating. Christ had risen! According to Patterson, at this point the missionary did not tell them to compose themselves and wait—the story was happening even now!

If the Bible truly is The Greatest Story Ever Told, then perhaps we need to celebrate the Happy Ending more.

12

And here's the wonderful thing—we're part of that story! We play an important role in God's Great Plan. This is *our* story! The Bible is our roadmap and our cast list. Knowing how these stories are used, how they're important, and what to watch for is important so we will know our parts in this great cosmic comedy/drama.

> Life is as simple as this. We are living in a world that is absolutely transparent, and God is shining through it all the time. This is not just a fable or a nice story, it is true . . . If we abandon ourselves to Him and forget ourselves we see it sometimes and we see it maybe frequently: that God manifests Himself everywhere, in everything—in people and in things and in nature and in events and so forth. So that it becomes very obvious that He is everywhere, He is in everything, and we cannot be without him. You cannot be without God, it's just simply impossible. The only thing is that we don't see it. (Thomas Merton, "A Call to Contemplation," *Essential Writings* [Maryknoll, NY: Orbis Books, 2000], 70)

Two

BEGINNINGS . . . ADAM AND EVE AND CAIN AND ABEL

➡ (GENESIS 1–4)

Every good story begins "There once was a man . . . " or "Once upon a time . . . " or even, "In the beginning . . . " This tells those who are standing just outside the warming fire, "Hey! Come on in! Something wonderful is about to happen." It's the narrator's hospitable way of inviting us into a new world.

The book of Genesis has at least three narrators telling this tale—and many of the tales still to come in this remarkable book. Scholars have called these narrators the *Elohist*, the *Yahwist*, and the *Priestly* writers. Whenever the Elohist writes, he (or she) uses the noun *God* exclusively. When the Yahwist account is being read, watch for the use of the noun *the LORD* (for "YHWH"). The Priestly writer also has a number of markers that enable scholars and linguists to surmise that he (or she) wrote certain passages. Each writer has a slightly different approach or agenda. Whoever wove the stories together (and for centuries it was assumed that it was Moses) into one long, incredible narrative did a masterful job. This is good stuff.

Genesis 1:1–2:25

Of the two creation accounts in Genesis, the first (1:1–2:4) is the most famous—a glorious, rapturous cosmic song whose subject matter is nothing less than the creation of the universe:

15

In the beginning when God created the heavens and the earth, the earth was a formless void and darkness covered the face of the deep, while a wind from God swept over the face of the waters. (Genesis 1:1-2)

In many commentaries, the Hebrew word for "wind" is also translated as "breath."

Modern writers have fallen in love with the idea that God spoke or *breathed,* or even sang the universe into existence. In *The Magician's Nephew,* the first book of C. S. Lewis's Narnia stories, Digory, the Cabby and his horse, the witch, and the self-consumed Uncle Andrew have found themselves observers at the moment that the great lion Aslan sings the song that calls the cosmos into being:

— KR KRAFT —

GOD'S DAY-TIMER

> Then two wonders happened at the same moment. One was that the voice was suddenly joined by other voices; more voices than you could possibly count. They were in harmony with it, but far higher up the scale: cold, tingling, silvery voices. The second wonder was that the blackness overhead, all at once, was blazing with stars. They didn't come out gently one by one, as they do on a summer evening. One moment there had been nothing but darkness; next moment a thousand, thousand points of light leaped out—single stars, constellations, and planets, brighter and bigger than any in our world. There were no clouds. The new stars and the new voices began at exactly the same time. If you had seen and heard it, as Digory did, you would have felt quite certain that it was the stars themselves who were singing, and that it was the First Voice, the deep one, which had made them appear and made them sing. (New York: Macmillan Publishing Company, 1970, 99)

In *A Wind in the Door,* from Madeleine L'Engle's *A Wrinkle in Time* quartet, the mysterious *farae,* who are at the center of all living things, sing at the moment of their Deepening:

16

We are the song of the universe. We sing with the angelic host. We are the musicians. The farae and the stars are the singers. Our song orders the rhythm of creation. (New York: Farrar, Straus and Giroux, 1973, 180)

J. R. R. Tolkien has a similar creation story in *The Silmarillion*, his prequel to *The Hobbit* and *The Lord of the Rings*, where Eru, the One, also called Ilúvatar, creates the Ainur, the Holy Ones. It is the Ainur who sing Creation into being:

Then the voices of the Ainur, like unto harps and lutes, and pipes and trumpets, and viols and organs, and like unto countless choirs singing with words, began to fashion the theme of Ilúvatar to a great music; and a sound arose of endless interchanging melodies woven in harmony that passed beyond hearing into the depths and into the heights, and the places of the dwelling of Ilúvatar were filled to overflowing, and the music and the echo of the music went out into the Void, and it was Void. (Boston: Houghton Mifflin Company, 1977, 15)

Back in Genesis, God's singing continues for seven *days* until all of creation is completed and the Prefect Creator pronounces Creation to be *good*.

The second account (2:5-25, by the Yahwist) reverses the order. In this creation story, the LORD creates the Garden of Eden first, then the first human, a Man. When the Man has named all of the creatures and plants, the LORD gives him a companion, the Woman, although they are not yet named (*adam* means "man" or "humanity"). She is created from his *rib* (although the Hebrew is so obscure, we're not really sure *what* the word here actually means) as his co-equal partner.

And so it goes for an undetermined length of time: Man and Woman, enjoying each other's company in a

"THE WAY I SEE IT, THERE ARE TWO KINDS OF PEOPLE IN THIS WORLD."

paradise on earth and daily communing with their Creator. There has never been a time like it since.

17

Genesis 3

Into this earthly paradise comes temptation, in the form of a snake or serpent, revered in the Middle East as somehow immortal, since it is the only animal that sheds its skin. The snake, who also represents our own rebellious nature, is a worthy adversary, not because it is such a convincing liar, *but because it tells the truth*—or at least *part* of the truth.

One day, the man and the woman are in this garden *together* (as the text takes pains to point out) and the snake casually engages the couple in a conversation. Here's one version of that little *tête-à-tête*:

"Did God sssay, 'You ssshall not eat from any tree in the garden?'"

"No," she answers, "God said we can eat of the fruit of *any* tree in the garden, save for one."

"Which one?"

"That one," she says innocently, "the one in the middle. God said if we even touched it, we'd die."

The man nods absently. *That's a good-looking tree, too*, he notes mentally. *Why have I never noticed it before?*

"I've got newsss for you two," the snake says brightly. "You won't die. That'sss not what God isss sssaying. He'sss sssaying your old sssself will die. Instead, once you eat some of that juicy ssstuff, your eyesss will be opened! In fact, you'll be like God becausssse you'll know the difference between good and evil."

The man and woman look at each other in amazement.

"Cool!" they say in unison.

So the Bible says they walk over to the tree together, grab a couple of pieces of

> It's important to note here that Genesis 3:6 points out that " . . . she took of its fruit and ate; and she also gave some to her husband, *who was with her,* and he ate." This one little misunderstood verse (I added the italics) has been used for centuries to somehow *blame* women for all evil in the world and has been employed as a bludgeon to "show" that women are weaker and therefore need to be dominated. As we'll see throughout this book, that's a misuse of the original story, plain and simple.

fruit, and munch happily away—together.

"The snake's right," the man says. "We didn't die!"

"And we now know good from evil," she responds. "Meanwhile, do you

Reluctant Prophets and Clueless Disciples

feel a draft? Let's sew some fig leaves together."

The snake was right about something else. The man and the woman *are* now self-aware. They know—for the first time—that they've been naked, and they're ashamed of it. They know—for the first time—that they've disobeyed their Creator, and they're ashamed of their actions. So when the LORD God comes strolling through the Garden and calls for

them, they're too embarrassed to come out of hiding. But it's hard to keep stuff from Someone who is Omnipotent! Soon, the whole sordid truth comes tumbling out.

Had the man and the woman 'fessed up immediately, they might have escaped some of the tough times to come. Instead, they did what most of us do in these situations; they rationalized their actions by trying to blame someone else. The woman blames the snake; the man blames the woman. The LORD God will have none of it and pronounces a series of terrible judgments:

1. Snakes will lose their arms and legs, have to crawl around forever, and become the instant blood enemies of humanity.
2. Women will have terrible pain in childbirth and men will spend most of their lives trying to dominate them.
3. Men will spend their lives trying to tease a living from the unforgiving soil.

This is a curse that will last until the flood of Noah, nine generations later.

To make matters worse, the LORD God expels them from the Garden of Eden—not, as is usually assumed, for eating of the fruit of the Tree of

19

Knowledge—but to keep them from eating of the fruit of the Tree of Life and becoming immortal like God! To keep the disgraced couple out of the Garden—and to keep out all of their descendents, for that matter—the LORD God places cherubim and a flaming sword to stand guard over the Garden for all eternity (see 3:20-24). (The cherubim were apparently angel-like creatures with a human face, a lion's body, and massive eagle's wings—check them out again in 1 Kings 6:23-28 and Psalm 18:10.)

Genesis 4:1-16

O, my offense is rank, it smells to heaven;
It hath the primal eldest curse upon 't,
A brother's murder!
(William Shakespeare, *Hamlet,* Act III, Scene 3)

The trials aren't over for our heroes. They eventually have children, first Cain then Abel. In the traditions of the Middle East, the first-born inherits the ancestral family lands, so Cain becomes a great farmer—no small feat in this mostly arid country. Abel, the second son, as was the usual custom, becomes a shepherd, most likely herding sheep and goats. The time comes to offer sacrifices to the LORD. Cain offers his fruits and vegetables and grain; Abel offers the fattest first-born lambs of his flock. For some unexplained reason, the LORD rejects Cain's offering while relishing Abel's sacrifice. Cain is first devastated, then furious.

"Hey! Why are you Mr. Pouty-Face this morning?" the LORD asks Cain.

Reluctant Prophets and Clueless Disciples

"You know why," Cain mumbles.

"True. I know everything," the LORD responds. "And you know that if you do good stuff for the right reasons, it will be embraced. But if you're doing stuff just because it looks good on the surface, then we've got problems. My desire for you, old friend, is that you resist that temptation. Comprende?"

This is a hard saying in the original text. Perhaps the LORD is implying that Cain didn't offer the best of his harvest as a sacrifice. Perhaps the LORD always prefers animal sacrifice to vegetable offerings. Perhaps there was something amiss in Cain's heart during his sacrifice: resentment, bitterness, envy. The text doesn't say. But Cain continues to seethe with hurt and resentment.

At last, Cain can't stand it any longer. He invites Abel out in the fields, where he murders him in cold blood. And just as the LORD did in the Garden of Eden, there follows a curious sequence where an All-Seeing and All-Knowing God feigns ignorance of man's folly:

"Hey Cain! Where's Abel?" the LORD asks one day.

"How should I know?" Cain snaps. "That's not in my job description, pal. I'm a farmer, not a babysitter."

The LORD answers with a voice that rumbles through the ground like a 6.0 Richter scale earthquake: "Cain! I know what you've done! I can hear your brother's soul crying to me. You've killed him. And for what?"

Cain starts to respond, but thinks better of it.

"Since you spilled your brother's blood into the ground, the earth itself will hate you!" the LORD thunders. "Your farming days are over. The soil rejects you. You're going to spend the rest of your life contemplating your sin—a gypsy, a man without a country, without a home!"

At last, Cain sinks to his knees, the enormity of both his sin and punishment suddenly washing over him. "This is too much," he howls. "This isn't judgment, this is vengeance. You've taken everything from me . . . everything! You might as well kill me now—it's open season on me wherever I go."

But just as the LORD didn't kill Cain's parents in the Garden of Eden, and just as Jesus will later forbid others from stoning the woman caught in adultery, the LORD will not allow his creations to be murdered.

The LORD muses that this is probably the case, and so puts some kind of mark on Cain as a warning. Again, just what the "mark" is has been a source of much debate. But Cain apparently wears it for the rest of his life, even as he flees with his wife into the Land of Nod (which means "wandering"), east of Eden.

21

Still, it is from flawed Cain (and his unnamed wife, whom we won't meet until 4:17) that the storytellers who told the tale of the Genesis weave the fabric of the generations that follow. Most of the Old Testament involves disputes involving younger and older brothers. The story of Cain and Abel is only the first such incident.

The Next Generations . . .

As for Eve and Adam (he's finally named in chapter 5), they have one more son, Seth, and it is through Seth that the genealogies are followed through to Noah. Adam and Eve disappear from the narrative in chapter 5. Adam is said to have lived to the age of 930; Eve is never mentioned again.

The stories of Adam, Eve, Cain, Abel, Seth, and ultimately, several more unnamed daughters and sons raise more questions than they answer. Where do the wives of Cain and Seth come from? What do some of these incredibly ancient stories mean? Is being a shepherd somehow better than being a farmer?

For later writers, such as Paul, Jesus Christ comes as another *first man* to undo the damage done by Adam. But for our purposes, Adam and Eve gracefully exit center stage, to live their apparently long lives in obscurity, watching as their children, grandchildren, and great-grand-children for many generations fill the world they left behind. And in that, they are two of the greatest tragic figures in the entire Bible.

A modern analogy would be rock superstars or famous movie stars that flame brightly for a time only to see their careers fizzle out just as rapidly. They are then sentenced to spend the rest of their lives in purgatory, doing infomercials and *oldies* shows in suburban malls, while younger stars take their places. They once had it all. Now all they have are their memories.

For Adam and Eve, how much more keenly must they feel their loss? They live on for hundreds of years after their expulsion from the Garden. They will never again know the sweet joy of a daily, intimate conversation with God.

They make a poignant pair, never able to return to the Garden, always living with the knowledge of what they've done. Perhaps, from time to time, Adam and Eve creep close to the Garden, where the terrible cherubim stand in eternal vigilance, forever scanning the horizon, their faces lit by the flaming sword. They watch for long minutes then silently return home. What's left to say? The time for recriminations and blame has long since passed.

22

It is in the centuries following their exile from the Garden of Eden that Eve and Adam—whose name means "man" or "humanity"—become the most human of us all. Once you have touched the face of God, how insignificant and melancholy and hopelessly, unutterably banal the world must forevermore appear!

Like so many of us, they will spend the rest of their lives trying to get back to the Garden.

Three

NOAH
➡ (GENESIS 5:28–9:29)

See the bird with the leaf in her beak
After the flood, all the colors came out.
(U2, "Beautiful Day")

Sometimes a story can be told and retold so often that it loses all
meaning. It becomes white noise. When you already know the ending, it
is difficult to sit through the same old tale yet again—no matter how
accomplished the storyteller. Perhaps it is your father's favorite "war"
story, a story you've heard so many times you can recite it by heart. You
roll your eyes and look for a handy exit. For someone who has never
heard this particular yarn before, it has a thrilling immediacy. But for
everyone else, terminal boredom sets in.

That's the way it is for many us of when it comes to the story of Noah
and the Flood and the Ark. There have been countless movies, TV shows,
songs, plays, parodies, and comedy routines (Bill Cosby's "Noah" is still the
best!). As a result, this story has that same dull overlay of over-exposure.

To make matters worse, numerous cultures—some older than the Old
Testament—have very similar flood narratives, including our friend
Gilgamesh in his epic myths.

What possibly is yet to be gleaned from this old war-horse?

As it turns out, quite a bit.

A careful reading of this story reveals a complicated set of narratives,
each vying for dominance, each telling us a little more about the man
who is the ninth descendent from Adam. He is the last of the *old patriarchs*, figures so impossibly ancient that they tower over all who follow
them; stories of such antiquity they were known to some of our earliest
ancestors. Not only are Noah's exploits nearly superhuman, he lives as

long as a demi-god, 950 years. (But not as long as his grandfather Methuselah, who hangs around for an astonishing 969 years!)

The Noah cycle also includes the, always intriguing, barest mention of a mysterious third race abroad on the land in those days, the *Nephilim*, the "sons of God and the daughters of humans," preternaturally powerful warriors, a *super-race* who "were the heroes that were of old, warriors of renown" (6:4). There is only one other fleeting reference to these shadowy heroes—for a heart-stopping second as the Israelites approach the promised land in Numbers 13:33—then they disappear from the biblical record forever.

For a non-biblical story about the Nephilim, no one spins a better yarn than Madeleine L'Engle. The fourth and final book of her *A Wrinkle in Time* quartet, *Many Waters*, is set in a pre-flood Earth, when magic is real and unicorns can heal with their horns and mammoths are the size of poodles and Seraphim and Nephilim vie for control of human hearts!

Genesis 6:5—7:24

In the Genesis account, Noah appears in a decidedly prehistoric world—and what he sees isn't pretty. In the generations since Adam, the human race has degenerated into a cruel and lawless anarchy. What had flowered so beautifully in the Garden of Eden has sunken into appalling corruption. And the tellers of the story of Noah endow the Almighty with that most human of all emotions—regret. It *grieves* the LORD to see what has become of the creation that began with such promise in the Garden of Eden. Only Noah and his family have, some-

26

how, resisted the temptations of their society. Sadly, the LORD at last appears to Noah with a fearful decision:

I have determined to make an end of all flesh, for the earth is filled with violence because of them; now I am going to destroy them along with the earth. (6:13)

And, in the familiar words of the text, God gives Noah the exact specs of a strange craft, an ark, built to be a perfect cube, 180 feet on each side. The ark will hold Noah's family and enough animals to repopulate the planet once the floodwaters recede. The two traditions—the Priestly and the Yahwist—differ on many of the details, but the end result is the same, and it is told with beautifully evocative language:

In the six hundredth year of Noah's life, in the second month, on the seventeenth day of the month, on that day all the fountains of the great deep burst forth, and the windows of the heavens were opened. (7:11)

Noah and his family are in a pickle! They have doubtless endured months of taunting and abuse from their neighbors as the strange craft emerges from the desert floor. Even as the floodwaters rise, Noah must experience bouts of terror and uncertainty aboard the ungainly ark. Once again, the two accounts differ on the actual duration of the flood. And more awful than the cries and howls of their doomed neighbors outside the ark's doors must be the unearthly silence that follows when the rains finally cease.

To those who survived the catastrophic *tsunami* that laid waste to so much of the Indian Ocean basin, how vivid must the words "all the fountains of the great deep burst forth" now appear!

The business about all of the other ancient cultures having similar flood stories is actually quite comforting, when you think about it. It lends even more credence to the idea that this *really* happened, that somewhere in dim prehistory something cataclysmic like this *did* happen, and the few survivors kept this story alive as some kind of tribal memory. Is this a fragment of some devastating flood in the land of the flood-prone Tigris and Euphrates? Is it somehow linked to our earliest ancestors in the Nile valleys? In the eons when the glaciers receded, early humans battled repeated floods. Or is this story/memory older still? Could this be the unthinkable event that led to the formation of the Black Sea—as some archaeologists now believe? Or perhaps it happened just as the twin narrators of Genesis say it happened.

27

Genesis 8:1—9:17

In the fullness of time, a flawed creation has been scrubbed clean, and the waters begin their slow, almost imperceptible recession. Just as God's breath blew gently over the primeval waters at creation (Genesis 1:2), so now . . .

> God made a wind blow over the earth, and the waters subsided; the fountains of the deep and the windows of the heavens were closed, the rain from the heavens was restrained, and the waters gradually receded from the earth. (8:1-3)

The battered ark finally comes to rest on the mountains of Ararat, perhaps in what is now southeastern Turkey. Once again, Noah's response is recorded differently in the two accounts, but the most famous story has a dove being sent from the ark three times before it finally finds evidence

28

of dry ground. Noah and his brood have survived their ordeal aboard the foul, crowded ark and they rush to embrace the earth. Past them stream pairs of all animals—clean and unclean—out into the fresh new world. Gratefully, Noah sacrifices a burnt offering to the LORD, who makes a solemn covenant with the survivors:

> I will never again curse the ground because of humankind, for the inclination of the human heart is evil from youth; nor will I ever again destroy every living creature as I have done.
>   As long as the earth endures,
>   seedtime and harvest, cold and heat,
>   summer and winter, day and night,
>   shall not cease. (8:21-22)

The LORD blesses the children of Noah and sends them the first rainbow as a sign that God will never again be the cause of earth's destruction.

Genesis 9:18-29

In the days that follow, Noah and his sons Shem, Ham, and Japheth (their wives and children, alas, aren't mentioned by name) get back to work. Noah immediately plants a vineyard in the rich soil and when the first grapes arrive, makes wine. To celebrate, he drinks too much and falls asleep in his birthday suit! When the sons arrive and find their old father naked as the day he was born, they are embarrassed and cover him back up. When Noah awakes, he is furious and casts a venomous curse on Ham's son, Canaan. And that odd incident marks the abrupt end of the account of Noah: "All the days of Noah were nine hundred fifty years; and he died" (9:29).

While this history would explain to Old Testament listeners why Israel continually warred with its neighbors, it has puzzled readers ever since. Some unscrupulous politicians through the years have used this obscure passage to justify the enslavement of African peoples (and later, continued segregation of African Americans) by using later verses to connect Ham with Africa. But no reading of the account justifies such a racist point of view.

The Intriguing Question

So? What's the point of this outlandish tale? (Besides explaining the creation of the rainbow and why Israel found itself at war all of the time with the nearby Canaanite peoples.) While Noah is certainly a good example of someone who obeyed God willingly, the story appears to have little to say today.

To some readers, the straightforward statement in 6:6 raises the most intriguing question: "And the LORD was sorry that he had made humankind on the earth, and it grieved him to his heart." To be "sorry" here implies that an Omnipotent God, the All-Knowing Creator of the Universe, the Alpha and Omega, is capable of making a pretty significant mistake: "Oops. My bad. I'll just flood the whole thing and start over fresh."

But that seems in conflict with our understanding of a Perfect God, One who knows the future as well as the present. It certainly seems likely that humans can *grieve* the heart of God with their horrible actions, but can God really *regret* a decision or an action? If God can see the future, couldn't God have seen this coming?

I suspect the answer, at least part of it, is in the concept of free will. God doesn't want robots. God wants us to come willingly into God's presence. We're allowed the unfathomable luxury of choosing or rejecting God's love through Jesus Christ. Regardless of our decision (or decisions, since this is a life-long process), we know that God loves us. God's love remains constant. God never stops loving us.

We can accept that love and strive earnestly to do God's will.

Or we can ignore this precious gift until the waters have risen over the rooftops . . . and it is too late.

The choice—then as now—is yours.

Four

ABRAHAM
➤ (GENESIS 12–23)

> In old days there were angels who came and took men by the hand and led them away from the city of destruction. We see no white-winged angels now. But yet men are led away from threatening destruction: a hand is put into theirs, which leads them forth gently towards a calm and bright land, so that they look no more backward; and the hand may be a little child's. (George Eliot, *Silas Marner* [London: Heritage Press, 1953], 177)

Though Moses will get more ink in the pages to come, the figure of Abraham towers over the Old Testament. He is revered by three of the world's major religions—Judaism, Christianity, and Islam. Some Hindus even lump all those faiths under the broad heading of *Abrahamists*.

How influential is Abraham? Consider these random facts:

- Thousands of years after Abraham's death, Jesus tells a parable about a rich man in hell crying to heaven, where Father Abraham is comforting the abased beggar Lazarus.
- In the *Magnificat* of Luke 1:46-55, Mary remembers how the Lord helped "His servant Israel in remembrance of his mercy; as he spake to our fathers, to Abraham, and to his seed forever" (Luke 1:54-55, KJV).
- There are nearly twenty references in the New Testament to Abraham, ranging from Romans 4 where Paul refers to how Abraham was justified by faith and is the father of all true believers, to 1 Peter 3 where Abraham is honored because . . . well . . . Sarah honored and obeyed him.
- During the darkest days of slavery in the United States, slaves equate President Lincoln with "Fadder Abraham."
- A billion Muslims are commanded in their lifetimes to make the arduous *Hajj* to Mecca, to circle the Kaaba, the shrine God told Abraham (and his son Ishmael) to make in the Arabian Desert.
- The large, bustling Turkish town of Sanhurfa, thought to be Abraham's original home of Haran, still has a festival honoring Abraham, which draws tens of thousands of pilgrims, Christian, Jewish, *and* Muslim.

• And even today, bloody battles are being fought over the presumed burial grounds of Abraham and his family in the Holy Land.

But for all of this attention, the personality of Abraham is maddeningly elusive. Unlike those who come after him—Moses and David in particular—Abraham is a curiously passive follower. He rarely disputes with God, rarely complains. Instead, Abraham obeys. Which, while admirable from a religious standpoint, of course, makes for a wraith-like hero in an epic journey. We simply *don't know* Abraham. Consequently, while Moses and David are loved, Abraham is admired. And yet some of the Bible's greatest covenants are between God and this man. Everything in the Old Testament to this point has been prelude to Abraham. It is with Abraham that our story really begins.

> For me Abraham is philosophy, Abraham is culture. Abraham may or may not be historical. Abraham is a message of loving kindness. Abraham is an idea. Abraham is everything. I don't need flesh and blood. (Rabbi Menahem Froman, as quoted by Tad Szulc in "Abraham: A Journey of Faith," *National Geographic,* December 2001, 98)

The book of Genesis presents a clear, straightforward narrative involving the life of Abram, later known as Abraham. It has been traditionally thought that he was part of the great migration of peoples from what is now Iraq westward, about 2000 BCE. There were certainly migrations. And some groups from this region did end up in the areas mentioned in the Bible. However, from a historical/archaeological standpoint, it's probably just as likely that Abram and the people who later bear the name *Hebrew* emerged from the Canaanite peoples who already inhabited the hills of what is now Israel. And recently, scholars have moved the date for Abraham to about 1000 BCE—more than a thousand years later than previous estimates—because of the mention of camels, which weren't introduced into the Holy Land until about then (although it is possible that they were inserted into the original stories by later scribes).

But for story purposes, let's follow the account in the text. It's a great, epic story any way you slice it.

Genesis 12:4-20

The Bible says Abram, son of Terah, was born in Ur of the Chaldeans, one of the greatest cities of the ancient world, identified now to be a site in extreme southeastern Iraq, near Kuwait. (And since the Chaldeans don't arrive on the scene until early in the first millennium BCE, that's another clue that the most recent date may be the more accurate.)

All that remains of Ur today are straggling, cone-shaped huts and a few ziggurats to Sin, the Moon God of the era. But archaeologists have found the lavish remains of a thriving community, the heart of a rich and powerful civilization about the time of Abraham, a port city on the Euphrates, near the Persian Gulf, and a rich trading town of 12,000 people surrounded by a flood-fed plain with vast expanses of fertile land.

In an ancient world regularly torn by war, it was a safe, prosperous haven. Still, Terah inexplicably takes his son Abram and his grandson Lot and their wives—and doubtless a whole bunch of servants, in-laws, cattle, and donkeys—to the town of Haran, hundreds of miles away, near the modern-day border of Syria and Turkey. The extended family prospers. But, in the midst of it all, God tells Abram to leave once again:

> Go from your country and your kindred and your father's house to the land that I will show you. I will make of you a great nation, and I will bless you, and make your name great, so that you will be a blessing. I will bless those who bless you, and the one who curses you I will curse; and in you all the families of the earth shall be blessed. (Genesis 12:1-3)

33

That's it. No word about how or why Abram was chosen. No word about Abram's response. Abram appears. God talks. Abram obeys. But with this direct Word from the Almighty, Abram becomes something special.

After the journey from Ur to Haran—an extraordinarily ambitious (and dangerous) trip over mountains, through bandit-infested wildernesses, across deserts, and skirting marauding bands of the invading Elamite armies—the jaunt from Haran to Canaan is a Sunday picnic. Abram, now a sprightly seventy-five, packs up his childless wife (the beautiful Sarai), his weasel-y brother's son (Lot) and Lot's wife (who is never given a name—let's call her Paris), and perhaps hundreds of related families, servants, and slaves and promptly caravans southward.

One problem: There are already *lots* of heavily armed Canaanites currently residing in Canaan. With God's blessing, Abram embarks on a series of highly symbolic (and perhaps a little mystical) stops at various cities that form the boundaries of what will become known as Israel by King David's time—Sechem (in the north), Bethel (in the central highlands), and eventually, Hebron (in the far south).

There follows a strange, off-kilter story that seems more like a digression or alternate tradition than an integral part of the Abram/Abraham narratives. Because of a famine:

1. Abram and his brood journey to Egypt for food
2. The Pharaoh covets the gorgeous Sarai
3. To save his own skin, Abram convinces Pharaoh that Sarai is his sister, not his wife
4. Pharaoh takes Sarai into his harem
5. Pharaoh showers Abram with riches
6. God punishes the Pharaoh and his people with plagues because he's appropriated another man's wife
7. Pharaoh fusses at Abram (who is lucky to escape with his life—see the story of David and Bathsheba later)
8. Pharaoh sends Abram and Sarai on their way, loaded with gifts
9. Sarai goes back to living in a tent and eating charred goat flesh after living in the palaces of the Pharaoh
10. Readers thousands of years later are left wondering what the heck to make of this story

Genesis 13:1–18

Back to our tale: Abram, now richer, if not all that much wiser, heads back up to Canaan, to a place between Bethel and the ancient city of Ai.

34

By now, Lot's holdings of sheep and cattle have increased dramatically, too. Soon, their shepherds and herders come to blows over the limited water and pasture in the area. Abram offers Lot a sweetheart deal: "You choose: the well-watered, fertile, plain of the River Jordan, complete with the happenin' cities of Sodom and Gomorrah with their trendy nightspots; or the rugged, barren hills of Judea." Lot's no fool, he takes the sure thing. God, however, once again promises the peacemaker Abram that he'll found a great nation. Meanwhile, Sarai, who has been uprooted twice, plopped in a harem, and now exiled to the wastelands, *still* keeps her peace.

Genesis 14:1-24

But Lot's greed doesn't do him much good. Open warfare erupts among the various principalities in and around the Jordan Valley and a coalition of four kingdoms from the east overruns the area and, coincidentally, seizes hapless Lot. Abram hears of his nephew's plight, raises a pretty sizable army of his own, defeats the bad guys handily, frees his nephew, and heads home. The account, which is older than most of the text around it, is intriguing enough, but it also sets the stage for one of the most mysterious figures in all of the Old Testament.

Upon his return, Abram is met by Melchizedek, King of Salem and—apparently—a priest of Abram's God! Nothing is known about Melchizedek beyond this cryptic passage, and yet he has become an important symbolic figure in both Judaism and Christianity, either as a cosmic figure or as a forerunner of Christ or both! The author of the New Testament book of Hebrews says that Abram acknowledges Melchizedek's higher priesthood and tithes (gives a tenth) of his belongings. Melchizedek, which he translates as either "king of righteousness" or "king of peace," is, the author of Hebrews says: "Without father, without mother, without genealogy, having neither beginning of days nor end of life, but resembling the Son of God, he remains a priest forever" (Hebrews 7:3).

(The author appears to be arguing that Jesus is like Melchizedek and therefore above the then-current priestly orders.)

Regardless, God once again blesses and rewards Abram for his faith.

Genesis 16:1-15

Chapter 16 contains one of the pivotal events of the entire Old Testament, an event that has touched and will continue to touch billions of people. Abram and Sarai are childless. According to the custom of the day, Sarai offers Abram her young Egyptian slave-girl, Hagar. Abram wavers—has he not trusted the LORD all this time? And hasn't the LORD promised that Abram will be the father of nations? Why should he stop believing now?

At last, however, he agrees and Hagar soon conceives. Not surprisingly, Abram is then very quickly caught in a power struggle between the barren wife and the very pregnant slave girl. In his old age, the once-decisive Abram waffles yet again. He finally allows Sarai—who has obviously reached her breaking point—to drive Hagar and her child into the wilderness. Once there, at the end of her rope, an angel appears to Hagar and blesses her, telling her that she too shall be the mother of nations. In the Muslim world, Hagar and Abram's son Ishmael becomes the founder of the Arab nations, and their time in the desert establishes their millennia-old bond with the harshest deserts.

Apparently, Abram later repents of his harsh action, because we'll see in the next chapter that Ishmael is back in his father's tent. As a slave, Hagar doesn't have much say in all of this, yet she may be the toughest person in the whole sordid story. She survives a couple of banishments, raises a confident, powerful son, and gets personal attention from God.

Genesis 17:1-18:15

But that still doesn't settle Abram and Sarai's original problem—they're still childless. In the next couple of chapters, God appears to Abram once again and tells him that he'll be the father of a great people. To commemorate this event, God changes his name to Abraham (and Sarai's to Sarah) and institutes the rite of circumcision for infant boys. "Oh, and by the way, you better get some cigars, Abe, because you're a daddy."

In one account, Abraham—who has just been called *blameless* by the narrator—cracks up at the news. He falls on the tent floor laughing. "Hey! You kiddin' me? I'm 99! Sarah's only a spring chicken at 90—how are we supposed to have kids?!" (In another account, it is Sarah who bursts out laughing uncontrollably.)

God reminds Abraham (and, presumably, Sarah) that a late pregnancy

36

really isn't much of a stretch for Someone who has created the universe. Abraham admits that God has a point.

God then tells Abraham that their new son will be called "Isaac." So Abraham takes Ishmael (now age 13) and "all the slaves born in his house or bought with his money, every male among the men of Abraham's house" (17:23) and circumcises the lot of them, followed by the grand finale—he circumcises himself . . . at age 99! The account doesn't say it, but I suspect it was very quiet in the tents of Abraham in the weeks that followed.

Genesis 19

The narrator now takes us away from this scene of domestic bliss and returns to the story of the clueless nephew Lot and his wife Paris. This is one of the most famous stories in all of Scripture—the destruction of Sodom and Gomorrah. Just as it is tempting to read God's favoring of the shepherd Abel over the

How Abraham ended up with circumcision.

farmer Cain, and Abraham's decision to live in the hills over Lot's decision to live on the fertile plain, as proof that God somehow favors ranching over farming, it is tempting to read the upcoming destruction of Sodom and Gomorrah as somehow representing God's judgment on ALL cities. Fortunately, that argument doesn't wash. God *loves* cities— and the people in them. (One of the most touching moments in the New Testament is Jesus' tender lament for Jerusalem in Matthew 23:37.)

Still, in this case, Sodom and Gomorrah have got to go. Abraham, ever the peacemaker, pleads their cause. Perhaps that conversation went something like this:

37

"Suppose," Abraham says, "there are 50 righteous people in these towns? Would You nuke 'em if there are 50 good people?"

"Nope, I won't nuke it if there are 50," God replies.

"Forgive me, Big Fella," Abraham says, "but I've got to be sure. How about 45? Will you lower the boom on Sodom if there are 45 good people there?"

"Nope," God says, "I'll spare it if I can find 45 good people."

"Um, how about 30?"

"Sodom is spared if I can find 30."

"Twenty?"

"No nukes for 20."

"Ten?"

"I will spare Sodom if I find 10 good and righteous people in Sodom," God says. "You, Abraham, however, are really annoying me. How about a lightning bolt between the eyes?" *(I made that last part up completely.)*

Alas, there aren't even ten good people in the whole city.

Meanwhile, oblivious to this cosmic drama, Lot and Paris are quite happy in Sodom, enjoying the all-you-can-eat buffets and $1 movies. Suddenly, two angels appear and the couple springs into action—

hospitality is one of the sacred trusts in the Middle East to this day. Word of the visitors leaks out to the wicked people in Sodom, who demand that Lot and Paris surrender their guests. Lot refuses and—in an action that appears unspeakably horrific today—offers his two young daughters instead! Enraged, the mob turns on Lot, who barely escapes back into his house to safety.

What Happens in
Sodom & Gomorrah
Stays **in**
Sodom & Gomorrah!

Rex Rubenzer

The two angels instruct Lot and his family to flee—God is about to destroy these horrible cities. Since his two soon-to-be sons-in-law scoff, Lot dawdles until morning, when the angels roughly push Lot, Paris, and his daughters out of town. As the little band dashes out of the gates, the skies open up and pound Sodom and Gomorrah into ash. At the last second, Paris looks back—despite a clear warning not to peek from the angels. She is instantly transformed into a pillar of salt.

In addition to explaining—in a folkloric way—how the area around the Dead Sea became a lifeless waste of salt deposits and bubbling asphalt pools, the story of Lot is once again a cautionary tale about the importance of obedience.

Alas, it is followed by another one of those curiously repugnant little scenes that pop up from time to time in the Old Testament, this time involving Lot and his daughters, inserted mainly to explain how two of Israel's ancient enemies—Moab and Ammonites—came into being.

Genesis 20–21

A new author—the so-called Elohist—takes over the story here and repeats many of the stories of Abraham, but with a different slant. Even the Pharaoh who mistakenly thought Sarah was Abraham's sister gets his reputation scrubbed clean. And poor Ishmael doesn't return to Abraham's tent, but spends his days living in the wilderness, where he becomes a skilled survivalist.

Genesis 22

The thread detailing the birth of Isaac finally returns in chapter 22 and—like the sordid tale of Sodom and Gomorrah—it is familiar not just to Jews, Christians, and Muslims but to both people of different faiths and people with no faith around the world.

It's also a troubling story, particularly in light of the fact that one of the religions that most tempted the Israelites for much of their history was the worship of the blood-thirsty demon-god Moloch, who demanded of his adherents the sacrifice by fire of their firstborn children. Moloch is denounced throughout the Bible, and yet God *tests* Abraham by commanding him to sacrifice Isaac.

39

Again, we're not told how Abraham responded to God's command. All we know is that he obeyed. He takes his beloved son deep into the wilderness, builds an altar, and binds Isaac. Just as Abraham raises his knife to kill Isaac, an angel, speaking for God, intervenes:

> Do not lay your hand on the boy or do anything to him; for now I know that you fear God, since you have not withheld your son, your only son, from me. (Genesis 22:12)

The traditional site of Abraham's altar is the magnificent Dome of the Rock, an Islamic holy place on the tip of Mount Moriah. It is here that Solomon and Herod will someday build their temples as well.

Some questions to ponder:

- Does an Omnipotent God already know what Abraham will do?
- What is Isaac thinking about God in all of this? Does this frightening event permanently scar Isaac?
- Does this sound like the action of a God known for his overwhelming love for his creatures?
- Is this something from such a vastly different culture that we shouldn't try to judge God—or Abraham—by modern standards?

It is a sobering moral dilemma of the highest order and sets the stage for the final days of Abraham.

Genesis 23

In the hands of the narrator, the next significant event is the death of Sarah, a deeply symbolic—and political—act. Abraham, remember, is still

40

technically an alien in the land. When he comes to purchase a burial site, the local inhabitants (called Hittites), out of respect for his moral authority (and power), instead give him a cave in or near what is now Hebron, where a towering Islamic mosque now commemorates the supposed burial site. This little scene will have profound implications thousands of years later as the various parties in the Holy Land try to work out their differences over this very ground.

Abraham's Legacy

After a respectable period of mourning, Abraham remarries and has a passel of more kids—and eventually dies at age 175. His sons Isaac and Ishmael bury him next to Sarah in the same caves of Machpelah in Hebron. The account simply says: "Abraham breathed his last and died in a good old age, an old man and full of years, and was gathered to his people" (25:8).

For all of the heroic stories, less is known of Abraham than virtually any other significant Old Testament figure. The oral traditions that preserved these stories were not concerned much with Abraham the man. He rarely speaks. He rarely questions. He only obeys.

In the end, it is not so much Abraham's life that is instructive as it is his legacy. Three of the world's great religions still honor him in their highest pantheons. His descendents are, indeed, as numerous as the stars in the sky. And while it is never stated explicitly, his single-minded devotion to God establishes the blueprint for a revolutionary concept—monotheism, a single God, a Supreme Creator, an All-Powerful Being, yet One still willing to have the most intimate conversations with one of his creations:

"OK, God. What about this? What if there are only 5 righteous people in Sodom—and one of them was kind of iffy? Would you spare it for 5 righteous men? Whaddaya say?"

"Abraham . . . "

Rock o' my soul in de bosom of Abraham
Rock o' my soul in de bosom of Abraham
Rock o' my soul in de bosom of Abraham
Lord, rock o' my soul.
(African American Spiritual, "Rock O' My Soul")

41

Five

ISAAC AND REBEKAH
➡ (GENESIS 24:1–28:5)

Well, Abe says, "Where do you want this killin' done?"
God says, "Out on Highway 61."
(Bob Dylan, "Highway 61 Revisited")

One of the great things about the Old Testament is that virtually all of its heroes have feet of clay. The patriarchs and matriarchs of the nation of Israel often behave like spoiled little whiners. Fortunately, our God is big enough to work with broken and wounded vessels, but you sometimes have to wonder what the Almighty thought about some of the actions of his followers.

Take that self-consumed pair, Isaac and Rebekah. Their neediness creates a blood feud that continues today and provides an excellent primer for parents—mainly, what *not* to do.

Genesis 24:1–67

In Abraham's last days, he makes his oldest, most trusted servant (probably Eliezer) swear that he'll find a suitable wife for his son Isaac. While Abraham's family continues to prosper, they are still aliens living in a foreign land, surrounded by Canaanites who worship an array of disturbing gods. So Eliezer travels to Nahor in Aramnaharaim (traditionally somewhere in modern Syria), founded by one of Abraham's brothers years ago. In Nahor, Eliezer prays to the LORD for success in his quest. Lo and behold, he bumps into the beautiful Rebekah. Eliezer asks Rebekah for lodging for the night which, in the wonderful tradition of so much of this part of the world, is swiftly granted.

At Rebekah's house, Eliezer meets her brother Laban and promptly tells him all about Abraham's command and his "chance" meeting with Rebekah at the well. Laban is impressed and agrees—Rebekah should travel with Eliezer to meet her future husband Isaac. Once Rebekah arrives in Canaan, the two are immediately married. The text says Isaac loves her, but *doesn't* report Rebekah's feelings on the matter. So it's not exactly a great love match, but what can you do?

Genesis 25:19-34

Still, Rebekah is soon great with child—actually, children—and it's a difficult pregnancy. In desperation, she prays to the LORD, who responds:

> Two nations are in your womb,
> and two peoples born of you shall be divided;
> the one shall be stronger than the other,
> the elder shall serve the younger. (Genesis 25:23)

These words don't comfort Rebekah much, but she perseveres. When the twins are born, Esau appears first, all hairy and red. Close behind, still clutching Esau's heel, is the much smaller Jacob. Unfortunately, the parents soon choose their favorites—Isaac loves the rough-and-tumble Esau, while Rebekah lavishes what love she has on the quiet, sensitive Jacob.

Long years pass. Esau becomes a manly man, a hunter, impulsive, and powerful. Jacob is something of a mama's boy and a bit of a schemer. One day, Esau has been out hunting—unsuccessfully—and is forced to return home empty-handed, famished, and more than a little grumpy. He finds Jacob in the kitchen, stirring up a pot of red lentil stew.

"Hey, girlie-man!" Jacob roars, "Gimme some of that stew. I'm starving—I could eat a horse!"

"Um, sure thing, big guy. But you know, I've been slaving over this hot campfire all day. How about *you* doing something for *me*?"

"Sure, whatever. Listen, I'm about to pass out from hunger here. What do you want?"

"Oh, nothing much. Just your birthright."

"My birthright? Who cares about a birthright—GIVE ME SOME STEW!"

"Bon appetit, bro. You want fries with that?"

But that's not the last we hear of that.

44

Genesis 26:1-11

Esau has a right to be hungry; the land is gripped in yet another famine. So old Isaac travels to meet with King Abimelech of the Philistines, who controls the rich coastal territories. But Isaac worries—like Abraham before him—that Abimelech will lust after the beautiful Rebekah. So he tells everybody that Rebekah is his sister.

Thus protected, Isaac asks that his people be allowed to resettle near Gerar. Abimelech approves the move. Many years later, however, Abimelech catches Isaac and Rebekah smooching and calls Isaac into his palace.

"Look, I don't know what kind of kinky thing you've got going here, Ike, but you told me Rebekah was your sister."

"Um, did I? Sorry. I was afraid someone would kill me and take her. She *is* a beauty, isn't she?"

45

"That's not the point. We could have gotten in real trouble with the gods here if someone had made Rebekah his wife!"

"Sorry, King. Won't happen again."

"I should say not. Meanwhile, I'm passing a decree—anyone who messes with you or the foxy Rebekah will have to face me."

"Thanks. You're a real pal."

Genesis 26:12-35

Now protected by the uncommonly merciful Abimelech, Isaac and his family prosper. In fact, they do so well that their Philistine neighbors begin to get jealous. Finally, Abimelech worries that he won't be able to protect Isaac much longer and orders them to leave. They strike camp and head north, but at each stop, Isaac's men are hassled by the Philistines. Finally, they reach the area around modern-day Beersheba. In time, Abimelech and Isaac renew their friendship and all is forgiven.

Things don't mend so quickly, though, between Esau and his parents, Isaac and Rebekah. Still smarting over the loss of his birthright and his mother's obvious favoritism toward Jacob, Esau marries two Hittite women, Judith and Basemath, and plots his brother's downfall.

Genesis 27:1-29

What happens next is a scene right out of a romance novel. Isaac's days are numbered. He's got cataracts and he doesn't remember things like he used to. Before he dies, he wants to make peace with Esau. He calls to Esau, asks him to whip up a mess of venison, and they'll have one last communal meal before he dies. Just like old times. Then he'll give Esau his blessing. Well, it's not an apology and it doesn't get back the birthright, but a blessing is a blessing, so Esau trots out to the wilderness with his bow and arrow.

Of course, Rebekah has been listening behind a tapestry in the tent. She conceives a dangerous plan and summons her pet Jacob. She orders Jacob to kill two young goats—one to eat and another to skin. Rebekah wants Jacob to disguise himself as Esau by wearing the goatskins. In his dotage, perhaps Isaac won't know the difference. Jacob protests half-heartedly but complies.

46

When all is ready, Jacob goes into Isaac's tent. With his mother's help, he manipulates the old man, who feels the goatskin on Jacob's arms and face. Warmed by the stew and the wine, Isaac blesses Jacob:

> Ah, the smell of my son
>> is like the smell of a field that the LORD has blessed.
> May God give you the dew of heaven,
>> and the fatness of the earth,
>> and plenty of grain and wine.
> Let peoples serve you,
>> and nations bow down to you.
> Be lord over your brothers,
>> and may your mother's sons bow down to you.
> Cursed be everyone who curses you,
>> and blessed be everyone who blesses you! (Genesis 27:27-29)

Genesis 27:30-40

Giddy with success, Jacob slips out the back way, just barely ahead of Esau. But it is too late for Esau. Jacob has already stolen Isaac's blessing. Great burly Esau breaks down completely and cries to his father, "Bless me, me also, father!" (27:34).

But Isaac believes that he cannot undo what he's already done. "Your brother came deceitfully, and he has taken away your blessing" (27:35).

Esau is on his knees by now, raging at his lying brother and begging his father for something, anything. "Have you not reserved a blessing for me?" (27:36).

Isaac has only this bitter prophecy:

> See, away from the fatness of the earth shall your home be,
>> and away from the dew of heaven on high.
> By your sword you shall live,
>> and you shall serve your brother;
> but when you break loose,
>> you shall break his yoke from your neck. (Genesis 27:39-40)

And, in fact, Esau *will* become the patriarch of Edom, the land just to the east of Israel, and the two nations will contend with each other for centuries. Under the armies of King David, Edom will eventually fall— only to rise again as an independent nation during the ill-fated reign of Jehoram.

Genesis 27:41-45; 35:27-29

From that moment on, Esau becomes Jacob's blood-enemy and he vows a terrible oath that—once Isaac is gone—he will wreak a terrible vengeance on his scheming brother. Once again, Rebekah overhears. And once again, she feverishly concocts a cunning plan to save her favorite. She manipulates feeble Isaac into sending Jacob away—to the land of her brother Laban—ostensibly in search of a suitable bride, but mainly to avoid Esau's wrath.

And the Rest of Their Story

This little soap opera marks Isaac's final act. The story now shifts to Jacob and his wives and the ultimate confrontation with Esau. Isaac's death is not found until the end of chapter 35, where he is "gathered to his people, old and full of days" (35:29) in Mamre (or Hebron). Jacob and Esau declare a truce long enough to bury their father.

Isaac's life is a curious footnote in the Bible. Nearly sacrificed by his father, he is a passive figure in a narrative dominated by stronger personalities, including Rebekah, Esau, Jacob, even his servant Eliezer. Isaac meekly tries to pass Rebekah off as his sister to save his own life, shows blatant favor to one son, then allows another son to steal Esau's birthright and blessing—and does nothing about any of it. In short, he's little more than a link between the more compelling stories of Abraham and Jacob.

As for Rebekah, we don't discover her fate until Genesis 49:31, where it is mentioned in passing that she has been buried by Jacob in the family cave at Machpelah, along with Abraham, Sarah, Isaac, and Jacob's wife Leah.

Rebekah is the much more interesting character of the two. The Bible account neither blames nor praises her schemes to see that Jacob prospers at Esau's expense, but her actions are somewhat troubling to modern readers today. She's certainly brave enough—she's willing to take full responsibility should her plan to fool Isaac go awry. And in a time when women had no authority, Rebekah found creative (if unscrupulous) ways to exercise power. Is she a deceitful woman? Or is this somehow part of God's grand plan for the future? Is she a champion of women and other second-class citizens (like younger sons), or simply someone who amorally deceives her husband for her own purposes?

48

Regardless, she is considered one of the four great matriarchs of Israelite history and her name is revered and cherished to this day. Perhaps it is best to remember her as her father Bethuel and brother Laban did, singing this song as she left the warmth and security of Nahor to ride into the wilderness to become a stranger's bride:

> May you, our sister, become
>   thousands of myriads;
> may your offspring gain possession
>   of the gates of their foes.
> (Genesis 24:60)

Six

JACOB, LEAH, AND RACHEL
➡ (GENESIS 28:10-35:26)

There is an ongoing debate on what influences children the most, *nature* or *nurture*. At the heart of the question is this, "Are there kids who are *naturally* good or bad—despite their parents' best efforts either way?" Or said another way, "Can kids be raised or *trained* to be good or bad because of their surroundings?" We all know people who have come from dysfunctional, toxic families and yet turned out splendidly. We also probably know people who came from loving, supportive Christian families who turned out to be holy terrors.

All of which brings us to Jacob. The son of a distant, troubled father and a smothering, doting mother, Jacob willingly betrayed his brother Esau on two separate occasions. Basically, the guy's a thief. But then, when you look at the track record of his parents and grandparents, you'll see a trail of casual betrayal, selfishness, and parental neglect—and they're the *good* guys!

The amazing thing about this story is that some of the people Jacob has hurt the most play powerful roles in his redemption.

Genesis 28:10-22

When we last saw Jacob, he was on the run from Esau, who had every right to want his brother's head on a platter. Jacob, it seems, is a man without honor. There is nothing he won't do to further his own ends. He knows he's badly hurt Esau, so he heads north, leaving Canaan as fast as his skinny legs will carry him. He finally drops from weariness and, using a flat stone for a pillow, falls asleep.

51

In the midst of his exhausted, tumultuous dreams, he sees a stairway open all of the way up to heaven! Hosts of angels ascend and descend in a constant stream. And at the top of the stairway stands the LORD, who speaks directly to Jacob:

I am the LORD, the God of Abraham your father and the God of Isaac; the land on which you lie I will give to you and to your offspring; and your offspring shall be like the dust of the earth, and you shall spread abroad to the west and to the east and to the north and to the south; and all the families of the earth shall be blessed in you and in your offspring. Know that I am with you and will keep you wherever you go, and will bring you back to this land; for I will not leave you until I have done what I have promised you. (Genesis 28:13-15)

Jacob awakens with a start and immediately consecrates this spot—which he calls *Bethel*—as a holy place for worship. This is an important psychological step for a group of nomadic peoples who have tended to carry their altars with them. Bethel remains holy ground until the advent of the temple in Jerusalem.

Jacob proceeds on towards Laban's territory and eventually meets some of Laban's shepherds, who introduce him to Laban's gorgeous daughter Rachel. Laban embraces Jacob as a kinsman and takes him home, where he meets Laban's older daughter, Leah, as well. You know where this one's going, don't you?

52

1. Jacob falls for the beautiful Rachel.
2. Laban says Jacob can have her *if* he works for him for seven years.
3. Jacob does.
4. At the end of the seven years, Laban pulls the old switcheroo . . . On their wedding night, he sends Leah into the darkened honeymoon tent instead of Rachel.
5. Jacob, who is obviously not the most observant of all patriarchs, is nonetheless miffed the next morning when he discovers the truth.
6. Laban responds, "Did I say Rachel? I meant Leah. For Rachel you've gotta work another seven years."
7. Jacob does.
8. Leah falls in love with Jacob anyway, but he doesn't dig her because, in those days before contact lenses, she has *weak* or *delicate* eyes.
9. Jacob loves Rachel.
10. Rachel, of course, is barren.
11. Leah, of course, is *very* fertile.

Got all that? It's the classic love triangle. Most marriage counselors now suggest that while marrying two women is not a recommended route to marital happiness, marrying two sisters is a sure-fire recipe for *disaster*.

Genesis 29:29–30:24

But there's more. Even though Jacob adores Rachel, Leah starts having his babies almost immediately. When it is clear that Rachel can't have any kids, she gives Jacob her maid Bilhah so that *she* can have Jacob's children in her place. Bilhah, who doesn't have any say in the matter, obligingly bears two children. Leah then one-ups Rachel and gives *her* maid Zilpah to Jacob so that he can have children with her. Jacob does. Finally, Rachel herself conceives and eventually has two sons. When it's all said and done, we've got twelve boys and one girl. If you need a scorecard to keep up with all of this begetting, maybe this will help:

RACHEL	LEAH	BILHAH	ZILPAH
Joseph Benjamin	Reuben Simeon Levi Judah Issachar Zebulun *Dinah	Dan Naphtali	Gad Asher

*(the lone daughter noted in the text)

53

Jacob, Leah, and Rachel

If you've read much of the Bible in the past, you'll recognize those names—they will become the names of the twelve tribes of Israel in the days ahead.

Genesis 30:25-43

Eventually, Jacob figures Esau must have cooled off by now and decides it is time for his extended family to return to the Promised Land. He and Laban strike a bargain: Jacob will take all of the speckled and spotted sheep and all of the black lambs; Laban will keep the rest of the flocks. But Laban—who has already tricked the dense Jacob once with the wife thing—has one last nasty surprise in store. He sneaks out and removes all of the speckled and spotted sheep and black lambs from his flocks and gives them to his sons, leaving Jacob with nothing. So Jacob does a little hocus pocus of his own with some tree branches and culls out the strongest of the animals. The text isn't exactly clear on exactly *what* happened, but Jacob (who is the Master of Sneaky) out-foxes the fox and eventually ends up with a huge flock of his own.

Genesis 31:13-21

Leah and Rachel then join in the fun, saying that their father cheated them of their dowries. Perhaps that's why Rachel sneaks back into her father Laban's tent and steals his household gods—as some kind of compensation for her perceived loss.

God has had enough. Jacob has another dream and the LORD tells him to quit fooling around and return home. NOW! Jacob gets the point. He gathers his brood and their flocks, pulls up his tents, and flees into the night toward the mountainous territory east of the Jordan Valley without leaving a forwarding address or paying his last electric bill.

Genesis 31:22-55

Although Jacob has a three-day head-start, an enraged Laban starts off in pursuit and catches him seven days later (When you've got that many kids needing regular pit-stops, travel is slow in any era!). Just

54

before Laban's men fall on the unsuspecting Jacob, God intervenes in a dream, telling Laban not to harm his wayward son-in-law. Still, Laban is furious and when his troops stroll into Jacob's sprawling camp the next morning, he gives Jacob the chewing out of his life. He's most angry about the theft of his household gods. Jacob doesn't know that Rachel has nicked them and invites Jacob to search the camp. But Rachel has hidden them in her saddle, where they go unnoticed.

Now it is Jacob's turn to be upset. He berates Laban for falsely accusing him. They argue for a while, but it is clear that their bonds are too deep to break. So instead of fighting, they make a covenant of lasting friendship at a place called Galeed. Laban kisses his daughters and grandchildren goodbye and returns home. And no one is the wiser about Rachel's little bit of *god-napping*.

Genesis 32

Despite all of the wonderful things that have happened to him, you get the feeling that Jacob is still the same shifty, me-first guy he's been all along. That's about to change. Before he can return home, he must pass through Edom, the land of his aggrieved brother Esau. Despite all of God's assurances, Jacob is panicked at the thought and sends messengers ahead to meet Esau. The messengers return saying that Esau is coming to meet them—with four hundred armed troops at his side! Jacob sends ahead lavish presents, whole herds of camels, cattle, and donkeys—but still Esau keeps coming.

That night, Jacob splits his tribe and sends his wives and children into hiding, leaving him alone by a small stream. Once again, his dreams are troubled and a curious incident follows:

> Jacob was left alone; and a man wrestled with him until daybreak. When the man saw that he did not prevail against Jacob, he struck him on the hip socket; and Jacob's hip was put out of joint as he wrestled with him. Then he said, "Let me go, for the day is breaking." But Jacob said, "I will not let you go, unless you bless me." So he said to him, "What is your name?" And he said, "Jacob." Then the man said, "You shall no longer be called Jacob, but Israel, for you have striven with God and with humans, and have prevailed." (32:24-28)

At some point during this epic emotional wrestling match, something changes in Jacob. That transformation is significant enough that the LORD changes his name from *Jacob* to *Israel*—which means, "God

55

strives." Whatever the cause of the conflict, Jacob/Israel emerges the next morning a better man. And should he ever be tempted to forget the lessons he learned that night, his persistent limp is there to remind him.

Genesis 33:1-17

It is a new man who faces his brother that morning. Jacob walks ahead of his family, abasing himself in Esau's presence—no longer out of fear, but in recognition of the many wrongs he has caused his brother. As for Esau, now a

Popular paintings always portray Jacob wrestling with an angel, but angels are infinitely more powerful than humans. Some commentators even suggest that the "man" is a river demon. Others prefer to view the struggle metaphorically. It is certainly a powerful image of man wrestling with his own inner demons—especially pride. Pride is a ferocious adversary, something all people must someday contend with. Left unchecked it morphs into the most dangerous thing of all—a self-love that so dominates a personality that there is no room for anything else, including the love of God.

powerful, respected tribal leader, he proves to be both gracious and forgiving. He happily meets Jacob's family and generously returns all of Jacob's gifts. Jacob, now thoroughly humbled by Esau's loving nature, pleads with his brother to keep the gifts. Shortly thereafter, the brothers part—only to reunite to bury their father Isaac a few years later, all transgressions forgiven, all wounds healed and past.

And the Rest of Their Story . . .

Jacob has a few more adventures in his old age and when he finally reaches his homeland of Canaan, his beloved Rachel bears him one more son, whom he calls Benjamin. But the childbirth is too much for Rachel and she dies. Jacob creates a pillar to mark her gravesite. And when—hundreds of years later—the Babylonians carry off the Israelites into captivity, the writer of Jeremiah uses, of all of the women in the Bible, Rachel for this beautiful allegory:

A voice is heard in Ramah,
   lamentation and bitter weeping.
Rachel is weeping for her children;

Reluctant Prophets and Clueless Disciples

she refuses to be comforted for her children
because they are no more. (Jeremiah 31:15)

This is the end of the stories of Jacob as an active participant. The cocky, self-consummate con artist has been transformed, in his old age, into a genial grandfather. And while he's a better man, he's still not perfect. He still favors his sons by Rachel, Joseph and Benjamin, over his other children. It is a misplaced favoritism that will have lasting consequences for his children and his children's children. The twelve tribes that will be named for the twelve sons spend the rest of the Old Testament fighting each other at least as often as they fight various Canaanites and Philistines. There is a long-standing jealously among the tribes that can be traced to Abraham and his sons and grandsons that, in the end, is partially responsible for their ultimate defeat.

Still, as Frederick Buechner is fond of saying, "God doesn't love people because of who they are but because of who he is" (*Peculiar Treasures* [San Francisco: Harper & Row, 1979], 58). It's called grace.

And even a flawed man like Jacob will become an important branch in the tree that ultimately leads to Jesus.

Seven

JOSEPH AND HIS BROTHERS
➡ (GENESIS 37–50)

Several generations of family dysfunction lead us, at last, to Joseph. Like the stories of Noah and the Ark and David and Goliath, the tale of Joseph and the Coat of Many Colors cuts across the ages. It is an epic, iconic story that poses two new questions for every one it answers. Even the film *Joseph (The Bible Collection)* can't quite condense this sprawling yarn into one nice and neat ninety-minute package. The Joseph of the book of Genesis refuses pigeonholing and narrow categorizations. His quest transforms a spoiled, self-centered boy into a confident, gracious, powerful man who deserves the title *hero*.

But it's a long way from brat to hero . . .

Genesis 37:1-11

When we left Jacob (by now called Israel pretty much all the time) and his sprawling brood, the old man was doting on Joseph, his eleventh son, but the first by his beloved Rachel. He loved Joseph so much, in fact, that he gave him a long robe with sleeves (the famed coat of many colors)—the clothing of royalty. Not surprisingly, the other brothers are miffed. Haven't they been out doing the grunt work of shepherding, farming, and fighting off bandits while Joseph is back at the *casa* being pampered?

Joseph is also something of a snitch. One day, at age seventeen, Joseph sees his older brothers doing something they shouldn't be doing and runs home to rat on them to his dad. To make matters worse,

Joseph is a dreamer and an interpreter of dreams. One day, he breathlessly tells his brothers about a dream he's had where they're all worshiping him. Still another time, he tells them of a dream where even the sun, the moon, and eleven stars bow down to him.

Do you get the impression that Joseph is oblivious, arrogant, or a little of both? No wonder the other boys despise him.

Genesis 37:12-36

Finally, the older brothers have had enough. One day, Jacob/Israel sends Joseph to check up on his siblings, who are shepherding way out in the wilderness. Standing under the hot sun, they see him coming. "Here comes the dreamer," one of them sneers. "Come now, let us kill him and throw him into one of the pits; then we shall say that a wild animal has devoured him, and we shall see what will become of his dreams" (37:20). Fortunately, older brother Reuben intervenes. He proposes that, instead of killing him, they strip off the flashy robe, throw him in a pit, and deal with him later. Perhaps Reuben has a plan to rescue his younger brother at a later date.

But once Reuben leaves to follow his sheep, the remaining brothers plot against Joseph once more. This time it is Judah who dissuades them. "Let's not murder him. Why not sell him to some traveling salesmen instead? Not only do we get rid of the little twerp, we'll make a little cash on the side!" When a caravan of Midianites passes by, that's exactly

60

what they do. When Reuben returns, he's distraught. The remaining brothers kill a young goat and smear Joseph's coat with its blood—that way it'll look like wild animals killed him.

When the remaining brothers return home and Jacob hears the bad news, he is inconsolable. (Unlike Joseph, Reuben does *not* squeal on his kin.) This leaves the other brothers doubtless pondering, "I wonder if he'd cry that hard if *I* was the one who'd died?" Even in *death*, Joseph makes a bad impression!

The Midianites eventually sell Joseph to Potiphar, one of the officials of the (unnamed) Egyptian Pharaoh.

Still, it's hard to muster much sympathy for Joseph to this point. He's been a pampered daddy's boy all of his life. And serving Potiphar was certainly better than what other slaves in those days were doing—hauling the ten-ton blocks needed to make the pyramids in the Egyptian summer!

Genesis 38

The text leaves Joseph for all of chapter 38 to tell the ancient (and really weird) story of another one of Joseph's older brothers, Judah, his wife Tamar, and some hanky-panky that eventually leads to the birth of Perez, one of the ancestors of David and—eventually—Jesus.

Genesis 39

OK, back to the main event—and Joseph. The LORD is obviously on the hard-working Joseph's side. Still just a teenager, Joseph prospers under Potiphar, who eventually sets the young slave running his household affairs. But Potiphar's wife—who is never named, either—has her eye on the good-looking Joseph and repeatedly tries to entice him into an affair. Joseph nobly resists.

Finally, one day when no one is around, she grabs him. Joseph wriggles free, leaving his garment in her hands. Her pride hurt, Potiphar's wife puts on one of the great acting jobs of the Old Testament. She howls in fear and pain. When the other members of Potiphar's staff rush in, she claims that Joseph tried to rape her. Only Joseph's history of great and loyal service keeps Potiphar from killing him outright. Why would his wife lie? And Joseph is thrown into the royal jail.

61

Once again, the narrator tells us that the LORD was with Joseph (besides, the narrator notes, he was "handsome and good-looking" [39:6]). Joseph again quickly becomes head toady for the chief jailer and eventually takes over the prison while the chief jailer goes snorkeling in the Nile (or whatever they did for fun in those days).

Genesis 40

Years pass. Eventually, a couple of the pharaoh's favorites find themselves tossed in the slammer as well—his cupbearer (which, as we'll see in the story of Nehemiah, is a big deal) and his baker. When they have vivid, troubling dreams, they turn to Joseph who has, by now, established himself as a big-time dream interpreter. The cupbearer dreams about—surprise, surprise—wine. Joseph says the dream indicates that he'll soon be tapping kegs for the pharaoh again. But the baker's dream is about—you guessed it—bread. This time, Joseph interprets the dream to mean that the baker will hang in just three days. Both dreams promptly come true in the next few days.

Genesis 41

Two more years pass and now it is the Pharaoh who is having dreams. His dreams are more like nightmares—seven skinny cows eating seven fat cows and seven skinny and diseased ears of corn eating seven fat and juicy ears of corn. (If he ever had the dream where he was late for a final exam in a class he'd never attended all semester and he can't find the classroom—that particular dream isn't mentioned in the text. I *hate* that one.) None of the Pharaoh's magicians can interpret the dream and the Pharaoh becomes increasingly antsy.

Finally, the fat old cupbearer remembers Joseph in the prison. (That's the problem with being cupbearer—the mind is the first thing to go.) Pharaoh summons Joseph from the prison and tells him his weird dream. "This one is easy," Joseph says. "The dreams both mean the same thing—there'll be seven years of good harvest, followed by seven years of serious famine."

The magicians are shocked and embarrassed. Pharaoh tells Joseph to continue. Joseph is feeling his oats now, so he starts to lecture the most powerful man in the world:

62

Now therefore let Pharaoh select a man who is discerning and wise, and set him over the land of Egypt. Let Pharaoh proceed to appoint overseers over the land, and take one-fifth of the produce of the land of Egypt during the seven plenteous years. Let them gather all the food of these good years that are coming, and lay up grain under the authority of Pharaoh for food in the cities, and let them keep it. That food shall be a reserve for the land against the seven years of famine that are to befall the land of Egypt, so that the land may not perish through the famine. (Genesis 41:33-36)

Pharaoh likes Joseph's advice so much that he promotes him to his second-in-command on the spot. He loads Joseph up with *bling-bling* and expensive clothes, and gives him his own souped-up chariot (four-horsepower, spoked wheels, and lifetime roadside assistance). But he's not through yet. The Pharaoh even gives Joseph a politically powerful wife, Asenath, daughter of Potiphera, one of the high priests. Joseph is now the second most powerful man in the country.

In the years that follow, Joseph's predictions come true. Likewise, he proves his worth as an administrator. When the worldwide famine strikes, Egypt has so much grain stored that it can sell its surplus (at a tidy profit, I'm sure) to the hungry of all the surrounding nations. Joseph (and Asenath) even find time to produce a couple of sons, Manasseh and Ephraim.

Genesis 42:1-25

Things in Canaan, however, aren't so peachy. In fact, Joseph's brothers and their families are starving. In desperation, Jacob sends the remaining brothers (except for his new favorite, Joseph's younger brother Benjamin) to Egypt to buy, beg, borrow, or steal enough grain to live on. What follows is one of the great passages in the Old Testament. For one of the very few times in the Bible, the writer portrays a range of complex emotions, giving us a rare insight into the heart and mind of one of our heroes.

The brothers are brought before Joseph, now arrayed in all of his royal finery. They don't recognize him. Joseph, however, recognizes them. Something has happened to Joseph since he was the proud and preening youngest son, parading around in his coat of many colors. Perhaps it was prison; perhaps it was the impact of his sudden ascension to a position of power and authority. The *old* Joseph might have enacted a terrible vengeance on his helpless brothers. Instead, Joseph decides to teach them an unforgettable lesson.

"Who are you bozos?" Joseph pretends to snarl.

"Um, we're foreigners," Simeon says unconvincingly. "We're from France."

Reuben pokes him in the ribs. "What my idiot brother meant to say is, we're from the Upper Transjordan region, a land of simple, *very* peaceful shepherds barely out of the Iron Age with absolutely no weapons of mass destruction, save for the odd slingshot, and we're looking for groceries, your highness," he says quickly.

Joseph rises and shouts at his groveling brothers: "Lies! You're sneaking spies and you've come to snoop out my defenses. Admit it!"

"Not bad," Joseph thinks to himself. *"When this Assistant King gig is over, maybe I ought to look into acting."*

"Spies? You've been given erroneous information by the anti-Canaan faction in your cabinet," Reuben whimpers. "Groceries. That's all. Groceries. We're in the midst of the Mother of All Droughts. We're reduced to eating tree bark . . ."

"At least it helped clear up my rash," Simeon says brightly.

Reuben pokes him again—harder. "No, your Worshipfulness. We're just dumb but transparently honest, mostly illiterate sheepherders, the sons of a single father. Be honest; does this guy even look smart enough to be a spy?"

Reuben motions to Simeon, who is contentedly scratching both of his armpits simultaneously.

Joseph stiffens at the mention of his father, whom he has not seen in many, many years.

"Nope," he roars, "you can't fool me. Spies—the lot of you, including the dumb one! They're the most cunning spies of all!"

The brothers see Joseph's soldiers edging dangerously close, swords at the ready.

Reuben makes a desperate decision. "Honest to Yahweh, your almightiness, we're just a band of twelve brothers." His fear makes him stutter and heave. "Well, that's not *exactly* true. Our kid brother is back home in the Transjordan with our old man and one was, um, *lost* years ago."

"One is lost," Joseph thinks. *"Has my father thought me dead all these years?"* He wants to throw down his crown and embrace them, but determines to finish the lesson instead.

"You compound lies with lies! Well, I know just how to determine whether or not you're telling the truth." Joseph's voice is soft now, a dangerous hiss. "Bring me your baby brother as a hostage—think of him as

64

a guarantee for your good behavior. One of you bumbling morons can go fetch him. The rest of you will stay here as my, ah, guests in our luxurious, air-conditioned dungeons. Or you can die on the spot. Your choice."

The brothers, helpless, agree.

With a wave of his hand, Joseph has the brothers roughly bound and thrown into prison. Only now do they understand what Joseph must have endured at their hands so many years ago.

After three agonizing days, he comes to the prison and has his interpreter make a new demand. One of them must stay while the rest go to fetch baby brother.

Huddled in their dank cell, the brothers talk urgently among themselves: "Boy, we're really paying the piper now," one says. "Yep, the chickens have really come home to roost," says another. "No question about it," says another. "We blew it big time. Joseph begged us to spare him. Did we listen? Nooooo."

By now, Reuben, the sole voice of reason back in the wilderness, has heard enough. "Dagnab it! I told you guys nothing good would come of this, even if Joseph was a spoiled, self-centered little twerp. Now I've got to pay for your bone-headed actions! Here's another fine mess you've got me into!"

The brothers sadly agree. Now they must choose the hostage to leave behind. The dungeon is filthy, crawling with rats, and littered with the bones of previous prisoners. It will be a painful, difficult decision.

Simeon looks up from playing hacky-sack with a small skull. "Hey! Why is everybody looking at me?"

Reuben's words have struck deep in Joseph's heart. Even as he continues the charade of pretending not to understand their language, he walks away so they can't see his tears. Once he has composed himself, Joseph returns and orders Simeon bound as the hostage, then imperiously sends them on their way. He also orders that their bags be filled with grain and—unbeknownst to them—tells his servants to surreptitiously return their money.

Genesis 42:26-38

The remaining brothers sadly make the trip back to Canaan through the Sinai desert. What is Father going to say? At a rest stop, one brother finds that his money has been returned. Now they know they are doomed. One brother sinks to his knees and wails, "What is this that God has done to us?" (42:28).

When they at last reach home, their worst fears are realized. When they tell Jacob of the Egyptian ruler's accusations and demands, the old man is beside himself with grief.

"I am the one you have bereaved of children: Joseph is no more, and Simeon is no more, and now you would take Benjamin. All this has happened to me!" (42:36).

Again, it is Reuben who takes charge. "You may kill my two sons if I do not bring him back to you. Put him in my hands, and I will bring him back to you" (42:37).

But Jacob will have none of it. "My son shall not go down with you, for his brother is dead, and he alone is left. If harm should come to him on the journey that you are to make, you would bring down my gray hairs with sorrow to Sheol" (42:38).

Genesis 43—44

In the end, of course, Jacob has no choice. His people are starving. He sends the brothers back to Egypt once again, this time with Benjamin, and a few pitiful presents, hoping to win the harsh Egyptian ruler's favor. The trip to Egypt must have been a somber and silent one, each brother lost in his own thoughts.

When Joseph sees his beloved brother Benjamin, he orders his stewards to throw an elaborate feast for the befuddled brothers, including Simeon—who is delighted to be released from the dungeon. Joseph is still too overcome with emotion to greet Benjamin properly. Still, at the banquet table, he orders Benjamin's place to overflow with the finest food and drink. And, perhaps because of his rank, he does not eat with his foreign guests.

On the brothers' departure, Joseph does a curious thing. He orders a precious silver cup hidden in Benjamin's pack amid the grain. When the still-confused brothers are several miles out of town, he orders his servants to race after them and to accuse them of theft. They are to search the bags of grain—where they'll find the silver in Benjamin's pack. In short, he wants Benjamin framed. The brothers are rudely dragged back to Joseph's palace and confronted with their *guilt*.

Abasing himself before Joseph, Judah offers the brothers up as slaves, if only Joseph will spare their lives. But Joseph only wants Benjamin. This is the key moment. Will the brothers sacrifice Benjamin to save their own skins just as they once sacrificed Joseph? Their future hangs on their response.

66

But, like Joseph, the remaining brothers have changed as well. In truth, all of the sons of Jacob have grown up. Judah desperately pleads their cause. They've already lost one brother due to their cruelty. If Benjamin doesn't return with them, their father will die of a broken heart. He begs Joseph, "Take me as your slave instead."

This is what Joseph has been hoping to hear. The remaining sons of Jacob have passed the test, they know of the supreme importance of family, loyalty, and fidelity.

Genesis 45

Joseph clears the room of his servants and soldiers. With tears streaming down his face, he reveals himself to his brothers. "I am Joseph, whom you thought lost." They stand speechless, in shock. Joseph? Alive? Here? Now?

That which was meant for evil, has once again—through God's providence—been turned into good. Joseph tells them that there are five more years of drought and famine ahead and—with the Pharaoh's generosity and support—urges them to return to Egypt as honored guests. Loaded down with presents and grain, the brothers return to Canaan with the news their father has longed to hear.

Jooseph and His Brothers

Genesis 46—50

And so ancient Jacob and his sprawling tribe migrate to Egypt, where the Pharaoh richly welcomes them.

At the ripe old age of 147, Jacob senses that his time is near and begs Joseph to allow him to be buried among his ancestors in Canaan. The final chapters of Genesis detail Jacob's legacy and his final words to his sons—an ancient prophecy/prayer laced with archaic words and phrases that even modern translators struggle with. Still, it is clear that Joseph orders Jacob's body to be embalmed in the custom of the Egyptians. The brothers carry Jacob to the cave of the field at Machpelah, near Mamre. This is the cave Abraham bought from Ephron the Hittite. Here are buried Abraham and Sarah, Isaac and Rebekah, Leah, and Jacob's beloved Rachel—and now Jacob.

After a long period of mourning, all of the brothers return to Egypt.

Chapter 50 ends with the death of Joseph, himself 110 years old. He too requests that he be buried in Canaan, but not before he offers a prophecy of his own, "I am about to die; but God will surely come to you, and bring you up out of this land to the land that he swore to Abraham, to Isaac, and to Jacob" (50:24). With his final ounce of strength, Joseph makes his surviving brothers swear an oath: "When God comes to you, you shall carry up my bones from here" (50:25).

Genesis Reflections

The story that began with the sin of Adam and Eve comes to a melancholy, somewhat disturbing end with the death of Joseph. The course of the book of Genesis takes a host of surprising twists and turns: heroes who act like villains, villains who behave honorably, and chosen people who consistently vex and confound their God, who stumble blindly down an uncertain road, carrying the baggage and sin of generations on their shoulders. Perhaps the greatest single miracle of all in Genesis isn't the Creation; perhaps it is the willingness of a Perfect God to continually forgive an Imperfect Creation.

In other words, *us.*

Reflecting on the Book of Genesis, which is so heavily dominated by men who don't seem to know how to be fathers (and the women who have to live with them), who pass on their dysfunctions and prejudices and problems to their sons and daughters, it's a wonder that *any* of the

68

so-called Patriarchs and Matriarchs were able to muddle through at all. It may be that what's *not* said in these pages is as important as what's actually said. At some point, I believe, Isaac forgives Abraham. Jacob and Esau forgive Isaac. Rachel and Leah forgive one another. And Joseph and his brothers forgive Jacob. And maybe even Dinah forgives her father and brothers. They *have* to forgive at some point.

When you get a minute someday, go to the video store, and rent Sherman Alexie's magnificent *Smoke Signals*, one of the best movies about forgiveness and redemption ever made. It's the story of two friends, Victor and Thomas Builds-the-Fire, young Coeur d'Alene Indians, living near Spokane, Washington. Victor's father Arnold accidentally sets the fire that kills Thomas's parents. Arnold struggles with guilt and alcoholism until he eventually leaves Victor and his mother Arlene. One day, Victor and Arlene receive word that Arnold is dead. Victor and Thomas then must travel to Phoenix to retrieve Arnold's ashes.

Thomas's final voice-over is adapted from Dick Lourie's poem "Forgiving Our Fathers." As Thomas speaks, we see Victor scatter his father's ashes in the Spokane River, allowing himself to cry and grieve over this father's death for the very first time:

> Do we forgive our fathers for leaving us too often or forever when we were little? Maybe for scaring us with unexpected rage or making us nervous because there never seemed to be any rage there at all?
>
> Do we forgive our fathers for marrying or not marrying our mothers? For divorcing or not divorcing our mothers? And shall we forgive them for the excesses of warmth or coldness?
>
> Shall we forgive them for pushing or leaning? For shutting doors? For speaking only through layers of cloth, or never speaking, or never being silent?
>
> Do we forgive our fathers in our age or in theirs? Or in their deaths? Saying it to them or not saying it? If we forgive our fathers, what is left?
>
> ("Forgiving Our Fathers" reprinted from *Ghost Radio,* copyright 1998 by Dick Lourie. Used by permission of Hanging Loose Press.)

Ultimately, this is one of the great themes of the entire Bible. Without God's forgiveness, without our forgiveness of others, *without our forgiveness of ourselves*, nothing is possible. Never has been, never will be. Without forgiveness, as Thomas Builds-the-Fire asks, "What is left?"

With the death of Joseph, so closes the book of Genesis. His quest is finished. But for his descendents, a long nightmare is just beginning. For with the beginning of the book of Exodus, we meet a man named Moses.

69

Eight

MOSES

➡ (EXODUS, LEVITICUS, NUMBERS, *AND* DEUTERONOMY!)

Moses supposes his toeses are roses
But Moses supposes erroneously.
(Arthur Freed, "Moses Supposes" from *Singin' in the Rain*)

No one in the Old Testament has more written about him than Moses. And yet we know precious little about him. His tumultuous life consumes the better part of three books (Exodus, Numbers, and Deuteronomy), and yet he is an enigma to us today. He's also the subject of one of the niftiest stories in the Bible, a sweeping yarn that contains all of the elements of a great epic—violence, romance, wars, the supernatural, treachery, sex, miracles, burning bushes, and people dancing like maniacs around a golden calf—not to mention that whole business with the Pharaoh and the parting of the sea.

In fact, Moses's life *has* been made into a movie—several movies. The most famous is *The Ten Commandments* (1956) with old-time movie star Charlton Heston. Heston's Moses is heroic, noble, and larger-than-life. It was followed in 1980 by *Wholly Moses* starring diminutive English comic Dudley Moore (best known for *10* and *Arthur*), as an honest but bumbling man swept quite against his will into Something Important. In 1996, Moses (the voice of Val Kilmer) was re-imagined as a romantic, angst-ridden teenager in the animated film *The Prince of Egypt*. And in 1998, *Moses*, a reverent mini-series that closely followed the biblical account was released. It starred Ben Kingsley (who won an Oscar as Gandhi in the movie by the same name) and went far beyond the whole "parting of the Red Sea" thing. It was also pretty darn dull.

Four radically different portrayals of Moses—taken together, perhaps they give us a reasonably accurate picture of this complex man.

Exodus 1:1—2:10

The Moses birth narratives are famous even to folks who have never cracked a Bible in their lives. Since the heyday of Joseph and the whole Coat of Many Colors thing a few generations earlier, the Hebrews have gone from being the apple of one Pharaoh's eye to brutalized, over-worked slaves in another Pharaoh's service. And when this particular Pharaoh notices the accelerating birth rates of this particular captive people, he orders all male babies executed. It's genocide, pure and simple. When Moses is born, his mother, in desperation, launches him on the Nile in a basket. He's saved by one of Pharaoh's daughters, who sees to it that he's raised in the courts of the most powerful, most educated kingdom in the world.

Exodus 2:11—14

The account jumps ahead twenty or thirty years to Moses as a young adult. From a historical standpoint, we know that Semitic leaders' sons were raised in the palaces of the new kingdom to ensure their (and their fathers') loyalty. What has happened in Moses's life over those intervening years is probably lost forever, but from his actions in the decades to come, we can infer a few things about young Mr. Moses. He's neither wholly Hebrew, nor wholly Egyptian; conflicted and confused about his identity and his destiny. He's stubborn, impulsive, headstrong, even reckless. He's not a natural leader. And he's prone to violence and rash acts—traits that both hinder and help him in the days to come.

One day, while wandering around the pyramids, Moses sees an Egyptian overseer savagely beating a Hebrew. Enraged, he kills the Egyptian—but only after looking to see if anyone is watching. The next day, he sees two more people fighting, only this time it's two Hebrews. He breaks them up and shouts at the aggressor, "Why do you strike your fellow Hebrew?" (2:13). In response, the bully sneers at Moses. "Who made *you* ruler and judge over us? Do you mean to kill me as you killed the Egyptian?" (2:14). Obviously, Moses hadn't been as sneaky the previous day as he'd originally thought. With that, he hightails it out of Egypt, the law on his trail. Not an auspicious debut for Israel's greatest leader!

72

Exodus 2:15-25

Moses flees to Midian and marries the beautiful Midianite Zipporah, daughter of Jethro (also called Reuel). They have a son, whom they name Gershom, which translates as "I have been an alien residing in a foreign land" (2:22)—a theme that will recur throughout Moses's life and, I think, crucial in understanding the man.

The first Pharaoh finally dies but his successor is worse. He turns life on the Nile into a living hell for the Hebrew people. Not that Moses, in far-off Midian, minds much. He's content tending his father Jethro's herds, enjoying all of the perks of being a priest's son-in-law. It seems likely that Moses would have been happy to stay in Midian. But God has other plans. In this, Moses is like Neo (*Matrix*) or Frodo (*The Lord of the Rings*). Your destiny is not always of your own choosing. Moses, Neo, and Frodo will spend much of their lives grappling with their respective destinies.

Exodus 3:1-17

While driving his sheep by Mt. Horeb, Moses sees the now-famous burning bush. He is curious: "I must turn aside and look at this great sight, and see why the bush is not burned up" (3:3).

This is a pivotal moment, not just in Moses's life, but also in the life of the Israelite nation. Alas, Moses's first conversation with Yahweh—who orders him to return to Egypt and free the enslaved Hebrew nation—doesn't go well. This is *not* the destiny Moses had in mind. He whines, "Who am I that I

73

should go to Pharaoh, and bring the Israelites out of Egypt?" (3:11). God assures him everything will be OK. Still reluctant, and maybe stalling for time, Moses then asks the Lord for his *real* name. God tells him, "I AM WHO I AM" (3:14), then adds that there are great victories still to come and that the wonderful land of milk and honey is just waiting for the Hebrews to come and pluck like ripe grapes.

Exodus 4:1-9

That's still not good enough for Moses. He's sweating bullets, grasping at rhetorical straws: "But suppose they do not believe me or listen to me, but say, 'The LORD did not appear to you'" (4:1). Exasperated, but with infinite patience, God gives Moses three *tools* that will *authenticate* his call to the Hebrews: a miraculous staff that can turn into a snake and back again, the ability to turn one of his hands *leprous* at will, and the ability to turn water from the Nile into blood. The miraculous staff, incidentally, will eventually be more trouble than it is worth.

Exodus 4:10-17

Seeing that God will not be thwarted, Moses is desperate now and starts begging: "O my Lord, I have never been eloquent, neither in the past nor even now that you have spoken to your servant; but I am slow of speech and slow of tongue" (4:10). Moses abjectly implores God to send someone else. God—now a little testy—relents and selects Moses's brother Aaron to be his spokes-prophet. Like the staff, Aaron will cause many more problems than he solves in the years to come! In retrospect, Moses was better off *before* he started all that wheedling and cajoling.

Exodus 5-6

Finally, Moses and Aaron head to Egypt. The now distraught Hebrews are in dire straits but are still reluctant to accept the leadership of this strange pair. So Moses dutifully does the three signs with the three tools. With the Hebrews' grudging blessing—after all, how much worse can things get, right?—the two finally get on Pharaoh's calendar for a quick confab over latte. Chapter 5 details the first of Moses's and Aaron's several

74

disastrous encounters with Pharaoh. Pharaoh not only doesn't listen, he doubles the workload on the Hebrews yet again. The Hebrews immediately blame Moses. This blaming business is another theme that will run, not just through Exodus, but through most of the books that follow for another oh, say, three thousand years.

The tag-team of Aaron and Moses gingerly approaches Pharaoh again. Moses, now 80, is forced to do the whole rod-into-snake routine again with even less success. Nothing. Pharaoh won't budge. The Israelites stay. The Bible says that God "hardened" (4:21) Pharaoh's heart, which is probably a very early, fairly primitive understanding of how God works. God doesn't do evil stuff. Nor do we need God's help to think and do evil things. We're pretty good at that all on our own, thank you. Regardless, that's how the writer (or writers) of the Moses Cycle of stories interprets his actions.

Exodus 7:1–12:36

All of which sets the stage in chapters 7–10 for the Plagues, a strange, disturbing sequence—conviction, renunciation, and new plague—that repeats time and time again. God attacks the Egyptians with everything from fleas to boils to the kitchen sink—*nothing* will change Pharaoh's heart. Nothing, that is, until the horrific Death of the Firstborn, a plague so terrible that it's hard to imagine that a Loving God could conceive of— much less execute—it. This is the crux of chapter 12, a ritualistic event so potent and so powerful, it remains one of the central tenets of Judaism today and is marked by the Feast of the Passover.

OK, BUSTER, YOU'VE GOT ONE MORE CHANCE TO EXPLAIN THESE PLAGUES... AND THIS TIME, I DON'T WANT ANY OF THIS "YAHWEH MADE MY HEART HARD" NONSENSE... YOU GOT ME?!!

When Pharaoh rejects Moses's—and more importantly, God's—requests a tenth and final time, God strikes down the first-born of Egypt.

The Hebrews avoid the massacre by instituting the sacred ceremony of the Passover with the sacrifice of the Passover lamb and swabbing the lamb's blood on their doorways. Of the resulting anguish, verse 30 is a marvel of understated horror—" . . . there was a loud cry in Egypt, for there was not a house without someone dead." Only then does a grieving Pharaoh permit the Hebrews to leave—but not before the Hebrews *plunder* their Egyptian neighbors of their gold and silver (12:35-36).

Exodus 12:37—14:31

Thus begins another one of those defining events in the history of Israel—the Exodus. The account says that the Hebrews hastily depart, not even allowing for their bread to rise. (This mass evacuation is the origin of two more beloved Hebrew liturgical celebrations, the Festival of the Unleavened Bread and the Consecration of the Firstborn.) Chapter 12 claims that six hundred thousand men—perhaps two to three million people—pour out of Egypt on that night, though those numbers are difficult to explain or support today. However many there are, they are led in a generally eastward direction, by a pillar of clouds by day and a pillar of fire by night, into the vast, inhospitable Sinai desert.

Let us pay tribute here to one of history's densest human beings—ol' Pharaoh. It's not enough that his economy is ruined, a tenth of his people have died, and everybody is suffering from boils the size of hen's eggs. He changes his mind and defiantly gives chase to the straggling Hebrew migration. Along with an unbeatable army, at his disposal is the most feared, most unstoppable weapon in the ancient arsenal, six hundred chariots—the Sherman tanks of their day. The trouble with being told you're a god all of your life is that you begin to think you're smarter than God.

An army of this size on those barren wastes raises a dust plume that reaches into the stratosphere. And at the rear of the drawn-out Hebrew column, they *know* this isn't a pizza delivery truck bearing down on them. Instantly, the people blame Moses again: "Oh, this is just great. Man, we were better off in slavery in Egypt making bricks without straw than suffering a hideous death under the wheels of Egyptian chariots. I told you this was a bad idea. But did you listen to your mother? No!"

76

I like Moses's answer: "Do not be afraid, stand firm, and see the deliverance that the LORD will accomplish for you today; for the Egyptians whom you see today you shall never see again. The LORD will fight for you, *and you have only to keep still*" (14:13-14, italics added). That last clause probably means "you won't have to lift a finger in your own defense." But I take it to mean, "If you will all *just shut up*, God will take care of this thing."

You know the punch line. Crowded by the Red Sea (or Reed Sea), so close now they can hear the thunder of Egyptian chariots on the hard-baked desert floor, the Hebrew people howl in fear. Moses stretches out his hand and staff and the sea opens! Great winds hold the waters back while curious fish enjoy the spectacle—like Sea World in reverse!

Emerging from a supernatural fog, the armies and chariots of Pharaoh expect to see a cowering mass of refugees. Instead, they see the grand avenue open before them, a dry throughway splitting the sea in twain. Thanking their gods Isis or Ra or Anubis, the Egyptians storm into the breach. Just as the last Hebrew staggers through, panting, on the other side, Moses—at God's command—stretches out his staff to allow the waters to return. In a single panicked, horror-stricken moment, the chariot-drivers and the rest of Pharaoh's army see the giant walls of water like an unfathomable tidal wave crash down on them.

It must have been a bittersweet triumph for Moses, the Rev. Raymond Bailey once suggested in a sermon. Moses had been a Prince of Egypt; some of those who drowned were doubtless once his best friends.

> When Israel was in Egypt's land
>   Let my people go!
> Oppressed so hard they could not stand
>   Let my people go!
> Go down, Moses,
> 'Way down in Egypt land—
> Tell old Pharaoh
> To let my people go.
> (African American Spiritual, "Go Down Moses")

Under Moses's astute leadership (he was, after all, educated "in all the wisdom of the Egyptians," says Acts 7:22), this band of mud-brick-making migrant workers now head resolutely out into one of the worst deserts in the world. They're now home free, right? It's a no-brainer. With God's support, they'll just stroll across the Sinai and claim what God has promised them. Only it doesn't work that way. Some of it is Moses's fault and some of it is the people's fault—and all of it is uncomfortably familiar to life today.

77

Exodus 15—16

In chapter 15, our band begins its journey into the wilderness—with non-stop complaining. Right off the bat, the water's bad in Marah and Moses must perform a miracle to sweeten it. A few days later, the Hebrews complain again about the food: "If only we had died by the hand of the LORD in the Land of Egypt, when we sat by the fleshpots and ate our fill of bread; for you have brought us out into this wilderness to kill this whole assembly with hunger" (16:3). Thus follows the miracle of the manna and the quail. Each morning, God covers the ground with "manna," apparently a sweet, grain-like substance that could be baked into bread and *manna*cotti. For the carnivores, God also provided vast flocks of quail. Again, Moses, through Aaron, gives them the ground rules: "When the LORD gives you meat to eat in the evening and your fill of bread in the morning, because the LORD has heard the complaining that you utter against him—what are we? Your complaining is not against us but against the LORD" (16:8). The people will munch on manna for the next forty years or so. It's the original Sinai Beach Diet.

"There will be a 40 year layover in Sinai, Mr Moses."

Reluctant Prophets and Clueless Disciples

Exodus 17:1-13

And so it goes. It's not long before the Hebrews are complaining again about the water. By now they're experts: "Oh woe is us. We'd rather be well-fed and well-watered slaves in Egypt than die here in the desert. Moses, you've got to be the worst leader in the history of the world." Moses, who knows a thing or two about complaining, vents: "Why do you quarrel with me? Why do you test the LORD?" (17:2). Then, to God: "What shall I do with this people? They are almost ready to stone me" (17:4)! And once again, God commands Moses to do a miracle, striking a rock with the same staff and once again, water gushes forth.

Moses's next major test is a battle with the Amalekites, descendents of Esau. It's also our first introduction of Joshua, Moses's main general. But God puts a peculiar prerequisite on this battle. As long as Moses holds his hands out steady with the magical staff of God, Israel wins. When the arms wobble, Israel loses. So Aaron and Hur physically hold 'em up until the Amalekites are defeated.

Exodus 19-23

Fresh from their victory, the Israelite caravan trudges towards Mount Sinai, where God commands Moses to ascend to the summit. God appears to Moses in a thick cloud, surrounded by volcano-like trappings and a voice like thunder (see 19:9-25). While he's on the mountaintop, thousands of feet below the people tremble in fear and beg Moses *not* to let God speak directly to them. Moses says, "Do not be afraid; for God has come only to test you and to put the fear of him upon you so that you do not sin" (20:20), and disappears deeper into the mysterious thick darkness, closer to God, where he is given the Ten Commandments and additional laws concerning the altar, silver idols, the release of slaves, violence, property, restitution, social and religious laws, justice, sabbatical years, festivals, and finally—if they do all of these things—free passage into Canaan.

Exodus 24-31

This is followed by an interesting passage, 24:9-11, where Moses, Aaron, Nadab, Abihu, and seventy elders are allowed not only to see

God (who has feet, because they notice the sapphire stone pavement beneath them), but also eat and drink in God's presence! This never happens again in the Bible, by the way. Moses and Joshua then go even further up the mountain to get the famed Ten Commandments stone tablets, leaving the people to fend for themselves. Not a wise decision.

"Then everything else is okay, right?"

Moses receives more laws regarding offerings in the temple, the Ark of the Covenant, the Table for the Bread of the Presence, the Lampstand, the Tabernacle itself, the Framework, the Curtain, the Altar of Burnt Offering, the Oil for the Lamps, Vestments for the Priesthood, the Ephod, the Breastplate, the Other Priestly Vestments, the Ordination of the Priests, the Daily Offerings, the Altar of Incense, the Half Shekel for the Sanctuary, the Bronze Basin, the Anointing Oil and Incense, and the Sabbath Law and the Two Tablets of the Covenant. This takes forty days; as you might imagine, Moses's shorthand is pretty rusty, particularly when chiseling big words into stone.

Exodus 32:1–33:5

Back on the plain, though, the people are getting restive and, led by Aaron, melt down their gold rings to build—of all things—a golden calf, and begin to party.

Somewhat annoyed, God tells Moses he's going to destroy the Hebrews. Moses loses his stutter and eloquently begs his hotheaded God to cool off:

80

"O LORD, why does your wrath burn hot against your people, whom you brought out of the land of Egypt with great power and with a mighty hand? Why should the Egyptians say, 'It was with evil intent that he brought them out to kill them in the mountains, and to consume them from the face of the earth'? Turn from your fierce wrath; change your mind and do not bring disaster on your people." (Exodus 32:11-12)

He also reminds God, who appears a tad forgetful, of his promises to Abraham, Isaac, and Israel.

At last, God cools down and Moses takes the tablets and meets with Joshua, who alone is patiently waiting a little further down the mountain. Joshua is worried—he thinks there is a battle brewing down in the camp. But Moses knows better: "It is not the sound made by victors, or the sound made by losers; it is the sound of revelers that I hear" (32:18).

Sure enough, as they near the camp, Moses and Joshua see the golden calf and dancing. In one of the most famous scenes in the Old Testament, Moses throws the Ten Commandments to the ground, burns the calf, and makes the Hebrews drink the ashes in water. Aaron blames the people, rationalizing his actions, "Hey, you know these people— they're just naturally evil. They made me do it." Moses inexplicably buys Aaron's lame excuses.

One of many horrific scenes of the life of Moses follows. Moses stands at the gate of the camp and shouts: "Who is on the LORD's side? Come to me!" (32:26). All of the sons of Levi immediately join them and Moses says,

THIS NEXT SONG GOES OUT TO ANYONE WHO'S EVER BEEN A SLAVE IN EGYPT, OR WORSHIPPED A GOLDEN CALF, TO ANYONE WHO'S EVER WANDERED THE DESERT FOR YEARS ON END...

© 2002 ROGER JUDD

Thus says the LORD, the God of Israel, "Put your sword on your side, each of you! Go back and forth from gate to gate throughout the camp, and each of you kill your brother, your friend, and your neighbor." (Exodus 32:27)

When they're done, about three thousand people are dead. Moses then says, "Today you have ordained yourselves for the service of the LORD, each one at the cost of a son or a brother, and so have brought a blessing on yourselves this day" (32:29).

By now, Moses surely must be thinking, *"These people are not ready for freedom. They were born slaves; they'll die slaves. They can't handle this. To the hot and stinky place with the lot of them."* But instead, he returns to God's presence and pleads, "Alas, this people has sinned a great sin; they have made for themselves gods of gold. But now, if you will only forgive their sin—but if not, blot me out of the book that you have written" (32:31-32).

Still somewhat miffed, God spares the Israelites, sends a plague on

If we believe the Bible is true, does this sequence—and many more like it still to come—mean we worship a bloodthirsty God? Are we like those who believe God or Allah or Krishna or whoever calls us to kill non-believers even if they're members of our own families? A couple things to consider here: The writers of these books are probably working either during or after the Exile, following the destruction of Judah and a long period of exile as slaves under a foreign idolatrous power, either Babylon or Persia. All they have left is their faith and heritage. We're not living in captivity or slavery today, so what does this have to do with us? We have trouble rationalizing wholesale slaughter.

At the same time, while we may not feel a slaver's whip on our backs, we do live in a consumer-obsessed, bottom-line culture, one preoccupied with national security, sex, physical beauty, and any number of other ephemeral trends. This story might be a good time to ask, "What do we have to contend with; what do we have to exorcize in our lives in order to live as true followers of the Risen Christ?" When you think of it that way, the death here is death to self, not death to infidels. Perhaps we should read bloody stories like these as cautionary tales for our own lives. What are your idols? What needs to *die* in your life before you can truly be more like Jesus?

Reluctant Prophets and Clueless Disciples

them, and then tells them the harshest words of all—"You'll never live to see the Land of Milk and Honey, only your children will." God even calls them a "stiff-necked people" (33:5).

Exodus 33:6—40:38

Demoralized, the ragged band moves deeper into the desert, while Moses returns to the mountain for the last time, where God gives him a second copy of the Ten Commandments, with slight variations from the first batch.

This time, however, when Moses returns, he is physically changed, his face glows (a bad translation once rendered that as an indication that Moses had "horns," thus the famous statue of Michelangelo) and for the rest of his life, he always wears a veil or mask over his face, unless he is talking to God (see 34:29-35). Moses oversees the building of the tabernacle (with Aaron, who has apparently gotten off scot free for the whole golden calf episode). The glory of the LORD enters the Tabernacle and it leads the people deeper into the desert where—and they don't know it yet—they'll spend the next forty years.

Leviticus

Our story is interrupted here by the book of Leviticus, which consists mostly of highly detailed rules for Hebrew life. It's a manual for the priests and forms the center of the Torah. Moses pops up only three times in Leviticus and none of the stories move the narrative forward.

Numbers 10

The book of Numbers picks up fourteen months after the exodus from Egypt and begins with a long census. The Moses story at last resumes at the end of chapter 10 with the breaking of camp and the Israelites again following the cloud by day and the fiery pillar by night.

So you wanna go back to Egypt, where it's warm and secure
Are you sorry you bought the one-way ticket when you thought you were so sure?

You wanted to live in the Land of Promise, but now it's getting so hard
Are you sorry you're out here in the desert, instead of your own backyard?
Eating leeks and onions by the Nile
Ooo, what breath—but dining out in style!
Ooo, my life's on the skids
Give me the pyramids!
("So You Wanna Go Back to Egypt," lyrics by Keith Green. © Birdwing Music/BMG Songs. All Rights Reserved. Used by permission.)

Numbers 11

Chapter 11 begins with complaining and that complaining continues through chapter 25—pretty much non-stop.

"I still say we should have worked within the system!

The *rabble* is sick of manna and fondly remembers the fish, cucumbers, melons, leeks, onions, and garlic of Egypt. Finally, Moses blows up and complains to God too—about his burden of leadership: "I am not able to carry all this people alone, for they are too heavy for me. If this is the way you are going to treat me, put me to death at once—if I have found favor in your sight—and do not let me see my misery" (11:14-15).

God hears Moses and gives the people meat—quail, *lots* of quail—so much quail, the Bible says, that you'll eat it "until it comes out of your nostrils and becomes loathsome to you" (11:20). The LORD allows Moses

84

to appoint seventy elders to help him rule—and even puts some of his spirit on them. Just for good measure, God hits the Hebrews with another plague for their whining.

Numbers 13—14

Chapter 13 offers yet another famous story in the history of the Hebrew nation. As they finally near Canaan (the long-promised Land of Milk and Honey), Moses sends twelve spies into Canaan to scope out the territory and the inhabitants. Among those they encounter are the *very* tall Anakites. Remember the Nephilim from Genesis? This is them. (Later on, David will kill an Anakite from the town of Gath, Goliath. Perhaps you've heard of him.) Shaken, ten of the spies urge the Hebrews to pull out. Eating quail is one thing; nobody said anything about fighting giants! Only Joshua and Caleb urge the people to take control as God has promised they can. Once the people hear these reports, they—you guessed it—complain: "Woe is us! It's better to be back safe as slaves in Egypt eating leeks than to die here!" They even begin the process of electing a captain to take them back.

God—and who can blame him?—is furious and, once again, is about to destroy them when Moses, once again, begs for mercy. Moses shrewdly plays the *Egypt card*, saying, "Hey, the Egyptians will laugh at you if you kill the Hebrews after saving them oodles of times." We know Moses isn't a coward because then he even quotes Scripture to God:

> And now, therefore, let the power of the Lord be great in the way you promised when you spoke, saying,
> > "The Lord is slow to anger
> > And abounding in steadfast love,
> > forgiving iniquity and transgression,
> > but by no means clearing the guilty,
> > visiting the iniquity of the parents,
> > upon the children
> > to the third and fourth generation."
> Forgive the iniquity of this people according to the greatness of your steadfast love, just as you have pardoned this people, from Egypt even until now. (Numbers 14:17-19)

Somewhat mollified, God agrees, but again decrees that *none* of the people who have seen his glory and miracles will see Canaan, except for Caleb and Joshua. Instead, they'll wander in the wilderness until that

85

generation dies—about thirty-nine more years. Disappointed and a little peeved, the Israelites attempt to take it out on the Amalekites and Canaanites. But they do so without the Ark of the Covenant leading them and are easily defeated.

Numbers 20

More complaining, more miracles follow—the budding of Aaron's staff, the death of Miriam in chapter 20, and still more grumbling by the Israelites that, once again, they don't have water or figs or pomegranates. I'm reminded here of Stanley Hauerwas's prayer: "Zealous God, we confess, like your people Israel, that we tire of being 'the chosen.' Could you not just leave us alone every once in a while?" (*Prayers Plainly Spoken* [Downers Grove, IL: InterVarsity Press, 1999], 44).

In response, Moses is told to "command" (20:8) the rocks to produce water. He assembles the people and asks this odd question, "Listen, you rebels, shall we bring water for you out of this rock?" (20:10). He then strikes the rock twice and water gushes out, enough for the people and their livestock.

But this is *not* just another miracle. Something has gone terribly, terribly wrong. God told Moses to "command" the rock, *not* strike it. This little incident infuriates the LORD, who thunders at Aaron and Moses, "Because you did not trust in me, to show my holiness before the eyes of the Israelites, therefore you shall not bring this assembly into the land that I have given them" (20:12)! That's it. After all of this—and there's more to come—Moses will not see Canaan. *Ever*.

Did I miss something here? So Moses tapped the rock—big deal? And *Teflon* Aaron, who has weaseled out of repeated punishments in the past, does nothing this time but even he's splashed with Moses's backwash—finally! What gives? Moses has either said or done something wrong. What's up? Moses's vague rhetorical question prior to the miracle can be read various ways:

- Is he claiming that *we* (that is, Moses and Aaron) *and not God* will be responsible for making the water flow?
- Is he publicly, after all of this time, *doubting* the LORD's ability to perform yet another miracle? Asking something like, "Do you think we (including God now) are *really* able to bring water from this rock?"— implying the obvious NO answer?

86

- Perhaps the sin isn't in the question, but *how* he bashes the rock. Perhaps Moses has come to rely on the supernatural powers of his staff. As in: "Sure, God can command the water to flow, but he still needs a little help from my trusty magical wand here."
- It could be that, while Moses thinks he is venting his frustration at his people when he strikes the rock, it's really God he is lashing out at. A merciful God is giving these obnoxious people water and Moses's behavior is perilously close to blasphemy.

Who knows? Whatever the reason, Moses's response to God's punishment, if any, is not recorded. But the Waters of Meribah must have been the bitterest pill of all for Moses. The chapter ends with the death of Aaron, Moses's closest friend and last remaining ally from Egypt.

Numbers 25

More compelling, disconcerting stories follow—more complaining followed by a plague of poisonous snakes that are only stopped by Moses's bronze serpent, various and sundry small wars with small kings, and the wonderful oracles of Balaam's donkey—all of which deserve more space and attention than we can give them here.

By chapter 25, it's obvious that Moses is emotionally, spiritually, and physically exhausted. He appears unable, in Shittim in Moah, to stop the men from mingling with the Moabite women and worshiping Baal. Irate, God tells Moses to kill all the men. Just then, a well-known Israelite businessman brings a Midianite woman into his tent, in full view of everybody. An eager young priest named Phinehas kills them both simultaneously with a single spear. God is so pleased that he grants Phinehas's people perpetual priesthood. Phinehas's action stops another one of God's plagues against the Israelites, but not before 24,000 more people are dead.

Once again, what are we to make of this? Remember, Moses married a Midianite woman back in Exodus 2 without being condemned. (And in a few years, we'll have the story of Ruth, the Moabite woman, ancestor of Jesus.) The meaning of this apparently heartless butchery is lost in the mists of time, something we may not know until we sit at the feet of the Author of the Great Story.

Numbers 27

One of the most heart-rending scenes in the Old Testament follows in chapter 27. God tells Moses to climb a certain mountain in the Abarim range and see the land that God will give to the Israelites—the same complaining Israelites that you, Moses, have led for forty years: out of Egypt, through the desert, fighting every step of the way—but not to you. You, by the way, will die soon and join Aaron because you hammered the rock at Meribah. Moses doesn't argue or complain; instead he thinks first of his people. "Let the LORD, the God of the spirits of all flesh, appoint someone over the congregation who shall go out before them and come in before them, who shall lead them out and bring them in, so that the congregation of the LORD may not be like sheep without a shepherd" (27:16-17). God picks Joshua, then gives Moses a whole bunch more rules and regulations his people are to follow.

There's no peace for Moses in his final years. The Israelites war with the Midianites again, whom they defeat handily. But when the soldiers return with the women—some of the same women who back in chapter 25 seduced the Israelite men and led them into Baal worship—Moses goes postal. He tells them not only to kill all of the remaining Midianite boys but to kill all of the women, except of course the virgins. By the way, among those killed is the Prophet-for-Hire Balaam, who apparently incited the Midianite women in the first place. This is yet another troubling chapter in our understanding of both God's will and the character of Moses.

The remaining chapters of Numbers include preparations for the conquest and additional laws and rules.

Deuteronomy 31-34

Which brings us to the poignant close of the Moses cycle in Deuteronomy. The forty years have passed. The epilogue contains the arrangements for Israel after Moses's death. It includes two poems: the Song of Moses (32:1-43) and the Blessing of Moses (33:2-29). After writing down everything that has happened since Egypt—including every tiny rule and regulation—Moses gives his book to the Levites, with this wry little aside:

"Take this book of the law and put it beside the ark of the covenant of the LORD your God; let it remain there as a witness against you. For I know well how

Reluctant Prophets and Clueless Disciples

rebellious and stubborn you are. If you already have been so rebellious toward the Lord while I am still alive among you, how much more after my death! (Deuteronomy 31:26-27)

And Moses finishes with another admonition, delivered in his most curmudgeonly manner:

For I know that after my death you will surely act corruptly, turning aside from the way that I have commanded you. In time to come trouble will befall you, because you will do what is evil in the sight of the Lord, provoking him to anger through the work of your hands. (Deuteronomy 31:29)

The beautiful Song of Moses, apparently a survivor of an incredibly ancient oral tradition, follows this. It includes Deuteronomy 32:18, one of several texts that refer to Israel's God as mother. Afterwards, God reminds Moses, *yet again*, that because of his failure at the Waters of Meribah, he won't be going into Canaan but will die on Mount Nebo, repeating almost exactly the account given back in Numbers 27:12-14.

Moses's life ends with the Final Blessing in chapter 33, a prophecy of what will happen to each of the twelve tribes. In chapter 34, Moses climbs the appointed mountain, where he can see Canaan but never, ever touch the soil. What must the old man have been thinking? *"It's not fair! You use us and discard us when you're finished. And after all I've done . . . "* The little stream that separates him from Canaan might as well have been the Pacific Ocean. The Lord sneaks in one final reminder of his failure with the whole striking the rock thing before Moses dies at age 120 and is buried by God in an unmarked grave. The final verses are worth savoring:

Never since has there arisen a prophet in Israel like Moses, whom the Lord knew face to face. He was unequaled for all the signs and wonders that the Lord sent him to perform in the land of Egypt, against Pharaoh and all his servants and his entire land, and for all the mighty deeds and all the terrifying displays of power that Moses performed in the sight of all Israel. (Deuteronomy 34:10-12)

Moses's Legacy

Thousands of years later, what are we to make of the curious, contradictory life and times of Moses? On one level, he's a failure and a murderer to boot. On another, the Moses cycle is a group of fables celebrating

89

and worshiping a bloodthirsty god. And yet, until Jesus, no other biblical figure will have this unparalleled access to Yahweh—twice out-arguing the Almighty and changing God's mind.

Moreover, Moses is often credited with inventing Israelite monotheism. Someday maybe we'll know how much Pharaoh Akhenaten's radical Egyptian monotheism—worshiping the Sun without images—affected Moses, if at all. It's probably not coincidence that two aniconic monotheisms emerged out of Egypt at about the same time.

Between the LORD and his people stands Moses, called The Lawgiver. He's much more than that. He's the liberator. He's neither wholly Hebrew nor wholly Egyptian, forever set apart from *both* peoples. The stranger, who marries still another alien, is forever a stranger in a strange land.

There are eerie parallels between the lives of Moses and Jesus. It has been pointed out that they were both eternal outsiders, refugees in Egypt, persecuted, and scorned. Both led bands of followers who generally didn't get what they were talking about. Both had intimate relationships with God. Neither ever had a place to call home.

But the story of Moses, taken as a whole, is something to celebrate, as Raymond Bailey once reminded his congregation in a sermon. If God could use bumbling, stuttering, mercurial Moses for God's glory, then God can certainly use you and me. Each and every day, we stand staring at the future from our own Mount Nebo, the opportunities limitless. Will God be able to use us half as well?

Nine

JUDGES
➡ (JUDGES 1–21)

The book of the Judges is a strange and sometimes fantastic interlude between the relatively straightforward stories of Moses and Joshua and the later stories of the rise of the monarchy under Saul, David, and Solomon. It incorporates ancient narratives of compelling (or at least plausible) historical accuracy next to wild and wonderful stories of super-men with superhuman hair! There are numerous internal inconsistencies chock-a-block with detailed accounts of specific battles in specific locations, led by intriguing, fully drawn heroes.

There is a significance difference in tone between the positive, can-do optimism of the book of Joshua and the much more melancholy book of Judges. Despite his many great victories, it turns out that Joshua actually couldn't quite subdue all—or even most—of the bad guys in the Promised Land. The Philistines, crowding eastward from the Mediterranean, and the lowland Midianites stubbornly resist all efforts by the various Hebrew tribes to dislodge them—in part because they're better equipped (with their fearsome chariots) and better organized. Consequently, the twelve tribes are relegated to the rugged hills and mountains that form the spine of modern-day Israel. For much of Judges, the Israelites are either suffering in bondage to the Philistines or facing overwhelming Midianite forces in the homeland.

In fact, this is one of the most depressing, disturbing books in the Bible. Slaughters, murders, and maiming mark the pages. The land is in chaos; the once-cohesive twelve tribes are just as likely to turn on each other as on the bad guys. The book ends with a near-genocide of the tribe of Benjamin by the rest of Israel. Chapters 17–21 even imply that the LORD has completely abandoned Israel. Why? The editors of these various stories, some incredibly ancient, repeatedly cite two reasons:

1. The people keep abandoning the LORD for the local deities.
2. As the refrain repeats throughout the book, "In those days, there was no king in Israel; all the people did what was right in their own eyes."

In short, this is a horrible time to be alive. Jewish tradition calls the stories in this book the "texts of terror." The Judges of the book's title are, in the end, total failures. It's no wonder that the Israelites will eventually cry for a king.

After the passing of Joshua in chapter 1—or maybe not, since he reappears briefly in a separate story in chapter 2—there is bloody anarchy in the land. Without the strong leadership of the Moses/Joshua team, the once-cohesive twelve tribes quickly degenerate into squabbling petty chiefdoms, disputing pastures and cities among themselves. The authors of Judges place these failures on the heads of the people, for continuing to lust after the Canaanite gods—especially the fertility god Baal—and for repeatedly abandoning Yahweh.

Thus begins a long decline where the tribes regularly leave Yahweh to follow Baal, are punished by Yahweh, cry for help, are forgiven, and then are delivered by Yahweh—over and over again. In response to their ongoing distress, Yahweh calls up and anoints various charismatic leaders to handle the various problems as they arise. Most are minor personages, barely worth a mention. A few receive more notice from the compilers of Judges, though the accounts are distressingly skimpy: Othniel, the left-handed warrior Ehud, and Jepthah, the son of a prostitute. Three of the judges, however, present rich (and sometimes infuriating!) story cycles for modern readers:

1. The remarkable woman judge and prophet Deborah
2. The brilliant military commander Gideon
3. The outrageous, almost mythic exploits of Samson.

I'll be post-feminist in the post-patriarchy

DEBORAH

Deborah (Judges 4–5)

Deborah (which means "honeybee" in old Hebrew) appears from nowhere, touched and anointed by God to serve as both prophet (the only person so dubbed in the book of Judges) and judge for the bickering tribes. She is immortalized by the narrative account from Judges 4 and the probably even older so-called Song of Deborah in chapter 5. She is nicknamed *The Fiery Woman*, perhaps for her temperament; and somewhere in the hill country of Ephraim, she sits and hears the thousand and one petty squabbles of these late Bronze-age peoples.

Judges 4:1-9

Deborah emerges at yet another time of great peril for the Israelites. They are mightily pressed by the more powerful Canaanites from the west, who are led by King Jabin and his general Sisera. At the heart of the Canaanite army is a fearsome contingent of nine hundred armored chariots and they have oppressed the Israelites for twenty years. In her wisdom, Deborah chooses a modest man named Barak to lead the defense—an army drawn mainly from the tribes of Zebulun and Naphtali. God advises Deborah to muster Barak's army on Mount Tabor. Deborah plans to draw the enemy to a pass between Taanach and the plain of Megiddo (which will figure prominently, not just in the New Testament book of Revelation, but into modern times as well!), which opens into the Jezreel Valley and where several small streams flow together to form *Wadi Kishon.* When Sisera and the Canaanites hear that the Israelites are on the move, they're thrilled. For years they've been trying to lure Israel into pitched battle on open ground where their chariots can have a devastating effect.

Barak is understandably nervous. This is suicide. Still, Deborah's got pretty good connections with the Big Guy Upstairs. "If you will go with me, I will go," he tells her, "but if you will not go with me, I will not go" (4:8).

Deborah the judge is touched but Deborah the prophet issues a prophecy: "I will surely go with you; nevertheless, the road on which you are going will not lead to your glory, for the LORD will sell Sisera into the hand of a woman" (4:9).

Notice that she doesn't specify *which* woman. Still, Barak happily agrees. He's one of those great guys to have on your team who's not worried about who gets the *props* as long as the job gets done!

Judges 4:10-16

On the plain below, the giant Canaanite army assembles, itching for slaughter. Above, on Mount Tabor, bolstered by Deborah's presence, the

93

men of Zebulun and Naphtali wait for Barak's command. Suddenly, the signal is given and thousands of Israelites—venting years and years of cruel persecution—come howling down the mountain. The Canaanite line holds, then wavers, and then breaks in fear and confusion. Amid the flood of panicked deserters, Sisera's chariots are less than useless. He bolts from his royal chariot and disappears into the melee. The Israelites now have the blood lust and mercilessly hack down their ancient foes.

Judges 4:17-24

Sisera stumbles, dazed and bloodied, into a nearby village of Kenites, who have remained neutral in the war so far. A woman named Jael takes Sisera into her house, gives him food and drink, and then sends him to bed. While Sisera sleeps, Jael sneaks into the bedroom and pounds a sharp tent peg into his temple, killing him instantly. Without Sisera, King Jabin is bewildered and indecisive. Barak and Deborah seize the advantage and take the battle to Jabin's palace, where they win a decisive victory. This campaign is particularly notable as the first recorded victory by the Israelites over the occupants of the plains.

Judges 5

True to Deborah's prophecy, "The Song of Deborah" (which, with its use of particularly archaic language, may be one of the oldest texts in the entire Old Testament) celebrates Israel's deliverance, not by the deeds of General Barak, but by the work of the Kenite woman Jael. Chapter 5 is a wild and evocative epic poem, full of thunder and fury and dark hints of non-Israelite gods and demons. It also adds one additional clue as to why the generally invincible Canaanite army bolted. It says (or implies) in verses 20-21 that an unexpected downpour aided the Israelites by cloaking their movement down the mountain, even as the flood-swollen Kishon River drowned the Canaanites and cut off their retreat.

Deborah's fate is not mentioned, but chapter 5 ends with a comforting note: because of the leadership of Deborah and Barak, Israel enjoys at least a generation of peace. Judges 5:7 gives her the ultimate title, "mother of Israel," so she was obviously greatly esteemed by her entire nation. But that's the last we hear of her.

It would be nice to know more about Deborah. While Jewish law actually forbade women from becoming kings or priests, there were few specific

Reluctant Prophets and Clueless Disciples

injunctions against women entering other professions or positions. Women generally didn't live as long as men in those days and most of their lives were spent caring for children. All of this makes Deborah's sudden ascendancy—and equally sudden disappearance—all the more interesting.

Gideon (Judges 6—8)

Gideon receives a little more editorial space than Deborah and emerges as a more complex figure. The text hints that he wasn't always a follower of Yahweh (he's sometimes referred to as *Jerubbaal* and his father, at least, was definitely a follower of Baal). Despite being well known for his great victory over the Midianite invaders, he makes a near-fatal mistake near the end of his life. Some scholars believe the Gideon cycle is an uneasy marriage between two often-conflicting traditions (which accounts for our hero's two names), and from a strictly storytelling standpoint, his narrative doesn't really work with the military campaign outlined in chapter 7.

Still, it's a rip-snorting tale, with as much action and adventure as a story of Robert E. Howard's Conan the Barbarian. And Gideon himself is a complex enough figure to warrant further investigation.

Judges 6:1—10

At some point after the passing of Deborah, the bad guys have once again gained the upper hand as the twelve tribes have, once again, fallen away from Yahweh. For seven years, Midianite raiders from the east have plundered their villages and stolen their crops and animals, forcing the Israelites to cower in the badlands and mountains. The storyteller compares the Midianites to an invasion of countless locusts, stripping the land bare in their wake, carrying off their booty on camels. Once again, the Israelites cry to the LORD for help. God sends an unnamed prophet to convict them of their idolatry.

Judges 6:11—27

When the time is right, God sends an angel to a man named Gideon (whose name, curiously, means "hewer" or "hacker" in old Hebrew) who

95

is covertly threshing his wheat in a wine press to hide it from marauding Midianites. He is a member of the clan or tribe of Manasseh and is—apparently—a pretty good debater:

When the angel says, "God is with you," Gideon replies, "Um, no disrespect here sir, but if that's the case—why am I sweating it out in the wine press while Midianite reivers have the run of the land?"

The angel nods. "Good point. But God has chosen *you* to deliver his people from them."

Like Moses, Gideon is reluctant to commit. He's not eager to lead *anybody* into battle against an army whose numbers have been likened to a swarm of ravenous locusts. "Maybe you've got the wrong guy, buddy," he says carefully (you can't be too sure with angels). "I'm from the weakest clan in Manasseh—and Manasseh is not in the same league as the big boys, like Ephraim, to begin with. You probably meant to tap somebody else."

The angel sighs. He/she/it has heard this line of argument before. "Oh, do be quiet Gideon. The LORD will be with you. Isn't that enough?"

It isn't. Gideon asks the angel to prove that he/she/it really *is* from God. (Can't be too hasty when you're about to battle a zillion Midianites.) By way of a test, Gideon whips up a batch of chicken and dumplings. The angel zaps them with fire then disappears from sight.

"Uh oh," Gideon thinks, *"that really was an angel of God and I have royally ticked the LORD off. I'm in big trouble now and I didn't even get to eat any of the chicken and dumplings."*

But the LORD forgives Gideon and tells him to tear down his father Joash's altar to Baal and to build another one to Yahweh next door. Gideon sneaks off that night and does the deed.

Judges 6:28-40

The altar was apparently a real tourist attraction in Ophrah because when the Ophrahites awaken the next morning and find it in ruins, the Chamber of Commerce is incensed. They do a little sleuthing and discover that Gideon is the culprit and—with torches in hand—quickly form an angry lynch mob. They march to Joash's tent with a noose, calling for Gideon's neck. But Joash confronts them, standing with his arms folded, on the edge of town.

"Whattsamatter, boys?" Joash sneers. "Did poor old Baal get his widdle feelers hurt? Tell you what—let's let Baal *hisownself* settle this. If he's a

Reluctant Prophets and Clueless Disciples

real god, like you say, he'll settle Gideon's hash. If not, you'll have to go through me first."

Did I mention that Joash has a big scimitar hanging from his silk belt? The mob cools down.

"Joash is right," one guy says. "See, there's Gideon walking around big as life and Baal hasn't fried him yet."

"OK, you win, Joash," another says. "I guess we'll have to start calling Gideon *Jerubbaal* now—'He who contends with Baal'—since he's apparently bigger than Baal."

Relieved and now emboldened, Gideon emerges from his father's tent, blows his trumpet, and sends messengers to the neighboring tribes: "It's time to kick some Midianite rear!"

It's getting close to harvest again, so the Midianites and their buds the Amalekites decide it's time to do a little grocery shoplifting in Israel. They mass their army, cross the Jordan, and camp in the Valley of Jezreel.

Gideon looks at his puny army and is once again assailed by doubts. He prays again to the LORD. "Um, forgive me here, but I really, really, *really* need to be sure what looks, for all intents and purposes, like a suicide attack is absolutely necessary," he says. "How about if I lay some fleece outside my tent tonight? If there is dew on the fleece but none on the surrounding ground, then I'll know this was your idea and not something brought on by all the garlic in that lamb stew I had for supper."

The next morning the fleece is sopping wet; the nearby land is dry as a bone.

"Um, forgive me here again, LORD, but can we make this best two out of three?" Gideon begs. "How about if I put the fleece out again? Tomorrow morning, if it is dry and the yard is wet, then I will absolutely, positively, unequivocally know that this hare-brained idea . . . um, I mean . . . *brilliant plan* is from you."

The next morning, after a sleepless night (you can hear the thousands of Midianites snoring from Dan to Beersheba), Gideon pops his head out of the tent. Yup. The fleece is dry but his yard is damp.

"Hoo boy," Gideon says to no one in particular. "I believe!"

Judges 7:1–8:21

Gideon/Jerubbaal leads his rag-tag little army to a hill overlooking the valley. Below them, as far as the eye can see, are the colorful tents of the Midianites. But God isn't satisfied and tells Gideon to trim down his army so that no one thinks that defeating the Midianites is *their* doing instead of *God's* doing. Gideon gulps loudly, turns to his men, and—like William Travis at the Alamo facing an overwhelming Mexican army—draws a figurative line in the sand. "OK boys, you see the odds here. Anybody who is having second thoughts about this little excursion, now's the time to opt out." About 22,000 soldiers from Gideon's original army of 32,000 skedaddle for home, thrilled and delighted at their luck.

God still isn't satisfied. "Still too many soldiers, Gideon. Take your remaining forces down to the Spring of Harod for water. Those who throw themselves on their bellies and lap their water up like dogs—they're your keepers. Those who kneel, and cup the water to their mouths are outta here."

Gideon obeys. At the Spring of Harod, only 300 of his soldiers do the "dog-lap" thing! But God is finally satisfied.

"Good. Now take the clay pots and trumpets from the 9,700, send 'em home, and give the pots and trumpets to the guys who are left behind."

By now, Gideon is totally freaked out. *This is madness!* But God allows him to overhear a dream told by one Midianite to another Midianite. This assures Gideon of an Israelite victory, which bolsters his confidence once again.

That night, Gideon hands out the empty clay pots, trumpets, and torches to his remaining men and divides them into companies of 100 each. He

98

sends each company to a different side of the Midianite camp. He instructs them, at the appointed time, to break their pots, blow their trumpets, and shout, "A sword for the LORD and for Gideon!" (7:20).

The Midianites never have a chance. Panicked, sleepy, confused, and blinded in the dark, they blunder into each other and flail away at real and imaginary enemies. In the days before radio transmitters, an extremely dangerous commando raid at night turns into a bloody rout. Gideon sends messengers to the tribes of Naphtali, Asher, and Manasseh to join in the fray. When the retreating Midianites surge toward Ephraim, Gideon sends messengers to the Ephraimites to join in the slaughter too.

But poor Gideon can't even enjoy the LORD's victory. The next morning, members of the powerful tribe of Ephraim are complaining that they weren't invited to the original battle. Gideon expertly extracts himself by bad-mouthing his own accomplishments. Exhausted (hacking and hewing is hard work—try it some time), his original army then pursues the remnants of the Midianite army, led by Zebah and Zalmunna, back across the Jordan. But Gideon's request for aid at the towns of Succoth and Penuel is rebuffed. The people are still afraid of the Midianites and require proof of Gideon's victory—the mutilated hands of Zebah and Zalmunna. Gideon darkly vows revenge on both towns upon his return.

Gideon at last catches the Midianites and once again—despite being outnumbered by nearly 15,000 men—launches a successful sneak attack and destroys the Midianite army, capturing Zebah and Zalmunna in the process. When the two Midianite leaders confess to having killed Gideon's brothers during the initial battle, he kills them as well. And, just for good measure, he goes back and levels Succoth and Penuel.

Judges 8:22-35

For the moment, Gideon is the toast of Israel. The people clamor for him to become their king—and have his children and grandchildren succeed him. Gideon wisely declines their offer of a dynasty, saying, "I will not rule over you, and my son will not rule over you; the LORD will rule over you" (8:23).

But something has changed in Gideon in the past few days. The modest young man in the wine press is somehow different. Perhaps he is flushed with his own power and glory. Maybe he believes his own press releases. Or it could be that he's somehow deceived. Regardless of his motives, he makes a curious demand of his people—"Give me a portion of the spoils of war and I will create an *ephod* to commemorate this historic day." The exact meaning of the word "ephod" is unclear—it may be something that is folded into a dress or robe or it could be a breastplate of some kind. But from the donations of Midianite booty, Gideon crafts a giant golden *something* and the entire nation happily worships it. Gideon's rash decision will have disastrous consequences.

Still, under his able leadership, the Israelites enjoy a rare generation of peace. Gideon stays busy at home with his many wives and concubines—he has, after all, seventy sons, including his favorite, Abimelech (translated, "My father is king"—an odd name for the son of a man who has staunchly *refused* the kingship). Gideon finally dies and is buried back at Ophrah. Alas, his legacy does not include Yahweh worship and the land soon lapses back into idolatry. As for daddy's boy Abimelech, he's an opportunist and murderous bully—an extremely bad combination, even back then.

Gideon's Legacy

As with many of the stories in the Old Testament, the question arises: What are we to make of Gideon? It appears that his story serves mostly as a powerful cautionary tale against the establishment of royal dynasties, at least until the time of King David. And yet, the Israelites, with only a couple of exceptions, had disastrous experiences with most of the judges. As long as Gideon follows the LORD, all is well. When he takes it upon himself to make the *ephod*, the end result is death for all but one of his sons and the senseless loss of life of thousands of Israelites. There may be a missing link between the *ephod* and the short and nasty reign of Abimelech, but that connection can only be inferred.

As for Gideon himself, like many of us, his legacy is somewhere between success and failure, with plenty of both along the way as we journey toward our final reward. For modern readers, here is a question the Bible asks time and time again—what is *your ephod*? What are you worshiping instead of God? Money? Vanity? Success? Popularity? Grades? If there's something in your life that you knowingly or unconsciously have made a higher priority than your relationship with Jesus Christ, it's never too late to reprioritize. It's never too late to let it go.

Samson (Judges 13–16)

Finally, we come to the story of Samson, he of the mighty sinews, flowing locks, and exceedingly dim bulb. Judges 13–16 tells a fantastic tale of a gentle giant whose greatest weakness is a pretty face. You've probably known someone a lot like Samson in your life. What exactly these campfire tales have to do with Israel, it's hard to tell. But Samson appears at a time when the Philistines—actually the Sea Peoples, a loose confederation of peoples displaced elsewhere in the Mediterranean who relocate along Israel's western coast—have conquered all of the twelve tribes. And Samson is the last major judge until Samuel, so his often outrageous yarn is worth examining.

Judges 13:1-19

Samson is given a miraculous birth narrative, much like those of other biblical heroes in both the Old and New Testaments. An angel appears to an unnamed woman in the land of the tribe of Dan. The angel tells the previously barren woman she's going to have a son; and that he's to be dedicated to the Nazirite sect, a group that eschews alcohol, unclean foods, and barbershops. When she tells her husband Manoah the good news, he requests a repeat visit by the angel, just to be sure. But even amid this fanciful story, there is a dark hint of what's ahead. The writer notes, "It is he who shall *begin* to deliver Israel from the hand of the Philistines" (13:5, italics added). Samson only initiates the long, harrowing process that will not end until King David's armies torch the remaining Philistine strongholds many years later.

Judges 14:1-20

Samson grows up big and strong and a little spoiled. One day he sees a beautiful Philistine woman and tells his mom and dad that he wants her for a wife, even though she doesn't believe in the LORD. Manoah is disappointed in Samson's decision but arranges the marriage. What follows is one of the more bizarre stories in an often-bizarre book. Samson is attacked by a lion, which he casually kills and tosses aside. After wooing the Philistine woman, he returns to find the lion's carcass filled with honeybees. Samson scoops out a glob of honey and continues on his way home. Just to make the wedding ceremony more interesting, he proposes a riddle to the invited Philistine guests—with big prizes to the one who can guess the answer:

> Out of the eater came something to eat.
> Out of the strong came something sweet. (14:14)

While that isn't exactly great poetry, it is probably better than the limerick he might have used:

> This is the story of Samson the man
> Who once killed a big lion in Dan
> As quick as you please
> It was filled with some bees
> So Samson scarfed up some honey by hand.

When the wedding guests can't guess the riddle, Samson's blushing new bride turns on the tears. She begs and wheedles, pouts and threatens, nags and sweet-talks for seven days. Finally, Samson gives in and tells her . . . and she promptly tells the still-befuddled guests, who tell him:

Reluctant Prophets and Clueless Disciples

What is sweeter than honey?
What is stronger than a lion?
Neener, neener, neener. (14:18—Okay, okay. The last line isn't really in the Bible)

Samson goes ballistic:

If you had not plowed with my heifer,
you would not have found out my riddle! (also part of 14:18, really!)

He rushes into the Philistine city of Ashkelon, kills thirty Philistines, and robs them to pay his debt. The bride's father, obviously worried about a guy who'll kill thirty people on a bet, gives his wife to the guy who had been Samson's best man at his wedding. Now *there's* a loyal wingman for you!

And the point is . . . well, I don't know what the point is, except that some of the oppressive Philistines get terminated.

Judges 15:1-8

When we next see Samson, he has cooled down. He stalks back into Philistine country and demands to see his wife. But her father explains that, from their perspective, there has been a legal divorce. "Say, why not take her younger sister, Samson? She's prettier anyway."

But Samson will have none of it. He scours the countryside and catches three hundred foxes, sets fire to their tails, and watches in satisfaction as they destroy the Philistine crops. (Obviously, this passage was written before the advent of PETA—People for the Ethical Treatment of Animals. However, a sister organization, PETA—People for the Eating of Tasty Animals—already had active chapters throughout the ancient Middle East.) Now it's the Philistines' turn to be outraged. When they discover who the arsonist is, they go and kill, not just Samson's wife and hapless best man; they torch her father's place too! Samson—who has conveniently forgotten how this whole debacle actually got started—vows vengeance on the killers and promptly slays them all. He then heads for the hills.

Judges 15:9-20

Things are now getting out of hand at a rapid clip. Screaming for blood, the Philistines muster and attack the Judean village of Lehi

103

(which, curiously, means "jawbone"). When the reeling Judahites ask why, the Philistines blame the carnage on Samson. The men of Judah wisely seek out Samson and take him, bound and gagged, to the Philistines. Who needs this grief? But Samson breaks free and, grabbing the first jawbone of an ass he sees lying around, slays a thousand Philistines or so (a better translation is "a military unit" of uncertain size). Samson's exploit is immortalized in an ancient scrap of poetry inserted at this point by the compilers of the book of Judges:

> With the jawbone of a donkey,
>   heaps upon heaps,
> with the jawbone of a donkey
>   I have slain a thousand men. (Judges 15:16)

For good measure, since slaying and slaughter are such thirsty work, the LORD splits a rock and a stream gushes forth. Satisfied, the account says that Samson returned home and became a judge over Israel for the next twenty years.

Judges 16:1–31

Sunday school teachers generally don't spend much time on Samson's next escapade—a rendezvous with a Lady of the Evening in the town of Gaza. Once again a shapely leg snares him and once again his fabled strength gets him out of hot water.

But Samson's most famous exploit is the whole business with the luscious Delilah (which may mean, in old Arabic dialects, "to flirt"), still another tempting Philistine woman. This time, Delilah tries to coax not the answer to a riddle but the source of his incredible strength out of our love-struck hero. Samson fools her a couple of times but on the third try—after some serious pouting and nagging—he relents. The secret is in his uncut hair. Delilah spills the beans to the "lords of the Philistines," who pay her handsomely for the information. Shortly thereafter, the Philistines shear the "seven locks of his head" (16:19), bind him, blind him, and force him to push a grinding mill like an animal.

Day after day, Samson pushes the stone wheel, listening to the taunts of the Philistines, suffering from the overseer's lash, and—most importantly—growing out his hair. Finally, when the lords of the Philistines hold a festival day for their god Dagon, they call for Samson, their great enemy, to entertain them. Hour after hour, they torment him, like a great,

104

chained bear, until Samson edges his way to the pillars of the temple. At that moment, Samson whispers a prayer: "Lord GOD, remember me and strengthen me only this once, O God, so that with this one act of revenge I may pay back the Philistines for my two eyes . . . Let me die with the Philistines" (16:28, 30). Even in his last moments, Samson can't get it right. He doesn't pray for the deliverance of Israel or to prove that Yahweh is more powerful than Dagon—instead he prays for selfish reasons. Still, God agrees and Samson's strength floods back. He topples the pillars, killing everyone inside.

Samson's Legacy

With that great cinematic ending, it's an endlessly fascinating yarn. Hollywood has made several bad movies about Samson and Delilah. Now that special effects have come so far, it could be time for a remake, starring Dolph Lundgren, the Rock, or even Howie Long as the big, lovable—if terribly naïve—lug. (Unless you wanted to go for a comedy, in which case you'd cast Danny DeVito or Jack Black.)

Um . . . so what exactly *are* we to make of Samson? He's not a military leader. He acts alone, usually out of spite. You probably wouldn't want to take serious issues of the law to Judge Samson either—he was apparently more interested in wine, women, and song. He does kill a lot of Philistines. In fact, the account says that the temple toppling killed more Philistines than he'd killed in the rest of his life combined. But it was that business with his first wife that brought the wrath of the Philistines down on Judah—an innocent bystander in the whole lion-honey-riddle incident—in the first place. In some ways, he resembles the archetypal *trickster* figure of antiquity, a practical joker with tremendous strength, more than your standard, courageous Old Testament deliverer.

Ultimately, Samson's life exemplifies the struggles of the Israelites ever since they crossed the Red Sea—rebellion against God, repentance, and finally, redemption.

If that's the case, perhaps Samson is here as an example of what *not* to do. You certainly wouldn't want the governor of your state, for example, to be a muscle-bound action hero with good hair and a fatal attraction for the ladies . . . *uh, would you?*

Perhaps Samson is here because, at a time when the Israelites were enslaved to the Philistines, telling about the exploits of Samson around the campfire gave them hope. He was a larger than life hero, a Paul

Bunyan or Johnny Appleseed or John Henry. Like underdogs and captive peoples everywhere, the Israelites told and re-told the stories of Samson in the darkest days of their oppression. And with each retelling, perhaps his heroic deeds got just a little bit more heroic.

Or perhaps even here, though Yahweh is rarely mentioned, the listeners of long ago heard the subtext—that even in dark and dangerous times, God is *still* secretly working in our lives, even through fatally flawed characters like Samson. And more, that Samson's apparently lone heart-felt prayer, no matter how self-centered, is answered in his time of greatest need.

And the Rest of the Story

The final chapters of the book of Judges are perhaps the most unsettling in the entire Bible. Horrible things happen to innocent people. The land has degenerated into unfettered savagery. It's as if the LORD has turned away from Israel and the entire country has descended into barbarism. There are short snippets of stories here, though none to match the longer story cycles of Deborah, Gideon, and Samson. But these final tales are particularly repugnant to modern readers. It's as if the compilers of Judges were trying to make a convincing argument for a royal family by including the most bloodthirsty yarns and historical anecdotes they could find. Are these, too, cautionary tales? Or are they the ancient equivalent of horror stories, ghoulish tales best told around a campfire at night? The book of Judges is an uncomfortable link between the straightforwardly positive travels and conquests of Moses and Joshua, and the tales of the monarchy to come.

Whatever the reason, the apparently more familiar tales of Samuel, Saul, David, and Solomon that follow are a welcome relief from the nightmarish landscape of the final chapters of Judges.

May you live in interesting times.
(old proverb)

Reluctant Prophets and Clueless Disciples

Ten

KING SAUL

→ (1 SAMUEL)

Here is one of the great tragic heroes of the Bible, a Shakespearean figure, tormented and haunted by mistakes that—when compared to those of his successors—seem astonishingly minor. Saul never wanted the job or the power; he never benefited personally and was by all accounts a moral, highly religious man. He led his people bravely in war. He organized a loosely allied federation of twelve very suspicious tribes into the fledgling kingdom of Israel. He established the first royal bureaucracy and the first standing army. Saul protected and promoted a distinctively Hebrew identity for his people while surrounded by pagan nations and never once wavered in his faith in Yahweh. And despite the clearly biased account left by the historians of the king who deposed him, it is clear that Saul inspired love and devotion unto death.

Compared to some of his predecessors, we know quite a lot about Saul: "There was not a man among the people of Israel more handsome than he; he stood head and shoulders above everybody else" (9:2). The Bible generally does not comment on appearances, so he must have been pretty hot. He's self-effacing and humble (see 1 Samuel 9:21). And later we're told that Saul drafts Israel's first constitution, which means he was literate too—another rarity of the day. Finally, he is a Benjaminite—Israel's fiercest warriors (in Judges 19–20, Benjamin, the smallest tribe, takes on the other eleven tribes combined and nearly beats them!).

Then why is Saul a tragic figure with a tragic end? Like Macbeth or Hamlet, like Custer at the Little Big Horn or Davy Crockett at the Alamo? Like Moses, why does God punish him, even to his final hours? What—if anything—is his fatal flaw?

To find these answers, we need to read the story of Saul the Benjaminite, called "God's Mistake." One of the keys to Saul's story is, I believe, understanding the character of the judge and prophet Samuel. Like Sir Thomas More and King Henry VIII in the movie *A Man for All Seasons*, Saul's story is inextricably linked to Samuel.

1 Samuel 2–8

In 1 Samuel chapters 2–7, we see that, as *judge*, Samuel has served as the latest religious leader of a squabbling coalition of twelve proud tribes. In the tradition of the great judges, including Joshua and Deborah, Samuel provides both political leadership and a direct conduit to God.

It is Samuel, you may remember, who is raised in the temple under the old high priest Eli. And when Eli can't—or worse, won't—control his sons and heirs apparent, Hophni and Phineas, Samuel is tapped for the job. But in Samuel's old age, history repeats itself. The Israelites are increasingly turning to the gods of the Canaanites; the powerful Philistine alliance is again threatening and bullying the Israelites; and Samuel's own sons, Joel and Abijah, are as bad as Hophni and Phineas! Talk about *deja vu* all over again!

Still, Samuel obviously enjoys being judge, occasional military leader, prophet, and *de facto* king. But in recent years, the holy ark of the covenant had fallen into the hands of the infidels for the first time and, while it has since been rescued, the Hebrew people are at low ebb. In addition to the Philistines from the west, the Ammonites are pressing dangerously from the northeast. With Samuel apparently unable to right

Reluctant Prophets and Clueless Disciples

the seriously listing ship of state, the people finally reject his heavy-handed, apparently ineffectual leadership in favor of a *real* king at the beginning of chapter 8.

Samuel takes their cries for a king personally, although, by setting Joel and Abijah up to assume his mantle of judge/priest, he's already in the process of attempting to change the whole system of nonhereditary judgeship that ruled Israel for so long. Self-righteous as always, Samuel rails against the people's request, ominously predicting disaster—and sets about undermining whatever king they choose. From then on, Samuel is always lurking in the shadows, always looking for fault to denounce and condemn.

1 Samuel 9–11

Beginning in chapter 9, we are told that God chooses a young man named Saul. There are three different, apparently conflicting, accounts of how Saul is selected:

1. While searching for his father's lost donkeys, Saul encounters Samuel disguised as a seer, who inexplicably anoints him Israel's future king.
2. While telling the people how bad they are for rejecting him, Samuel says, "We might as well throw some dice and come up with a king." They do. Lo and behold, it's Saul, who is hiding in the luggage. (The modern-day saying "People get the government they deserve" may be worth remembering here!) In both stories, Saul doesn't act after hearing the news; he may be hoping it'll all just go away and he can go back to farming. When some "worthless fellows" *dis* their new king and don't bring him the presents due him, Saul holds his peace and doesn't punish them.
3. In the third version, we find farmer Saul plowing with oxen. Upon hearing the news that the Ammonites are gouging out eyes of captive Israelites at Jabesh-gilead, he angrily cuts up the oxen and summons Israel's warriors. Like Joan of Arc, the oppression of his people enrages Saul and he acts. (The question arises, of course, "Why wasn't Samuel leading the people until this point?") Under Saul's leadership, the twelve tribes break the siege of Jabesh-gilead and help their own people. Unlike a *lot* of those mentioned in this book, the people of Jabesh-gilead are grateful and honor Saul's sacrifices. Saul, meanwhile, returns to farming.

109

Whether there are three different narratives or a fractured version of a single story, Saul becomes the king (see 1 Samuel 9:21).

1 Samuel 12

At last, Samuel, like Moses, ends his public career with a long, self-serving farewell speech that further undercuts Saul's leadership. But unlike Moses (who promptly dies), Samuel never really leaves—he stays and stays and stays. Whenever Saul is called into action, Samuel appears.

1 Samuel 13–14

There is some text missing at the beginning of chapter 13, so we don't know how long Saul reigned, but apparently there were some pretty good years—no major wars, no major crop failures, and Samuel mostly stays off his case. Saul has a son, Jonathan, who is an even greater warrior than his father, and who leads the Israelites to a victory over the Philistine garrison at Geba.

Big mistake. The loss of the fortress infuriates the Philistines and they muster their greatest army yet, 30,000 chariots and 6,000 horsemen, and "troops like the sand on the seashore" (13:5), all armed with state-of-the-art iron swords and spears. King Saul calls the people of Israel together and assembles a much smaller force, armed with severely inferior bronze weapons. A fierce battle looms; the small nation's survival is at stake. As the Philistines press closer, Saul's tiny army—all volunteers—tremble and the people head for the hills.

But Saul is helpless because Samuel has insisted that he alone can perform the proper sacrifices that will bring Yahweh's blessing—and Samuel is nowhere to be found. He has made Saul promise to wait seven days; by the eighth day Samuel's unexplained vacation places all of Israel in jeopardy. Saul is caught between Samuel's insistence that only *he* can do the proper sacrifices, and the reality of the military situation, with soldiers deserting hourly. In desperation, Saul acts to save his nation and reluctantly offers a burnt offering to God. (Before we judge him, chapters 9 and 10 give plenty of evidence that a king has near-priestly status and *can* perform some priestly functions.)

Samuel must have been nearby. Maybe he was testing Saul; maybe he was showing his displeasure with this *king* situation; maybe he was trying to undermine Saul. But if Saul doesn't do the sacrifice, he loses his army. If he *does* do the sacrifice, he loses his dynasty. Saul chooses to save his people, even though his army is now down to 600 men fighting against a technologically advanced enemy.

When Samuel finally strolls up a day late, he casually asks Saul what he's done—as if he doesn't know. Saul answers him straightforwardly:

> When I saw that the people were slipping away from me, and that you did not come within the days appointed, and that the Philistines were mustering at Michmash, I said, "Now the Philistines will come down upon me at Gilgal, and I have not entreated the favor of the LORD"; so I forced myself, and offered the burnt offering. (1 Samuel 13:11-12)

This doesn't sound to me like someone who is willfully disobedient. Samuel, whose power has been usurped, is enraged and he pronounces the judgment that Saul's children—including the wonderful, heroic Jonathan—will never assume the throne.

Devastated, Saul nonetheless bravely confronts the overwhelming Philistine forces. He devises a bold plan and splits his small army even further. Meanwhile, Jonathan and a companion slip out for a bit of guerilla warfare on the side. Jonathan's sudden appearance in the seemingly impregnable garrison panics the complacent Philistines. What looks like a massacre of the Israelites suddenly turns into a rout of the Philistines.

Years of oppression mean that there is a blood lust in the air and, at a particularly bloody moment, Saul screams, "Cursed be anyone who eats food before it is evening and I have been avenged on my enemies" (14:24). Alas, a famished Jonathan, who is busy hacking away at Philistines on the other side of Ephraim, doesn't hear the king's edict and nibbles a bit of honeycomb later in the day. Fortunately, the people of Israel talk Saul out of killing his own son.

In the years to come, Saul proves to be an able commander. Leading his mostly Benjaminite army, he defeats the kingdoms of Moab and Edom, the Ammonites, Philistines and Amalekites, and the kings of Zobah. He returns to Benjamin after each battle, content to avoid the lavish trappings of monarchy.

1 Samuel 15

Saul's second *failure*, however, is even more costly. In 1 Samuel 15:1-9, before Saul fights an old nemesis, the Amalekites, again, Samuel shows back up and delivers a message from the LORD of hosts: "Kill 'em all—men, women, children, ox, sheep, camel, and donkey." This Saul does, but he saves the best of the animals (and spares King Agag of the Amalekites) as a praise offering to Yahweh.

The writer of 1 Samuel then includes the following lines, which certainly sound—at the very least—curious to modern ears: "The word of the LORD came to Samuel: 'I regret that I made Saul king, for he has turned back from following me, and has not carried out my commands'" (15:10).

This would imply, at least to an Old Testament reader, that an omnipotent God is capable of making a mistake or at the very least, the LORD isn't a very good judge of character! The best way to handle the passage is to assume that it is probably from a very old source or tradition and instead take it to mean that God is disappointed in Saul's character—or that Samuel is trying to retain power.

Still, this second *failure* is pretty clear-cut. Saul hasn't learned from his previous lesson: You've got to follow instructions from Yahweh (and Samuel) *exactly*. God and Samuel are both furious, even though Saul saved the best animals as a sacrifice to the LORD—*not* for his personal gain.

There's an interesting bit of insight into Saul's personality found here. As Samuel rails at Saul, he says, "Though you are little in your own eyes, are you not the head of the tribes of Israel?" (15:17). Again, this sounds like a reluctant hero, an insecure man who is only trying to do what's right. The verses make it clear that Saul is stunned by Samuel's reaction to his proposed sacrifice. His response is one of the most poignant passages in the whole Bible:

> Saul said to Samuel, "I have sinned; for I have transgressed the commandment of the LORD and your words, because I feared the people and obeyed their voice. Now therefore, I pray, pardon my sin, and return with me, so that I may worship the LORD." Samuel said to Saul, "I will not return with you; for you have rejected the word of the LORD, and the LORD has rejected you from being king over Israel." As Samuel turned to go away, Saul caught hold of the hem of his robe, and it tore. And Samuel said to him, "The LORD has torn the kingdom of Israel from you this very day, and has given it to a neighbor of yours, who is better than you. Moreover the Glory of Israel will not recant or change his mind; for he is not a mortal, that he should change his mind." Then Saul said, "I have sinned; yet honor me now before the elders of my people and before Israel, and return with me, so that I may worship the LORD your God." So Samuel turned back after Saul; and Saul worshiped the LORD. (1 Samuel 15:24-31)

Not content to strip him of his crown and dynasty, Samuel adds the extra twist of the knife, telling Saul that "his neighbor," the unnamed new

112

king, "is better than you" (15:28). There is something tremendously moving about a man so gutted with shame and a need for forgiveness that he desperately clutches at the robe of the man who has despised him his whole life.

The author adds one last insult in the final line of the chapter: "And the LORD was sorry that he had made Saul king over Israel" (15:35).

1 Samuel 16

This leads us to chapter 16 and the introduction of that neighbor, David. The stories of a youthful David—including the whole business with Goliath (whom David may or *may not* have actually killed—see 2 Samuel 21:19 and 1 Chronicles 20:5)—are as well known as the stories of baby Jesus in Bethlehem. Still, there is something a little creepy in the picture of David—who already knows he has been anointed king—playing the lyre to soothe the troubled soul of the man he's been chosen to replace.

As the days pass, Saul sinks into depression—in fact, it sounds like a classic case of manic-depressive personality disorder—"the spirit of the LORD departed from Saul, and an evil spirit from the LORD tormented him" (16:14). Saul's pain is understandable; God has turned his back on him and Saul's beloved Jonathan will not succeed him.

113

1 Samuel 17–21

David's mercurial personality is a popular topic of writers, who often laud his courage and faith. But David was ambitious too. When he hears the giant Goliath challenge the Israelites to produce a champion (and the ordinarily brave Saul is all but paralyzed by depression), David's first recorded words are shrewdly calculating: "What shall be done for the man who kills this Philistine, and takes away the reproach from Israel?" (17:26). In short, "What's in it for me?"

Still, the people love him. David becomes a superstar, winning greater and greater victories under the inspired leadership of Saul's general, Abner. David becomes a blood brother with Jonathan and marries Saul's daughter, Michal. Saul's mental degeneration is such that he frequently doesn't recognize David and twice attempts to kill him—although each time the Bible notes, somewhat cryptically, that "an evil spirit sent from God" prompted the act.

1 Samuel 22–24

Slowly, David builds a cult of personality around himself, and open warfare erupts between David's and Saul's factions. David heads to the countryside and assembles an army composed of "everyone who was in distress, and everyone who was in debt, and everyone who was discontented" (22:2). In another time, these people would be called bandits or rebels. In this nasty civil war, the fortunes wax and wane and each side commits atrocities. David has a chance to kill Saul, but refuses (see chapter 24). Meanwhile, Saul must contend with both David's rebellion *and* the Philistines. It is an impossible task for one already in the throes of madness.

1 Samuel 25–26

Samuel at last dies in chapter 25 and is buried in Ramah. For such a significant personage, the author of 1 Samuel barely allots two sentences to his death. Instead, he turns the account to David, who has been supporting his army by demanding protection money from the people in the area—much like the Mafia.

114

At the news of Samuel's death, David responds by making a foray to the lands of the husband and wife team, Nabal and Abigail, demanding even more money. Nabal refuses. But Abigail, who knows what kind of damage David's raiders can do, buys David off. When she tells her husband what she's done (and how much it costs), he conveniently dies. David promptly adds Abigail to his harem.

David later has a second opportunity to kill Saul, but passes—in part because of Abigail's wise warning about "bloodguilt" (25:26). From there, David goes on to serve one of Israel's enemies, the murderous King Achish of Gath. David lies to Achish, saying that he's plundering Israel when his bandits are really plundering Philistine cities!

1 Samuel 28

Sensing the weakness in the small monarchy, in chapter 28 the Philistines assemble their largest army yet for a *final solution* to the Hebrew problem, led by King Achish and his new bodyguard, the turncoat David. They see an opportunity here for serious *ethnic cleansing*. Saul's army is in disarray, badly outnumbered and still fighting with primitive weapons. He prays to Yahweh for guidance, but God doesn't talk to *losers*. He tries casting of the holy lots; he consults God's other prophets—nothing.

So Saul assembles what's left of his army, still mostly men from Benjamin, on Mount Gilboa. But there are ghosts here. It was by a spring on Mount Gilboa that Deborah and Barak led the Israelites to a stunning victory over Sisera, Jabin, and the Philistines (see Judges 4:15–5:21). It was here, at the Battle of Jezreel, that Gideon's three hundred defeated the hordes of the Midianites (see Judges 7). And years later, King Josiah will die on the plain at the foot of this mountain, fighting the Egyptians (see 2 Kings 23:29). Perhaps Saul is praying for one last miraculous intervention by Yahweh at this holy spot.

Despite his black depression and fatalism, Saul thinks *only* of his fickle people. He bravely undertakes a dangerous mission, traveling eight difficult and dangerous miles through enemy territory to Endor. Saul's goal is a well-known witch—a medium who can talk to the dead—who can tell him what to do. He disguises himself, since he's already issued a royal edict forbidding such activities with witches and warlocks. The woman recognizes him, but he assures her it's OK—and, "by the way, could you call up Samuel's ghost?" However she accomplishes the feat—séance, magic, or necromancy—this witch must be pretty good:

The woman said to Saul, "I see a divine being coming up out of the ground." He said to her, "What is his appearance?" She said, "An old man is coming up; he is wrapped in a robe." So Saul knew that it was Samuel, and he bowed with his face to the ground, and did obeisance.

Then Samuel said to Saul, "Why have you disturbed me by bringing me up?" Saul answered, "I am in great distress, for the Philistines are warring against me, and God has turned away from me and answers me no more, either by prophets or by dreams; so I have summoned you to tell me what I should do." Samuel said, "Why then do you ask me, since the LORD has turned from you and become your enemy? The LORD has done to you just as he spoke by me; for the LORD has torn the kingdom out of your hand, and given it to your neighbor, David. Because you did not obey the voice of the LORD, and did not carry out his fierce wrath against Amalek, therefore the LORD has done this thing to you today. Moreover the LORD will give Israel along with you into the hands of the Philistines; and tomorrow you and your sons shall be with me; the LORD will also give the army of Israel into the hands of the Philistines." (1 Samuel 28:13-19)

Death has apparently *not* smoothed out the rough edges of Samuel's personality—he's still a mean old coot. All we know is that he was "wrapped in a robe" (28:14), so we don't know if he looked like a reject from *Night of the Living Dead* or just a little dusty. Either way, it must have been terrifying. Samuel doesn't seem to care much about Israel. Instead, he seems to receive a charge from delivering a death sentence on Saul and his sons.

A lesser man would have fled (after first stopping by the palace and looting the royal treasury). Not Saul. Once again, repentant, emotionally shattered, and struggling with his own demons, King Saul finds the energy to carry on . . . for his people.

THANK YOU— FOR NOT BEING PERKY!

SAMUEL

1 Samuel 29—31

The author of 1 Samuel makes a curious decision here. Instead of plunging headlong into the climactic battle, chapters 29 and 30 recount more of David's exploits: fighting his battles, lying to King Achish, giving the stolen loot to the men, securing the support of the people in this part of the kingdom for his eventual ascension to the throne. David always plays both ends against the middle, plotting for the future and thinking ahead.

While David is off freebooting, Saul is left to defend the nation in the powerful chapter 31. If you know the battles of the Alamo and Sparta vs. Persia in the epic Battle of Thermopylae, this story has the same kind of resonance. Demoralized, with half the army off raiding with David, Saul's small army faces the mighty Philistines. King Saul is exhausted and literally demon-haunted; nonetheless, he leads them into battle one last time. The scene reminds me of the sequence in the third *Lord of the Rings* movie when the mad steward Denethor's son Faramir, who has never won his father's approval, leads his men on a doomed charge out of Minas Tirith.

It is a slaughter. The Israelite lines buckle under the assault and desperately fight their way back to the base of Mount Gilboa. Beautiful, heroic Jonathan, one of the great figures of the Bible, and all of Saul's other sons, die heroically defending their father. The Philistine archers send clouds of arrows into the air, grievously wounding Saul, who fights his way to the top of Mount Gilboa.

The Philistines hack their way up the hill through the last of Saul's royal bodyguard. Saul knows of the tortures and humiliations the Philistines inflicted on Samson when they captured him some years earlier. Now dying, he asks his armor-bearer to kill him. When he refuses, Saul denies the Philistines the pleasure of taking him alive and falls on his own sword. And across the valley, the cowardly Israelites who *didn't* come to his aid see Saul's fall and they flee as well.

The following day, the Philistines return to the battlefield and find Saul's body. Since they couldn't capture and torture him, they brutalize his corpse. They sever his head and send messengers throughout the Philistine countryside: one of their greatest enemies has fallen! They then nail his body to the wall of Beth-shan, a fortress in the Jezreel Valley.

I love the little coda that follows. The people of Jabesh-gilead, whom Saul had saved in the first act of his reluctant kingship, concoct a bold plan to honor him. They secretly ride deep into Philistine territory at night and retrieve the bodies of Saul and his sons. They return to Jabesh-gilead and give them a hero's funeral pyre, in direct defiance of their oppressors.

117

Saul's Fatal Flaw

Ultimately, Saul was an honorable failure as a king. He sought to do the right thing; when he failed, he repented. He never sought personal fame or fortune; he was steadfast even when he knew the outcome. He is, in sum, one of the greatest tragic heroes of literature.

So what was his fatal flaw? It certainly seems clear that he lacked the single-minded tenacity of a born leader. Saul was a people-pleaser. He was the ancient counterpart of a modern-day politician who conducts daily polls to determine his own *opinion* on controversial issues. Even his pursuit of David was half-hearted. Had he mustered a full army and enacted a scorched-earth policy—like the one that ultimately defeated the Apaches in Arizona and New Mexico—he might have brought David and his bandits to their knees. But Saul didn't have the heart to hurt innocent people. Perhaps the demands of power were too much for Saul, a genuinely reluctant king and hero.

David's grief over Saul's death in 2 Samuel seems authentic enough. He composes a mournful elegy in honor of Saul and Jonathan, and commands that the people learn it:

> Your glory, O Israel, lies slain upon your high places!
> How the mighty have fallen! (2 Samuel 1:19)

David's own troubles, despite all of his glory and exploits in the years to come, have barely begun.

Reluctant Prophets and Clueless Disciples

Eleven

KING DAVID
➡ (2 SAMUEL)

> King David and King Solomon
>   Led merry, merry lives,
> With many, many lady friends
>   And many, many wives;
> But when old age crept over them,
>   With many, many qualms,
> King Solomon wrote the Proverbs
>   And King David wrote the Psalms.
> (James Ball Naylor, "Authorship")

To retell the stories of David is to revisit your childhood. Even kids from only nominally Christian and Jewish homes know the stories of little David bravely guarding his sheep, playing his harp for King Saul, defeating the giant Goliath with only a slingshot, writing the greatest of the Psalms. In these stories, David is impossibly handsome and true, always the bravest of heroes, always the most loyal of friends. These tales have been told and retold so many times that—like the story of Samson—they blur almost into myth and sound more like the exploits of the ancient gods of Greece and Rome than someone of flesh and blood.

In fact, Biblical scholars have, for decades, tried to unravel the different Davidic storylines that the author (or authors) of Samuel and Chronicles have woven together to create a fast-paced yarn of epic proportions. Careful tracing of the language and syntax has identified various ancient story forms relating to the life of David—some more sympathetic to David, some decidedly less so. This is further complicated by the significant differences in the accounts of David's life and times among 1 and 2 Samuel, 1 and 2 Chronicles, and 1 and 2 Kings. There is even a case to be made that David actually joins the Philistines and is part of the final attack on Saul and Jonathan on Mount Gilboa!

But let's leave all that for the scholars, historians, and theologians. Let's instead take the riveting, roller-coaster ride of David as it is presented to us (more or less), and not attempt to decipher Akkadian cognates or the merits of proposed pro- or anti-monarchal sources. Taken as one, the various sources still create a picture of a wonderfully complex human being, who lived a life like few other men or women in all of history.

2 Samuel 2:1-11

Most of our story comes from 2 Samuel, beginning right after the death of Saul, which, by the way, does not automatically make David king of the empire, such as it is. There are many in the north (called Israel) that are loyal to Saul's heirs; still others regard David as little more than a bandit-chieftain for his raids as the personal bodyguard of the dreaded King Achish of the Philistines. What follows Saul's death reveals the pragmatic, bloodthirsty side of David—a man who moves swiftly to squelch opposition and clear his road to the united throne. First, however, he must get through Ishbaal, one of Saul's surviving sons. Ishbaal rules in the north, supported by Saul's craftiest commander, the brilliant strategist Abner. David bides his time, remaining in Hebron with his wives—including Ahinoam of Jezreel and Abigail, the widow of Nabal—and gathering support, especially in Judah.

2 Samuel 2:12-32

In time, Abner and a company of his fiercest fighters meet with David's commander and nephew Joab and his men, by the pool at Gibeon. But instead of open civil warfare between North and South, the two sides agree to a limited battle, perhaps because many of the best soldiers were comrades who had once served together under Saul and Abner. The short battle is ferocious—and decisive. David's men slaughter Ishbaal's men, who break and flee. Abner is chased by Asahel, Abishai, and Joab—the sons of Zeruiah, David's sister. Abner reluctantly kills Asahel, but the others stay in hot pursuit.

At last, Abner rallies his surviving Benjaminites on a small hill of Ammah; wounded and exhausted, they grimly form a single line to face Joab's much larger force. At the last moment, Abner desperately tries to stop the bloodshed:

120

Is the sword to keep devouring forever? Do you not know that the end will be bitter? How long will it be before you order your people to turn from the pursuit of their kinsmen? (2:26)

Joab pauses. Abner is right. The blood lust leaves him and he orders his men to return home. According to the story, he's lost nineteen soldiers, while Abner has lost three hundred sixty.

2 Samuel 3:2-21

The Battle of Ammah shifts the tide in David's favor and slowly families, clans, and cities loyal to the House of Saul desert Ishbaal.

During this lull in the civil war, David has kept *very* busy producing sons: Amnon (by Ahinoam), Chileab (by Abigail), Absalom (by Maacah, daughter of King Talmai), Adonijah (by Haggith), Shephatiah (by Abital) and Ithream (by Eglah).

Meanwhile, Abner, who is the real power in the north, runs afoul of Ishbaal when he moves in with one of Saul's former concubines—a not-so-subtle action designed to strengthen his position. Angered at Ishbaal's response, Abner, who is well aware that he's fighting a losing battle, sends messengers to David's camp. He's ready to switch allegiances. David's soldiers are delighted to have a veteran warrior like Abner on their side.

David has only one condition—Abner must bring David's first wife, Michal, Saul's daughter, with him. It was for Michal's hand that David gave King Saul the foreskins of a hundred Philistines. But during the war between Saul and David, Michal is apparently separated from her husband. In time, she marries again, this time to a man named Paltiel. David doesn't care—he apparently loves her still, or perhaps he sees it as a strategic alliance, furthering his claim to her father's throne. Abner is true to his word and when he defects, he brings both Michal and Paltiel. Paltiel follows his wife, weeping piteously. Once in David's headquarters at Hebron, David throws a feast for Abner and his men.

2 Samuel 3:22-4:12

But there are more intrigues afoot. Joab has been gone on a raiding party and upon his return, is astounded at the news that Abner has thrown in his lot with David. It's not hard to imagine their dialogue:

"That's right," David beams happily, "Abner is on our side. God has shown him the light. He wants to help me reunite our divided land."

Joab smacks himself on the forehead. *"D'oh!* Davie, if Abner has betrayed one king, what's to keep him from betraying another? Or maybe he's just here spying on you for Ishbaal. Don't you remember he killed your nephew Asahel?"

"Um, wasn't Asahel trying to kill *him* at the time?"

"That's beside the point, David. I can't believe you trust this guy!"

"Oh, do be quiet. Do you want to see the baby pictures of my latest half-dozen sons?"

But Joab is not that easily dissuaded. He sends for Abner, who innocently meets him, only to be stabbed to death in a dark alley by Joab and his brother Abishai.

David is flabbergasted. Everything he's done to heal the rift with Saul's still militarily significant followers may have been undone in a heartbeat. He loudly proclaims his innocence and grief, denounces Joab, orders a national day of mourning, and fasts for a couple of days.

Ishbaal is terrified—and rightfully so. Without Abner commanding Israel's army, he's virtually helpless. Within hours, two of Saul's former captains stroll into Ishbaal's tent, murder him while he's sleeping, and take his head to David. But instead of being happy about it, David orders both men killed, their hands and feet cut off, and their bodies hung from a tree. And the body count has only just begun.

2 Samuel 5:1-16

David now needs a new home for his new kingdom. For the first time, one man has united the larger, more economically powerful, ten northern tribes with the two, more pastoral, southern tribes—Judah and Benjamin. He chooses the seemingly impregnable walled city of Jerusalem, midway between the two tiny Hebrew kingdoms. His lightning blitzkrieg through the water shaft carved for the Spring of Gihon stuns the over-confident defenders of Jerusalem, who can mount only a token resistance. Now firmly in charge, he proclaims Jerusalem "the city of David" (5:9) and promptly proceeds to sire still *more* children: Shammua, Shobab, Nathan, Ibhar, Elishua, Nepheg, Japhia, Elishama, Eliada, and Eliphelet.

122

2 Samuel 5:17-25

Not surprisingly, the dominant power in the region—the Philistines—are not happy to hear that this former ally has installed himself as king, united the tribes, and set up shop in a formidable fortress in the middle of *their* territory. But with God's help, David's combined armies defeat several Philistine assaults and push them deeper into their own territory.

2 Samuel 6:1-23

Emboldened by his success, David decrees that the Ark of the Covenant must be moved to Jerusalem, where it eventually resides, but only after several misadventures. David is so thrilled that the Ark is coming to Jerusalem that he dances in front of it in wild abandon, in full view of the entire city. Verse 16 says he was "leaping and dancing before the LORD." For these precious moments, David is Little David again, a tousled-haired boy playing his harp, responsible for nothing more than a few sheep. But when highborn Michal sees David's giddy dance, the same verse goes on to say "she despised him in her heart." David's ritualistic dance precipitates a violent argument between the two. After it is over, David and Michal never speak again and David has lost his first and greatest love. From a political standpoint, this is a disaster. A child of this union would have united the warring royal houses of Saul and David and avoided much future bloodshed. Still, David's move consolidates his power; Jerusalem is now both the political and spiritual capital of all Hebrews.

2 Samuel 7-10

The next few chapters chronicle David's successes, both in the never-ending wars with the Philistines and on the home front. But this is David's last period of contentment. Forces are already on the move—some of his own creation—that fill his final years with heartbreak, betrayal, and pain.

By now, David has been in power a long time. He no longer leads his armies into battle, leaving the dirty work to his faithful nephews Joab and Abishai. It has been said, "Power tends to corrupt, and absolute power corrupts absolutely" (first attributed to Lord Acton in a letter to Bishop Mandel Creighton, April 5, 1887). David, who had sometimes been ruthless but was generally merciful, is now revealed to be little short of a despot, suspicious, and vindictive. His greatest problem may be simple boredom.

2 Samuel 11:1-26

While his nephews are waging war against the Ammonites and Arameans, David idly wanders about his lavish castle. Looking down from a parapet one day, he sees the beautiful Bathsheba bathing.

Overcome with lust, he sends for her. And whether it is consensual or not—few women dare resist the king—it's not long before Bathsheba, the wife of the brave warrior Uriah the Hittite, is pregnant. All of this happens while Uriah is away fighting for David in the siege of the Ammonite stronghold, Rabbah.

David now has a public relations problem. He sends for Uriah and covertly tries to get him to sleep with his wife so as to cover David's sin. But Uriah refuses to sleep in a perfumed bed while his men are dying on the walls of Rabbah. Exasperated, David sends a message to Joab via

Reluctant Prophets and Clueless Disciples

Uriah at the front, "At the right moment, pull back our troops, leaving Uriah alone." This is not the old David, who once attributed all of his successes to God's love for God's chosen people. This is a cruel and heartless David, one who sacrifices a noble friend on a whim.

There are few images more poignant in the Bible than that of weary, battle-scarred Uriah carrying his own death warrant to Joab. Was he curious about the letter's contents? Was he tempted to peek? Probably not—Uriah was too loyal, too trusting. And so, at the appointed time after a half-hearted assault on the walls, Joab callously abandons faithful Uriah, who dies valiantly, fighting for a king who doesn't deserve his valor. After an *appropriate* period of mourning, David takes Bathsheba as still another wife, and she dutifully bears their son.

2 Samuel 12:1-25

This is a small country. Bathsheba's comings and goings and sudden pregnancy, David's mysterious letter, and the murder of Uriah are probably common knowledge among the people of Jerusalem. Word reaches David's prophet-in-residence, Nathan. Enraged, Nathan tells David a harrowing tale of a poor man with a single ewe and a rich man with vast flocks of sheep. Just because he can, the rich man seizes the poor man's ewe and serves it to a guest. David rails at the injustice: "As the LORD lives, the man who has done this deserves to die; he shall restore the lamb fourfold, because he did this thing, and because he had no pity" (12:5-6).

In response, Nathan can barely hide the contempt in his voice: "*You* are the man!" (12:7). And further, the LORD decrees, because of David's actions, his family will be torn and tormented, his wives abducted and raped before him, and his child by Bathsheba will die. To David's credit, he immediately recognizes his sin and doesn't blame Nathan. The enormity of what he's done comes crashing down on him and he repents and fasts until the baby's death. The LORD forgives David, but doesn't revoke the sentence pronounced by Nathan. And while Bathsheba will eventually bear him another son—Solomon—David is haunted by his deeds to the end of his days.

The extent of David's conquests is hard to establish; it is likely his successors expanded the empire. David does extend his reach into the Negeb Desert, which enables him to tax the lucrative Arab spice trade and thus provides the source of much of Solomon's power in the years to come.

125

2 Samuel 13:1-29

Some time after the fall of Rabbah, when David is an old man, his life becomes sticky indeed. See if you can follow this sordid scenario, something right out of a daytime soap opera:

- His son Absalom has a beautiful sister, Tamar.
- Amnon, David's oldest and favorite—and Absalom's half-brother—falls in love with Tamar.
- Amnon enlists the help of Jonadab, the son of David's brother Shimeah.
- Shimeah and Amnon concoct a plan to have David send Tamar to Amnon.
- David does and Amnon rapes Tamar, then rejects her.
- David won't punish Amnon—after all, his actions with Bathsheba are only marginally different—plus, Amnon is his favorite son.
- Absalom vows revenge and bides his time for two years.
- Aided by his other brothers (and half-brothers), Absalom invites Amnon to a feast and has his servants kill the unsuspecting Amnon.
- David falls into mourning over Amnon.
- Absalom flees to a neighboring kingdom, Geshur, where he stays three years.
- Eventually, David gets over Amnon and starts missing Absalom.
- Meanwhile, the kingdom is going to pot.

2 Samuel 14:1-33

Finally, crafty Joab has had enough. He concocts an elaborate scheme, which gets Absalom first, back to Jerusalem, and eventually—he thinks—back into David's good graces. But something has changed in Absalom. Perhaps he still grieves over David's inaction regarding Tamar, perhaps the king of Geshur has warped his mind, or perhaps he has always wanted his father's throne. Absalom spends two years in Jerusalem, unable to see his father.

David finally relents and issues a royal invitation but, despite repeated entreaties at Joab's urging, it is Absalom who now refuses to come. Joab again intercedes and father and son at last make peace, though nothing will ever be the same between them.

Reluctant Prophets and Clueless Disciples

2 Samuel 15

By now, the embittered Absalom has a plan of his own. He slowly, carefully builds a power base among the Israelites and—after four more years—leaves and installs himself as a rival king in Hebron. Eventually, Absalom and his soldiers begin to move. There is panic in the streets of Jerusalem—Absalom and his armies are coming! David, his family (save for ten concubines, who stay to look after his palace!), his officials, and his followers flee Jerusalem. Only the Ark of the Covenant is left behind.

2 Samuel 16

Among those David and his band encounter during their flight is Shimei, still a friend of the House of Saul. Shimei boldly throws stones at David's caravan and bravely curses David: "Out! Out! Murderer! Scoundrel! The LORD has avenged on all of you the blood of the house of Saul, in whose place you have reigned, and the LORD has given the kingdom into the hand of your son Absalom. See, disaster has overtaken you; *for you are a man of blood*" (16:7-8, italics added).

Boy—bad news travels fast. David's officers want to kill Shimei, but David stays their hands. "Shimei is right, I *am* a man of blood—all that he says is true." And so the procession continues, soul-weary and foot-sore, toward the River Jordan.

After a triumphant entry into Jerusalem, Absalom, now supported by virtually all of the northern tribes, picks up two key allies: David's former advisors Hushai and Ahithophel, Bathsheba's grandfather, who still seethes with anger over David's despotism. Ahithophel advises Absalom to sleep with his father's concubines, again with the intent of showing the populace who is *really* in charge here. But Hushai, who is really a spy for David, works surreptitiously to undermine Absalom.

2 Samuel 17:1-23

Ahithophel suggests that Absalom again muster his army to chase the demoralized David and his followers while they're still near—but to kill only David and spare his army. Hushai counsels otherwise. David is a brilliant, dangerous leader, he says, it's better not to underestimate him.

Instead of moving quickly, it's better to delay and gather an even larger army. Absalom, despite Ahithophel's long service as an advisor and oracle, takes Hushai's bad advice. He will wait.

Still wanting to cover his bets, Hushai sends David word to cross the Jordan. Now given precious time, David rallies, provisions his men, and gains valuable allies of his own. Ahithophel alone sees what is happening. Absalom's only chance of defeating David is gone. Devastated, Ahithophel returns to his home and hangs himself. There is no place in either camp for a turncoat.

2 Samuel 18:6–16

When Absalom finally does mount a campaign, David is ready. He divides his army under three commanders—Joab, Abishai, and Ittai the Gittite—in the Forest of Ephraim. Without the counsel of Abner, Absalom blindly rides his army into David's trap. His superior numbers are useless in the dense forest. The battle turns first into a rout, then into a slaughter.

Absalom may have been many things, but a coward is not one of them. Even in defeat, he continues to fight on horseback until his luxurious head of hair is impossibly tangled in the thick underbrush. Joab's men refuse to kill Absalom, fearing David's wrath. Joab has no such compunction; there is already the blood of thousands on his hands. He stabs the helpless Absalom where he hangs.

2 Samuel 18:17–19:8

Once again, David is inconsolable. His lament is one of the most powerful in the Old Testament, "O my son Absalom, my son, my son Absalom! Would I had died instead of you, O Absalom, my son, my son!" (18:33). Even as hundreds of brave soldiers on both sides lie dying in the forest, David orders the nation into mourning. As for Joab, his blind faith in David is, at last, tested beyond reason. He shouts at his weeping king:

> Today you have covered with shame the faces of all your officers who have saved your life today, and the lives of your sons and your daughters, and the lives of your wives and your concubines, for the love of those who hate you and for hatred of those who love you. You have made it clear today that commanders

Reluctant Prophets and Clueless Disciples

and officers are nothing to you; for I perceive that if Absalom were alive and all of us were dead today, then you would be pleased. (2 Samuel 19:5-6)

Joab's voice turns from anger to barely concealed disgust:

So go out at once and speak kindly to your servants; for I swear by the LORD, if you do not go, not a man will stay with you this night; and this will be worse for you than any disaster that has come upon you from your youth until now. (2 Samuel 19:7-8)

Joab's harsh words stir the old king, who stumbles blindly to the gate and waves at his men as they return. David is installed, once again, as king of a united kingdom, though there is still much resentment in the north. It is a different David who returns to Jerusalem, one dispensing mercy to those who once opposed him. He is distracted, withdrawn, and barely able to function.

2 Samuel 20:1-22

Shortly thereafter, a man named Sheba, a distant relative of Saul's, rallies the disaffected northern tribes against David. David, still bitter over Joab's killing of Absalom, places his army under Amasa. But the wily old hatchet man won't be so summarily dismissed. Joab betrays Amasa with a kiss, plunging a knife into the unsuspecting Amasa's belly.

With Amasa dead, Joab and trusty Abishai then turn their attention to Sheba. Sheba's followers are no match for David's veteran, battle-scarred forces and they scatter. Sheba flees to the fortified town of Abel. Just as Joab is about to besiege it, the defenders quite prudently toss Sheba's severed head over the wall. This is not their fight! This is the last significant military action of David's reign.

2 Samuel 21-23

The next few chapters appear to be somewhat out of order, including events that apparently happened in the days following the death of King Saul. There is even an intriguing verse that claims that it is Elhanan, son of Jaareoregim of Bethlehem—not David!—who kills Goliath the Gittite (see 21:19).

129

2 Samuel 24

Chronologically, the story resumes with chapter 24 where David, once again against God's command, orders a census. When David repents, the LORD offers him a choice of punishments (reminiscent of the old childhood joke: "Would you rather be eaten by a hungry tiger or a starving lion?"). David chooses a three-day plague rather than three months on the run or a three-year drought. Still, another 70,000 people die because of David's disobedience.

1 Kings 1

The story of David comes to a pitiful ending in 1 Kings. David has not set a very good example. Most of his sons apparently have inherited his disdain for authority and the feelings of others. Even as David lies dying, unable to keep warm with still another beautiful young concubine, his son Adonijah (son of Haggith) decides to assume the throne. He forges an alliance with Joab but is unable to convince David's personal guard (his *Mighty Men*), the priests, or the Prophet Nathan to join him.

Instead, Nathan convinces Bathsheba that her son Solomon would be the better choice. Together, they tag-team the old king and convince him to throw his support behind Solomon. David orders the priests to anoint Solomon. When Adonijah hears this, he begs for mercy, which Solomon grants.

1 Kings 2:1-12

David's final words mark the strange inconsistencies of the man. At first he gives Solomon good advice, urging him to be faithful and just, and follow the LORD. But then he orders vengeance on his oldest and most faithful companion, Joab. David lists all of those Joab has killed, conveniently forgetting that most of the murders were done with, at the very least, *David's tacit approval*. Just as the great General Parmenio, the brilliant commander of both Philip of Macedonia and Alexander the Great, is killed by a lesser man, Solomon has Joab cut down like a dog. Joab's murder is an unbecoming, unworthy last will and testament for the old king.

David's last request is for Solomon not to spare Shimei, the man who cursed David when he fled Jerusalem—even though David had admitted

130

that what Shimei said was true and ordered his men not to harm him. Perhaps David feared Shimei's curse would extend to Solomon unless Shimei was exiled.

And that's it. "Then David slept with his ancestors, and was buried in the city of David" (2:10). The parallel account in 1 Chronicles says, "He died in a good old age, full of days, riches, and honor" (1 Chronicles 29:28).

David's Legacy

As with Moses, how should we judge the, sometimes maddening, mass of contradictions that is David? His sins certainly seem as great, if not greater, than those of Saul. And yet, the Bible says that God "loves" David, while Saul dies a horrific death, fighting for those who hate him. There is innocent blood on David's hands. He loves blindly and badly, an indulgent father whose per- missiveness causes disaster not just within his family but also to the nation at large. But when he dances in sheer, unadulterated joy at the arrival of the Ark of the Covenant, it's easy to see why the curly-haired shepherd boy steals Israel's heart.

The stories of David's youth are pretty and sanitized. He's like a colorful figure cut in felt and placed on a Sunday school felt board. But the stories of David as king exhibit a disturbing pattern: success, sin, abject repentance, and forgiveness. David's sins have far-reaching

131

consequences—he is never allowed to escape the consequences of his actions—but he is always, always forgiven.

Compared to proper and staid Solomon, jaded by riches and concubines, David the swashbuckling freebooter and king is the much more sympathetic figure. In his very public humiliations and repentances, as well as his very human sins, he is one of the easiest of the Old Testament figures to admire and identify with. That the greatest, most passionate Psalms are identified with him only strengthens his hold on our imagination.

And when Jesus rides into Jerusalem, the City of David, it is his bloodline as a descendent of David that is heralded and trumpeted above the ancient city's battlements and rafters.

> Little David play on your harp,
> Halelu! Halelu!
> Little David play on your harp,
> Halelu!
> Little David was a shepherd boy,
> He killed Goliath and he shouted for joy.
> Little David play on your harp,
> Halelu! Halelu!
> (African American Spiritual, "Little David")

Reluctant Prophets and Clueless Disciples

Twelve

THE PERSONAL TESTIMONY OF KING SOLOMON

➤ (1 KINGS 1–11)

I had it all—power, wealth, love, fame, wisdom, and the pleasure of my LORD. I oversaw the unified kingdom of Israel and Judah during the height of its greatest power and prestige. I was entrusted with the greatest building project of all time—the temple.

And yet . . . *and yet* . . . here I sit, a lonely and depressed old man. I see now that all of the things I strived for, all of the things I wanted so badly—*everything*—was vanity, as ephemeral as a puff of smoke.

I am feted around the world for my wisdom. Why can I not understand what fills my heart with such sadness?

Perhaps it began when—as a dutiful son—I fulfilled my father David's last requests. I ordered my toady Benaiah to kill the valiant, grizzled general Joab—Joab, who bore a dozen scars from fighting in my father's service, even when my father refused to leave his harem for the dusty and dangerous work of kingdom-building. I ordered Joab murdered even though he fled to the tent of the LORD—an inviolate place of refuge. By having him killed there, I set a dangerous precedent—the king is above even the LORD's law of asylum.

Nor did I show mercy to Shimei. He was exiled to live in Jerusalem in the Wadi Kidron for the crime of telling my father the truth. I decreed that the penalty for crossing the Wadi is death. Three years into my reign, Shimei went in search of some lost slaves. When I found out—what did I do? I ordered Shimei executed, eliminating the last link to Saul. Though I personally did not wield the sword, his blood was on my hands too.

Ironically, the completion of these bloody deeds marked the beginning of a long period of relative peace and prosperity for my long-suffering people. At the suggestion of my wise mother Bathsheba, I built on the conquests of Saul and David, not in constant military campaigns, but through a series of strategic marriages to the daughters of nearby kings, including the reigning Pharaoh of Egypt. I am smart enough to know that the only reason Israel flourishes is that neither Egypt to the southwest, nor the Persians, the Medes, or the Babylonians to the east are yet strong enough to contend for our little patch of desert. Still, these *alliance marriages* would cause me untold grief in the years to come.

It's true that I ended the ancient practice of worshiping Yahweh in the *high places*. Although I wonder what other choices were there for the common people in the countryside?

And it's true that the LORD visited me in a dream at Gibeon. In those days, the LORD was pleased with me and asked what I wanted in life. I was young and cocky then, of course, but watching my father struggle time and time again, invariably making bad choices, I knew I wanted something more for the life of my kingdom—and myself, of course. I was smart enough to know that I wasn't very smart. So I asked for a "discerning mind." It was the best choice I ever made in a life filled with questionable choices.

The LORD was happy with my answer, though, and said that not only wisdom but riches and honor would be mine as well.

For a time, the future seemed limitless, as if I were invulnerable, as if there was nothing I couldn't do, nothing I couldn't accomplish. Oh Yahweh, hear a foolish old man—forgive a foolish young man.

My newfound wisdom was tested early in my reign. Two poor prostitutes came to me, disputing over a child. Both had borne children, and one of the children had died tragically. Now both claimed that the remaining child was theirs. This case, at least, was ridiculously easy. I called for my sword.

"Divide the living boy in two," I thundered, in my best authoritarian voice. "Give half to the one, and half to the other."

I raised my sword menacingly—even my flunkies and the court parasites were aghast—but I had no intention of harming the child. Instead I watched their eyes.

One woman threw herself on the squalling baby. "Please my lord," she pleaded, "give her the living boy. Whatever you do, don't kill him!"

Song of Solomon

SOLOMON WAS A WISE OLD KING
LA DA DA DA, LA DA DEE DA
TWO LADIES DID A BABY BRING
LA DEE DA DEE, DA DEE DEE DA
IT'S MINE SAID ONE; NO, MINE, SAID THE OTHER
THEN HE SAID LET'S JUST SEE WHO'S THE MOTHER
LA DA DEE DUM, DA DUM DEE DA

WE'LL CUT THE LITTLE GUY IN HALF
LA DA DEE DA, LA DA DEE DEE
THE WISE OLD KING SAID WITH A LAUGH
HA HA HA HEE, HEE HEE HEE HO
NO NO SAID ONE, O.K. SAID THE OTHER
THEN HE SAID NOW WE KNOW WHO'S THE MOTHER
DA DUM DEE DUM, DUM DUM DEE DUM

The other woman smirked and said, "Good, it shall be neither mine nor yours. Go ahead, my king, divide it."

I lowered my sword. "Give the first woman the living boy," I said. "Do not kill him. She is the mother."

I glared at the other woman—who fled from my sight.

As I said, if only they all were that easy . . .

In the years ahead, the countryside conquered and my people united, I began an ambitious administrative plan, dividing the land into twelve more manageable administrative units, with twelve officers—each hand-picked by me. It seemed to work well. This enabled me to more efficiently assess and collect taxes. I tapped the trade routes going north and south, as well as the lucrative caravan routes to and from Egypt that passed through the southernmost reaches of my kingdom. With the tax revenue, I was able to raise and maintain an army ten times the size of the one mustered by my father.

And my court became a magnificent jewel, attended not just by the artists and leaders of Israel, but by the best and the brightest from surrounding kingdoms as well! The poets called it a golden age—and perhaps it was.

But the greatest treasure of my reign was that the LORD allowed me to build a temple. I spared no expense—how could I? The fact that it existed at all was a gift from the LORD. The finest cloth, the sturdiest woods, the most precious stones! The greatest craftsmen of the age flocked to Jerusalem to build the long-awaited temple. I wandered through the unfinished halls, giddy with delight, touching rare silks, breathing in the heady perfumes, marveling at the intricate bronze work, soaking in the dozen languages of the artisans as they truly created something worthy of the LORD! And at its center was the precious, priceless ark of the covenant, holding the greatest relics of our people—the stone tablets of Moses, a pot of manna from the wilderness, and Aaron's rod. In this way, the presence of the LORD took possession of the building and made it the holiest of holies on the earth. No nation on the face of the earth has ever seen more elaborate dedication ceremonies! And the LORD blessed the temple.

How do you top that?

What was left for me to do? Perhaps it would have been best if I had died at that moment—happy, fulfilled, feeling the love of the LORD.

But life goes on, doesn't it? You must continue the daily acts of living long after the sweetness is gone. What choice do we have?

Once the temple was completed, I turned to other, more mundane tasks. I built and rebuilt fortresses and walls

136

throughout the country. I enslaved the foreign peoples—those who were still living in Israel—for my elaborate building campaigns. I ensured that our armies were equipped with the latest weaponry: swords made of iron, spears of hardened wood, tipped with iron blades.

There was one thing else I built during this time, to my eternal shame. Nothing was good enough for my wife, Pharaoh's daughter. Her father's palaces dwarfed mine. Israel was still little more than a rural province compared to Egypt's might. She hounded me day and night, threatening, wheedling, cajoling, begging; whispering that should she not be pleased she would leave Jerusalem and its dust. So I built her a magnificent palace in Millo, hoping to be rid of her. Alas, if I had only known . . .

I received many visitors: kings, high-ranking representatives of Pharaoh, magi from the East, warlords, and exotic satraps. But none rivaled the Queen of Sheba, the royal representative of the powerful Sabeans who controlled the trade routes through Arabia and Africa. Although her official purpose was to establish trade relations between our nations, I suspect she was simply curious about this new kingdom springing out of the desert. She was effusive in her praise—and decidedly crafty in her bargaining! Still, we lavished each other with gifts, each trying to out-do the other. I vowed to visit her lands but never found the time. Not a day goes by that I don't think of her.

And I was bored. The land had been conquered—or so I thought. The temple had been built. The cities had been fortified; the rich trade routes tapped. No pleasure was denied me.

It had taken me decades, but I accomplished everything I set out to do. I was an old man and I was bored. Like my father, I suddenly found myself without a world to conquer. Like my father, my idleness brought only ruin and disaster to my people.

I had married seven hundred princesses from various lands—for the good of Israel, I constantly told myself. Along with the three hundred concubines, my court was a bloated, obscene pageant, a mass of milling people, all whispering, conspiring, and jockeying for position.

Many of my wives, some of whom I only saw at official functions, began to lobby for temples for their various gods. My favorite wives introduced me to their beloved deities: Astarte, Chemosh, Milcom, and—I am ashamed to admit—the voracious demon Molech, who requires the sacrifice of the firstborn child. I know my historians make excuses for me now; they say I was addled in my old age, but I knew what I was doing. Oh yes, I was quite aware. I sought to curry favor from these beautiful young princesses. I should have been searching for the LORD's favor. And, in my darkest hour, I built temples to their abominations.

One night, the LORD, who had been absent from my dreams for years, finally reappeared to me. The LORD had twice before warned me against this apostasy. But on this night, I knew no rest. The LORD thundered at me, telling me that because of my unfaithfulness, my precious Israel would soon be sundered, except for the tribe of Judah—and only that sop would remain because of the LORD's great love for my father. I was stricken, horrified, but it was too late—too late for anything. I had made my bed and now I must sleep in it.

In the days that followed, the LORD allowed enemy after enemy to assail Israel: Hadad the Edomite, who had been raised in the Pharaoh's courts; the Ephraimite Jeroboam, who led a bloody tax-rebellion by the northern tribes; and the desert marauder Rezon, son of Eliada, who savagely plundered and decimated my people from his fortress in Damascus. My armies fought bravely, but more and more of our taxes were poured into defense until virtually everything was expended on keeping our borders safe. I was forced to raise taxes again and again, and borrowed heavily from foreign rulers. In time, I was forced to sell my personal treasures. But the wars never ceased and my people groaned under the heavy tax burden.

And now I am old, too old to go into battle, too old to do anything. My eldest son Rehoboam will succeed me. He is a vain and self-important man, cruel and tactless. Mark my words—his callous, unthinking behavior will be the end of Israel.

There was a time when I was honored by kings for my wisdom. But that wisdom was just so much vapor. Now that I have

Reluctant Prophets and Clueless Disciples

reached the end of my appointed days, I have finally found true wisdom. I didn't find it in books or possessions or honor or glory. I found it—or perhaps, it found me.

What matters is the understanding that life is a journey, not a destination. What matters is how you treat others. What matters is that you earnestly petition the LORD's guidance, that you love the LORD with all of your heart, that you seek to do the will of the LORD. That alone is wisdom.

But I am too old to do much about it now. All I do is sit in my glittering palace and write laments and proverbs. My father wrote beautiful, joyous songs. I write of the black despair and hopelessness that I see as I eagerly await death.

I had it all . . .

Vanity of vanities, . . .
   vanity of vanities! All is vanity.
What do people gain from all the toil
   at which they toil under the sun?
A generation goes, and a generation comes,
   but the earth remains forever.
The sun rises and the sun goes down,
   and hurries to the place where it rises.
The wind blows to the south,
   and goes around to the north;
round and round goes the wind,
   and on its circuits the wind returns.
All streams run to the sea,
   but the sea is not full;
to the place where the streams flow,
   there they continue to flow.
All things are wearisome;
   more than one can express;
the eye is not satisfied with seeing,
   or the ear filled with hearing.
What has been is what will be,
   and what has been done is what will be done;
there is nothing new under the sun.
Is there a thing of which it is said,
   "See, this is new"?
It has already been,
   in the ages before us.
The people of long ago are not remembered,
   nor will there be any remembrance
of people yet to come
   by those who come after them.
(Ecclesiastes 1:2-11)

139

Thirteen

NEHEMIAH
➡ (NEHEMIAH 1–13)

If someone can write a book on Jabez's short prayer promoting American-styled capitalism, then there's an entire encyclopedia contained in the prayers of Nehemiah. His book is hidden away in the second half of the Old Testament, surrounded by bigger and more famous books. But for *story*, it's got 'em all beat. I must confess, however, that until the popular speaker Rev. David Peterson opened my eyes to him, I would have overlooked Nehemiah too.

There are some confusing chronological problems with the adjoining books of Nehemiah and Ezra. But essentially, the story is this: The last king of Judah has fallen to the Babylonians under King Nebuchadnezzar and many (but not all) of the Hebrew people (including the prophet Jeremiah) are marched off to Babylon in modern-day Iraq in about 587 BCE. Things are looking pretty bad for our heroes, the chosen people. Everything the prophets warned them about has come true. Because of their infidelity to Yahweh, Jerusalem and the temple are in ruins; they are slaves in a foreign land; the sacred artifacts in the temple are looted; and all of their Gentile neighbors are saying, "Nanny, nanny boo-boo. My god's bigger than your God."

But in the course of their captivity in Babylon, the Assyrians and then the Babylonians eventually give way to the Persians. At the time of these books, though, even their giant empire is under assault from several sides. So, about fifty years after the nations of Israel and Judah were forcibly marched to Babylon, King Cyrus institutes a new policy of allowing captured peoples to return to their homelands, thus creating (what he thought would be) compliant buffer states around his empire. There, in the rubble, the Hebrews eke out a hardscrabble life, much like the German people after World War II. The book of Ezra points out that the first wave of returning immigrants includes—very sensibly, I think—two hundred male and female singers (See Ezra 2:65).

Ezra himself is a scribe, a scholar who reads, interprets, and lives by the first five books of our modern Old Testament: Genesis, Exodus, Leviticus, Numbers, and Deuteronomy (known as the Pentateuch). He and his retinue of priests, servants, and still more singers made the trip in about fourteen weeks. Together, over the course of twenty years or so, under Ezra's leadership, they rebuild a scaled down version of the temple.

This brings us to the book of Nehemiah. Just as in Egypt with Joseph, the Hebrews—an industrious, highly motivated people—eventually find themselves in positions of power and influence in the foreign governments that originally enslaved them. Some Hebrews do so well that they never return and are absorbed in the vast Persian Empire forever—the ten so-called lost tribes. But a few, mostly from the tribes of Judah and Benjamin, still desire to return to the Promised Land someday.

One of them is Nehemiah, cupbearer to the recently installed King Artaxerxes. Even though folks in those days primarily drank wine at every meal, this doesn't sound like a particularly taxing job.

"How was your day at court, dear?"

"Exhausting! I accidentally sloshed some of the *Mouton Rothschild*, and then King Artaxerxes wanted some of the Reserve Cabernet Sauvignon from the lowest vault. Hey! Smell's great. What's for dinner?"

"Chicken with a nice red wine sauce."

"Ack!"

The cupbearer had other duties too. In a day when

142

poison was the popular choice for instituting regime change, the cupbearer was also the royal wine and food-taster. And since many kings in those days believed that wine consumption made them think more clearly (a common misconception held by many drinkers even today), they made most of their important state decisions while under the influence of a particularly fruity *Dom Perignon* with a delicate, almost impertinent fragrance of pears and walnuts. This meant the cupbearer was not only a busy guy; he was usually the king's best bud too.

In short, good work if you can get it.

Nehemiah 2

In the middle of another brutal day of sniffing wine and popping corks, Nehemiah hears from his brother Hanani, just returned from Judah. "Things are bad in the old country," Hanani reports. "Very bad. The walls are down and the neighborhood's gone to the Horonites."

Nehemiah is devastated and does what he always does when he's confronted with important information—he prays. (Not a bad course of action, by the way.)

Nehemiah prays, broods, and fasts for days, even while he's serving the king. This is not a good thing. A cupbearer is also charged with being the Royal Drinking Buddy. Displeasing the king is not how a bureaucrat gets on the Fast Track to Success. Still, when he's not snockered, Artaxerxes is apparently a fairly perceptive guy and notices.

"Yo—what's up, Nehemiah?"

"Nothing, my lord." He's scared now but forges ahead. "Um, actually there *is* something. I can't help but think about my still-devastated homeland, your Majesty. The walls are in rubble. Even the graves of my ancestors are laid to waste."

Fortunately, perhaps because the ravishing Queen Damaspia is sitting next to him, Artaxerxes is feeling gracious. He grants Nehemiah's request to go home, and even provides him with safe passage and supplies for the rebuilding job ahead. Just as modern-day businesses *loan* experts for the local United Way campaigns, Artaxerxes *loans* Nehemiah to Judah for the task of rebuilding the walls around Jerusalem.

Delighted that he still has his head, Nehemiah and his entourage head for Jerusalem. Despite the king's letters of safe passage, Nehemiah finds that—once he reaches Judah—not everybody's glad to see him. In fact, the surrounding forces—Sanballat and the Horonites, the Ashdodites,

143

Geshem and the Arabs, and especially Tobiah and the Ammonites—
like having a weak and subservient Jewish nation and they hassle
Nehemiah. But they're not going to cross Artaxerxes—for now. Still,
Nehemiah takes a politically prudent approach in chapter 2. He surveys
the damage to the city under the cover of darkness. Hanani was
right. The city is in ruins and the people are living like rats. Without the
shelter of the walls, they're susceptible to the depredations of all of
their enemies.

Nehemiah 3—4

The next day, Nehemiah announces his rebuilding plan to the Jewish
leaders in and around Jerusalem. The plan galvanizes the Jews and infuriates their neighbors. But Nehemiah is confident and the reconstruction
of the walls begins. Chapter 3 details which group of people rebuilds
which gates and walls. But by chapter 4, opposition is mounting steadily.
Sanballat and Tobiah stand provocatively with their armies and taunt the
Jews. At one point, Tobiah sneers, "That stone wall they are building—
any fox going up on it would break it down!" (4:3). More than the insults,
the presence of the armies understandably makes Nehemiah and his
friends very nervous.

His response as a good leader? Again—prayer, coupled with action:
"So we prayed to our God, and set a guard as a protection against them
day and night" (4:9). Nehemiah's orders reveal a strong understanding of
military strategy. He stations guards at the most vulnerable places in the
still-unfinished wall, he stations soldiers to guard the parts of the wall
closest to their homes, and he orders all workers to keep their weapons
close at hand even while they work.

Here's another good leadership tidbit: Nehemiah and his servants
worked alongside the workers, stood guard alongside the guards, and
"neither I nor my brothers nor my servants nor the men of the guard
who followed me ever took off our clothes; each kept his weapon in his
right hand" (4:23). (I'm guessing that after a few days of lugging stones
in the Jerusalem heat, none of the natives work too close to Nehemiah
and his men!) In short, Nehemiah is—as William Robinson, President
of Whitworth College says—"leading from the middle" (from a
lecture/Bible study at Laity Lodge, near Leakey, Texas, 2004). To
lead from the middle means you share the joys and sorrows of those
you lead.

144

Nehemiah 5

That trait is never more evident than in chapter 5. Things are going well: everybody's pitching in; the walls are going up. But between the external threats and the construction project, the daily business of life around Jerusalem has ground to a halt. Crops haven't been planted or harvested. As a result, the poor people have had to take out loans just to pay the king's taxes. When they are unable to pay, their own rulers are taking their children as slaves. Just a few generations out of slavery in Babylon, Jews are taking Jews as slaves!

Nehemiah is enraged. But before he takes action, he thinks it over—another good trait for a good leader; don't do anything while you're angry. He then confronts the nobles and officials. But here the narrative takes an interesting twist. Nehemiah discovers that his own family and servants have been lending money and grain, and charging the people interest as well. He's part of the problem! So instead of shaming or threatening the leaders, he calmly outlines what's happened and calls for complete restoration of everything that has been lost—and promises that he and his family will lead the way! Great leaders lead by example. (Not only that, in the twelve years he is in Jerusalem overseeing the rebuilding of the walls, Nehemiah and his significant entourage do not tax the local population for their own upkeep—even though he is responsible for the food and care of one hundred fifty people on a daily basis.) Apparently, this was not the case with the previous governors of Judah.

Nehemiah 6

Not that it's all downhill from here. The Jews are not a tight-knit, cohesive little group. Many stayed behind in Persia (and much earlier, in Egypt). There are daily conflicts between those who left and those who stayed, just as there are frightening tensions today in Iraq, Latvia, Estonia, Lithuania, Bosnia, and other places where people, displaced by one government, return to their original homes—only to face people settled in their place by the government thirty years earlier. What, if anything, does a Greek-speaking Jew from Alexandria have in common with an Aramaic-speaking Jew from Babylon, or with a Hebrew-speaking Jew from Jerusalem?

Nehemiah (as the governor of Judah) also must face down a fierce letter-writing campaign by Tobiah's followers, who seek to undermine his rule by spreading slander to the king of Persia. In fact, some of the

145

unscrupulous behavior and psychological intimidation used by Tobiah and Sanballat's people (no doubt with the blessing of their leaders) in chapter 6 provides a pretty good blueprint for the tactics used by political campaigns in modern times!

Nehemiah 7–9

Nehemiah's life and example reinvigorate the people. The Jewish state steadily grows and prospers, in part through Nehemiah's resettlement of many Jews inside the walls. Ezra reenters the picture in chapter 8. (Again, there is some confusion about whether Ezra and Nehemiah could have actually been contemporaries but—for the sake of the story—let's assume they were.) Amid the rubble, Ezra discovers a complete copy of the Law—the Pentateuch. Perhaps he had one all along, waiting for the completion of the wall, or a similarly significant day, to assemble the people and reread the words of Moses. Perhaps it has been compiled and edited for the first time in Babylon, as many scholars now believe. Regardless, at the newly restored Water Gate, in front of the nation, Ezra and his scribes retell the stories of Abraham, Isaac, Jacob, and Moses. For most of those assembled, this will be the first time they've heard the entire Pentateuch—and the results are electrifying. The reading is followed by a general revival in the land, as the people rededicate themselves to God.

Ezra rebuilt the temple. Nehemiah rebuilt the walls. But they built something even more important. They built a community. Their actions focus the spiritual, political, and economic power of the Israelites in Jerusalem. They unite a fragmented and demoralized people.

Many scholars trace the birth of modern Judaism to this moment. As such, it is a watershed moment in all of history. Dr. Lynn Tatum once told me in a Sunday school class that if Israel were to someday build a Jewish version of Mount Rushmore, it would contain the faces of Abraham, Moses, David, and Ezra.

Imagine, in some distant, post-apocalyptic future, surviving Americans gathering outside the Lincoln Memorial to hear their leaders reread a recently uncovered copy of the Constitution, a document of mythic proportions, one unheard and unseen in hundreds of years. That's the kind of impact this moment has.

146

Nehemiah 12

It's followed by an unusually fun and joyous event. Throughout Ezra and Nehemiah, the text repeatedly refers to "the singers" and their necessity in daily life. These are probably part of the religious chorus in the temple, but even in this hardscrabble existence, the Israelites know the importance of having singers around.

In chapter 12, beginning in verse 27, Nehemiah gathers all the singers from the villages they've built for themselves outside Jerusalem. Imagine! Whole villages of singers! It must have been like Motown or Nashville. He marches them around the walls until they surround the city—the world's first great mass choir!

> They offered great sacrifices that day and rejoiced, for God had made them rejoice with great joy; the women and children also rejoiced. The joy of Jerusalem was heard far away. (Nehemiah 12:43)

And not an overhead projector in sight . . .

147

Nehemiah 13

After a great feast, Nehemiah returns to Persia, where he could have lived out his life in palace luxury. However, there is an interesting coda to the story. In chapter 13, he hears that the current priest, Eliashib, has given one of Nehemiah's old archenemies, Tobiah, extensive rooms in the temple complex. Nehemiah petitions King Artaxerxes to return to Jerusalem one last time. He unceremoniously tosses Tobiah and his "household furniture" (13:8) out onto the street, orders the rooms purified, and scolds the officials.

When we last see him, Nehemiah is again ordering reforms—prohibiting intermarriage with non-Jews and most activities on the Sabbath—some of which endure to this day. Then he disappears from the biblical record. Presumably he returned to Persia and died there, much mourned by the king. Perhaps there is still a handsome tombstone buried deep under the shifting sands that now cover most of Babylon, a stone that marks Nehemiah's grave; a tombstone that tells of a man who received honor in one nation and helped save another.

Nehemiah's last words? One more poignant prayer: "Remember me, O my God, for good" (13:31). You can almost hear an implied "Please?" in there.

Nehemiah's Legacy

The book of Nehemiah is a textbook on good leadership. He was wise, he was adaptable, he listened to the voices of the weak and dispossessed, he countered justice with mercy, and he covered all of his important decisions with prayer.

From Nehemiah's (and Ezra's) time forward, the Jewish people will never again be tempted by idols. Like an addict who needs to reach bottom or have a near-death experience to truly want to reform, it takes the captivity to cure Israel from lusting after golden calves and demons that call for child sacrifice.

Eventually, the temple would be razed—yet again. And the Jews would be forcibly dispersed—yet again.

But lessons—and the victories—won by Nehemiah would never be lost.

Reluctant Prophets and Clueless Disciples

Fourteen

RELUCTANT PROPHETS

The Bible is jam-packed with prophets prophesying. There are powerful prophets who influence kings and nameless prophets who suddenly appear, dash off a few words of warning, and then disappear, never to be seen again. There are lots of angry prophets. There are prophets who work miracles. There are prophets who find that prophesying is hazardous to their health. There's a bald prophet. There's a prophet who loses his head. There are some female prophets. Some call Moses a prophet. John the Baptist was a prophet. There is a prophet who gives his kids crazy names. There are prophets who eat questionable stuff.

You have probably heard of some of the prophets: Isaiah, Jeremiah, Ezekiel, Deborah, Elijah, Elisha, Jonah, and Daniel.

AND WHAT AM I SUPPOSED TO SAY WHEN MY FAMILY ASKS WHY YOU'RE STILL A MINOR PROPHET?

HABAKKUK AT HOME

Some prophets that you may not have heard of have really cool-sounding names that sound like extras from a *Star Wars* movie: Obadiah, Nahum, Habakkuk, Zephaniah, Haggai, Zechariah, and Malachi.

Interestingly enough, for all of their differences, prophets have a lot in common:

First—Most prophets are reluctant.

Second—The activities of most prophets follow a pretty narrow formula:

1. Israel and/or Judah is going to Hades in a handbasket because of idolatry
2. The prophet calls for the nation(s) to repent
3. When Israel/Judah ignore the prophet's warnings, the prophet does something drastic to get their attention
4. Israel/Judah ignore the prophet again
5. God pounds Israel/Judah to get their attention using:
   a. Assyria
   b. Egypt
   c. Babylon
   d. Nineveh
   e. Rome
   f. Whatever nearby pagan kingdom is handy
6. The surviving Hebrews repent
7. The surviving Hebrews get involved with idol-worship again and the whole process repeats

Some of their visions may be utterly indecipherable to us today. Others seem chillingly apropos to life in the twenty-first century.

That said, there are glorious language, spectacular battle scenes, wondrous visions, *and* powerful apocalyptic prophecy in *all* of the prophetic books, especially the so-called Major Prophets: Isaiah, Jeremiah, Ezekiel, and Daniel. This is thrilling stuff.

The prophets themselves are a mixed lot—strident, goofy, compelling, and mystical. Virtually all suffer for their prophecies; some even give the ultimate sacrifice.

The prophets make up more than a third of the Old Testament. And sometimes, in their passion, they may repeat their warnings a few too many times for modern tastes. But even a few thousand years later, they're never dull. Jonah is a perfect example . . .

Jonah

Up to my ears
In bitter tears.
Can't believe I've sunk this low
As I walk the plankton
Inner sanctum.
Got outta Dodge,
Sailed on a bon-less
Bon voyage.
You said North,
I headed South.
Tossed overboard.
Good Lord, that's a really large mouth . . .
("Belly of the Whale," lyrics by Peter Furler/Steve Taylor/Work for Hire. © 2004 Ariose Music/Bob and Larry Publishing/Soylent Tunes. All Rights Reserved. Used by permission.)

Meet Jonah, the Old Testament's most unlovable old coot, the guy who had a close encounter with a whopper and cared more about castor beans than human beings.

The short book of Jonah is a delightful little yarn, one that features a God much more in line with the God of Jesus' teaching, a God who extravagantly loves both all people (not just *chosen people*, the Hebrews) and all of creation (not just humankind).

It's a fast-paced tale, one where events happen at an astonishing clip, told in active verbs, in a breathless, hyperactive voice, and laced with a decidedly comic tone.

If the stories of Moses are a mini-series, then the story of Jonah is a sitcom. It's got everything: a shipwreck, an epidemic of repentance, stray miracles, a big fish who does as he's told, and a reluctant prophet who grudgingly delivers one eight-word prophecy during the entire story, then pouts about it for the rest of the story.

That's right—Jonah is the Homer Simpson of the Bible.

Jonah 1:1-3

Our story begins in an indefinable place at an indefinable time. Our man Jonah—son of Amittai—is minding his own business when the LORD shows up.

"Go at once to Nineveh, that great city, and cry out against it; for their wickedness has come up before me" (1:2) the LORD booms.

Jonah's got a problem. Although we don't know when this story takes place, Nineveh is one of the all-time great blood-enemies of the Hebrews. They hate the Ninevites. Asking Jonah to preach salvation to the Ninevites is like sending Billy Graham to preach to Al Qaeda. All normal, Yahweh-fearing Hebrews despise the folk of the great, sprawling pagan metropolis to the north.

Rather than deliver his prophetic message, Jonah bolts. He heads down to Joppa and boards a boat heading west into the Mediterranean Sea.

Jonah 1:4-17

But for the LORD who created the universe, tracking down one grumpy, self-consumed prophet is no biggie. The LORD covers the entire Mediterranean in a vast storm. The hapless sailors cry to their various gods . . . Nothing. They toss the cargo overboard . . . Nothing. When that fails they try mindless panic . . . *Still* nothing.

Finally, someone notices Jonah, fast asleep in the hold, oblivious to the *perfect storm* raging around him.

The captain quickly figures something's up. He makes his way down into the leaky hold, now already knee-deep in seawater.

"Dude!" the captain shouts over the gale, "What in tarnation are you doing snoozing through this?! Wake up, man. Call on your god to save us. We've tried every other deity on the planet; maybe yours is the right one. YOO-HOO! We're drowning here!"

Jonah, apparently a man of few words back home, doesn't say much here either.

Meanwhile, up on deck, the sailors cast sacred dice trying to figure out who has turned Mother Nature against them.

When Jonah's name is mentioned, the dice come up *snake eyes*.

The sailors drag him to their quarters and pepper him with questions: "Hey! Sleepy head! Why is this happening to us?"

"Wake up; what are you—a professional mattress-tester?"

"Where's home?" "Who are your *homies*?"

Jonah chooses to answer only the last question. "I am a Hebrew . . . I worship the LORD, the God of heaven, who made the sea and the dry land" (1:9). He adds as an afterthought, "Oh yeah, one other little thing. I'm *fleeing* that particular deity—the One who made the earth, the skies, the cosmos, the universe, yadda yadda yadda . . ."

Jonah's apparently not a real *big picture* kind of guy.

152

By now the sailors, who are drenched and shivering, aren't in the mood to play "twenty questions."

"If that's the case, then what the heck did you do to cause the 'God of Heaven, who made the sea and dry land' to be so royally ticked off?!" By now, 100-foot waves are crashing over the tops of the sails. "What should we do?" they wail.

Here's one of the great moments in the Bible. Jonah sighs and as matter-of-factly as if he's ordering extra cucumbers for his gyro says, "Well, I guess you could pick me up and toss me into the sea. I suppose that would quiet this thing down. After all, I'm the guy who started this mess."

Hee hee hee . . . that Jonah; what a kidder . . . He reminds me of Eeyore from *Winnie the Pooh*, and Marvin, the depressive robot from *The Hitchhiker's Guide to the Galaxy*, all rolled into one.

This leaves the sailors and their captain in a pickle. If this lunatic's God really *is* the reason for this breezin', then who knows what the LORD will do to them if they chuck Jonah into the briny deep?

Just in case Jonah's not a fruitcake, they try to row to shore. But God throws in 150-mile-per-hour winds and a few more waterspouts for good measure.

At last, the sailors are out of options. They pray to Jonah's God, hoping to rationalize what they're about to do: "Please, O Jonah's LORD, do not let us perish on account of this idiot. And please don't hold us responsible for innocent blood if we throw him overboard which, by the way, apparently is what this guy really, really wants. Amen."

153

They grab Jonah and pitch him off the starboard bow.

INSTANTLY the clouds clear and the sea becomes as calm and flat as glass.

The sailors stare blankly for a moment then fall all over each other trying to offer a sacrifice to the LORD.

As for gloomy Jonah, the biblical account is characteristically terse:

"But the LORD provided a large fish to swallow up Jonah; and Jonah was in the belly of the fish three days and three nights" (1:17).

Jonah's reaction isn't recorded, but I suspect it was something like this:

"Great. I'm in the stinking belly of a big fish. Wonderful, just wonderful! I *knew* something like this would happen."

> Woke up this morning kinda blue,
> Thinking through that age-old question:
> How to exit a whale's digestion?
> It might behoove me to be heaved.
> Head out like a human comet.
> ("Belly of the Whale," lyrics by Peter Furler/Steve Taylor/Work for Hire. © 2004 Ariose Music/Bob and Larry Publishing/Soylent Tunes. All Rights Reserved. Used by permission.)

Jonah 2

Spending three days awash in gastric juices and dead fish was apparently the slap in the face Jonah needed. Chapter 2 is Jonah's prayer to the LORD, comparing the belly of the fish to *Sheol* (hell), and thanking the LORD in advance for saving him, which, by the way, he's quite ready for. "OK now, anytime, LORD, with the whole deliverance thing; I'm not going anywhere."

Early followers of Christianity will later adopt the three days and nights to symbolize Jesus' three days in the tomb and subsequent resurrection. Images from Jonah's adventure were often featured in early Christian art.

At the end of the three days and nights, the LORD tells the fish to hurl and Jonah—who by now *really* reeks and is probably pale from the stomach acid—is unceremoniously dumped on a beach. Welcome back.

Jonah 3

As Jonah is picking krill out of his hair, the LORD reappears and tells him, once again, to go to Nineveh and preach. Perhaps the ensuing dialogue went something like this:

154

"But look at me, LORD! I'm a mess! I'm covered with fish guts. And I haven't got a thing to wear."

"How about a white sport coat and a pink crustacean?" *(Author's note: Sorry, but I've waited years to use that line.)*

Eventually, Jonah trudges to Nineveh, which is huge. The account says it was so large that it would take a person three days to walk from one end to the other.

He finds an opportune spot and cries, "Forty days more, and Nineveh shall be overthrown!" (3:4).

Ever throw a rock in a pond and watch the ripples radiate toward the bank in all directions? That's the effect Jonah's one-sentence sermon has on Nineveh. It ripples through that great city like a shockwave. Friend shares it with friend; neighbor tells it to neighbor. A great revival spontaneously breaks out; the people immediately repent and begin a fast. Even the king is conscience-stricken. He declares a national time of mourning and prays desperately to Jonah's God, asking that Nineveh be spared. It's one of the great revivals in the entire Bible. And the LORD, in turn, spares Nineveh.

Jonah 4

Great story, right? Everybody loves a happy ending.

Everybody but old Jonah; he's miffed. He's beyond miffed. He rails at the LORD. He's just been an instrument in the salvation of one of Israel's most ancient foes. Everybody back home in Israel is going to be royally ticked off at him when he returns. "Who you gonna save next, Jonah?" they'll sneer. "Egypt? Babylon? We've got a name for people like you, pal."

Finally, Jonah, who says he'd just as soon die as return home, plops himself under a crude lean-to outside Nineveh, hoping against hope that maybe God isn't all that gracious after all and will smite Nineveh with nukes. Day after day he sits, waiting for the fireworks and mushroom cloud.

God, of course, plans to do nothing of the sort. Instead, the LORD causes a fast-growing plant (maybe a castor bean plant or gourd of some kind) to spring up, sheltering Jonah from the brutal Middle Eastern sun.

"Not bad," Jonah thinks, "I can watch the Technicolor destruction of Nineveh in style, now!"

But the very next day, God sends a voracious worm to weaken the plant and the noonday sun shrivels it down to nothing.

155

Jonah is in a real snit now. He demands that the LORD end his life. This guy *really* knows how to throw a pout!

God just laughs:

> You are concerned about the bush, for which you did not labor and which you did not grow; it came into being in a night and perished in a night. And should I not be concerned about Nineveh, that great city, in which there are more than a hundred and twenty thousand persons who do not know their right hand from their left, and also many animals? (Jonah 4:10-11)

And apparently—though the account ends here—Jonah *gets* it. Nineveh is not destroyed. Jonah goes home. The guys down at the pool hall welcome him back with open arms. And no one ever believes the greatest fish story ever told, no matter how many times Jonah tells it.

Except that no one can quite explain why Jonah's hair, eyebrows, and beard suddenly, inexplicably, turned snow white while he was gone.

And what's the deal with all of these clean-cut missionaries from Nineveh who are suddenly in town preaching about the LORD? What's up with that?

Jonah's Legacy

This is what publishers call a *chewy story*, because there is so much content to chew on. Unlike most of the earlier Old Testament books that preach that the Hebrews need to be a people apart, Jonah says that God loves *everybody.* Period. *Finito.* End of story. God even loves "many animals," as the last verse makes clear.

The book of Jonah reads like a hymn to creation. Everything on earth—the skies, the seas, the fish, the plants, even the hungry worms—has a place. They are all cherished by their Creator.

And in the middle of it, blind to the wonders and miracles all around him, is our curmudgeonly friend Jonah.

Jonah, who mopes and whines . . . Jonah, who finally—and reluctantly—does what God asks . . . Jonah, who—after all—sounds a lot like you and me.

156

OLD TESTAMENT CODA

Following the return from exile, and Nehemiah's rebuilding project, Judea (Judah, Benjamin, and some of the surrounding lands) remains a self-governing vassal of the Persian Empire for about two hundred years, before the Macedonian Steamroller, Alexander the Great, defeats the Persians. Alexander's greatest legacy, though, may have been the spread of *Koine* Greek, a language that would come to be spoken by most educated people of the day—and hasten the spread of the Gospel a few hundred years later.

Big Al the Great dies about 323 BCE and there is chaos in his far-flung empire. Two Greek dynasties fight for control of the area around Jerusalem, the Ptolemies (working out of Egypt) and the Seleucids (working out of what is now Syria). At one point, neither side is very strong and, after hideous repression under Antiochus IV, there is a widespread rebellion, led by the Maccabees, beginning about 128 BCE. Forty years later, there is a brief period of independence, a Jewish Spring, even though there are numerous splits within the country between those wanting a secular or religious state.

When the Romans under General Pompey arrive in 63 BCE, the little state is simply no match for the greatest war machine in the world. (Pompey later strives with Julius Caesar for sole control of the Roman Empire, but loses.) One of the Roman puppets, Herod Antipater, trying to curry favor with his simmering population, lavishly remodels and expands Ezra's temple around 20–10 BCE. It is this temple that a young Jesus, born during the Roman occupation, will attend in a few years.

The feisty Jews continue to rebel throughout this period, however, and both the Jewish state and the recently rebuilt temple are destroyed in 70 CE, about thirty-five years after the crucifixion and resurrection of Jesus.

157

Reluctant Prophets and Clueless Disciples

Fifteen

THE PERSONAL TESTIMONY OF MARY, MOTHER OF JESUS
➤ (LUKE 2; MATTHEW 2)

Mary, did you know this sleeping child you're holding
Is the great I AM?
(Mark Lowry and Buddy Greene, "Mary, Did You Know?")

I was just a girl, not quite fourteen. Joseph was much older, but I loved him very much. He was very handsome, too.

But one night, an angel appeared to me! He was both beautiful and frightening at the same time. It seemed like he was larger somehow than the entire room I was sitting in. You can imagine my terror.

And . . . he spoke to me. He said his name was Gabriel. His voice was like quiet, rolling thunder: "Greetings, Mary, you who are highly favored. The Lord is with you."

He must have seen me shaking with fear. "Do not be afraid, for you have found favor with God. You will be with child and give birth to a son and you will name him Jesus. He will be great and will be called the Son of the Most High. The Lord God will give him every throne of his father David and He will reign over the house of Jacob forever and his kingdom will never end."

I was trembling so violently, I couldn't speak, I couldn't move. I could still feel Gabriel's presence, even though I had kept my eyes closed the entire time. At last, I peered up at him. I had to squint because a bright light shone from him.

I said, "How can this be? I'm a virgin."

At first, I thought he was mad at me. I was afraid he might strike me down for daring to question him. His beautiful face was troubled. Now I know that Gabriel was not angry—he was just as frightened as I was. The most important message in history has just been delivered—and he's telling it to a skinny little girl shaking on her knees!

But I guess you don't get to be head angel by questioning the Lord. Gabriel smiled and said, "The Holy Spirit will come upon you and the power of the Most High will cover you. And your son will be called the Son of God. If your cousin Elizabeth has conceived, she who has been barren for so long, do you doubt the power of God? Nothing is impossible with God!"

I was in tears by now. I said, "I am the Lord's servant. May it all happen as you have said." I bowed before Gabriel and when I looked back up—he was gone.

But I knew, even then, that I was pregnant. I just *knew*.

Dear, dear Joseph, of course, was not thrilled with the news. Who would be? At first he was speechless, especially when I told him about the angel. Then he was sad, profoundly, desperately sad. He . . . he made plans to quietly end our engagement. I . . . I don't think he believed me . . . and I am not sure that I blame him. He did not want anyone to know. But he did not speak to me again that day.

That night, however, an angel appeared to Joseph as well. He assured Joseph that everything I had said was true. The angel said, "All of this is taking place to fulfill what the Lord had said through the prophet, *'The virgin will be with child and will give birth to a son and they will call him Immanuel—which means, God with us.'*"

I know Joseph meant to apologize the next day. It is difficult for men to apologize sometimes. But he did, in his own way. And he never doubted me again.

It was a good time to be alive in Nazareth. There was much work for Joseph. The Romans were always building something and Joseph was a master craftsman and builder. He all but had a monopoly on cabinet construction in Nazareth.

160

But to pay for those splendid roads and villas and aqueducts, the Romans needed taxes. And when they needed more taxes, they conducted another census. This one was a nightmare; it took ten years to complete and uprooted half of Israel. We all had to return to our hometowns to be counted. It was madness—whole tribes of people in transit. I've heard that one such census in Gaul took forty years to complete! Of course, it must be difficult to count people who don't want to be counted.

We complied—what else could we do? Even though I was due any day and Joseph would lose a valuable construction contract, we returned to Bethlehem. The roads were clogged and I felt every cobblestone all of the way up my spine.

To make matters worse, neither of us had any family left in Bethlehem and there wasn't a room to be had anywhere. All of the inns were full.

I'm afraid we must have looked a pitiful sight to the last innkeeper. I was as big as a house and we were both covered in dust. He said that travelers were sleeping in hallways and in tents on the roof—there simply was no room for us anywhere.

But he was a compassionate man and offered us a room in a small cave where the animals were kept. He let Joseph sweep it up and bring in some fresh straw. And with the little donkey and the oxen in their stalls, it was probably as warm as a room in the inn.

Through the night, the contractions

The Personal Testimony of Mary, Mother of Jesus

increased until finally, sometime before dawn, Jesus was born. I thought he was the most beautiful baby in the world. Now I know that *all* parents think their babies are the most beautiful children in the world! And he did all of the things babies do—he cried, he slept, and, sometimes, I think he smiled at us.

I barely remember the shepherds coming by that night, babbling something about a star. I do remember a funny old shepherd with a big belly and a bad knee.

We stayed in Bethlehem for two years. Joseph quickly got work and we moved into a small house once the crush of the census was past. We were in Bethlehem long enough to get another surprise. We'd heard wild rumors for several days of an astonishing caravan from the East entering Jerusalem. Three wise men, astrologers or kings, depending on whom you believe, traveled all the way from Babylon through the wild lands beyond the *Pax Romana.* They paid a courtesy call to that monster Herod to assure him of their peaceful intentions. I'm told he casually asked them, "Why have you come?"

They replied, "We are looking for the one called the King of the Jews. The prophecies in the ancient text foretold his coming. When the great star appeared, we took it as a sign. We have come to worship him. Do you know him, O king?"

Immediately, there was an uproar in the court and word spread like wildfire through Jerusalem. But that crafty old fox Herod kept his thoughts to himself. He nodded and said, "Of course. Allow me to assist you in some small way. Meanwhile, please refresh yourselves at my table."

Herod summoned all of his priests and all of the teachers of the law. Within minutes, they appeared from all over Jerusalem, huffing and breathless.

"Why was I not told of this King of the Jews?!" he roared.

The priests conferred and, with trembling knees, quoted the prophet Micah: "*And you, Bethlehem, in the land of Judah, are by no means least among the rulers of Judah; for from you shall come a ruler who is to shepherd my people Israel.*"

Enraged—how dare another king usurp his rule!—Herod dismissed his counselors and called the wise men into chambers. "Go and make a careful search for this child king," he said. "As

162

soon as you find him, report to me, that I may go and . . . *worship* him too."

Bowing, the wise men left. That evening, the star reappeared and led them directly to us! Can you imagine my surprise? We hear a knock and—just outside—is this giant, sprawling royal caravan that stretches halfway to Jerusalem!

Moments later, three gorgeously dressed men stepped forward with gifts and presents. They fell to their knees when they saw Jesus and worshiped him. Joseph and I were mute with wonder and awe. All through the night, they told us amazing stories of the great city with the two giant rivers where they lived, of their perilous journey through bandit-infested hills, and of the brilliant star that miraculously arose each night and led them further and further west.

They also told us what Herod had said. Joseph and I were

very much afraid for Jesus; Herod is infamous for his murderous rages. He's killed his brothers—even his own sons—to secure this very throne. But the wise men easily saw through his ruse. They were also warned in a dream not to return to Herod.

The very next morning, the wise men left, heading south, away from Jerusalem.

The frankincense and myrrh are long gone, but I've hidden

163

away and treasured one of the gold coins from Babylon. One of the wise men said it had once belonged to Daniel, whose writings they still study and revere.

We knew we couldn't stay in Bethlehem. Nor could we return to Nazareth; Herod's spies were everywhere. The angel spoke to us as well and instructed us to flee to Egypt. And so we did, using some of the gold to pay our way.

And when that . . . *creature* died, we returned to Nazareth.

I have never returned to Bethlehem. Herod was furious when he learned that the wise men had tricked him, so he ordered his soldiers to go to Bethlehem and . . . kill all of the baby boys under the age of two. After this slaughter, he left strict orders that no one should mention these murders—under the pain of death.

Every time I went outside, I saw that monster Herod's giant fortress/palace, looming darkly on the horizon to the east.

Sometimes, late at night, my dreams are haunted by the cries of those precious, innocent babies.

As for Jesus, he grew up strong and wise and brave . . . but then, you know the rest of the story. Don't you?

(This material is adapted and reprinted from *I, Jesus*, by Robert Darden. Originally published by The Summit Publishing Group, 1997. Used by permission of Tapestry Press.)

Reluctant Prophets and Clueless Disciples

Sixteen

THE COURT TESTIMONY OF OTHNIEL THE SHEPHERD

Official Court Record

(The shepherd was shabbily dressed, meek, and a tad fearful, particularly at first.)

You sent for me, magistrate?

Yes, I am Othniel, son of Jephunneh. Occupation? As you can plainly see, I am but a humble shepherd—a humble, *law-abiding* shepherd—magistrate. May I inquire as to the charges against me? Disturbing the peace?! Magistrate, on my father's honor, I have never disturbed the peace! Oh the others, from time to time, may pool their pitiful wages for some cheap wine from Cana, but I swear to you I have *never* abandoned my flocks. It is a sacred duty, one that has been handed down in an unbroken chain from David himself. Why the mere thought of leaving my helpless charges in the hills to go to some broken-down tavern in Bethlehem fills me with revulsion. I'd rather . . .

Sorry, sir. Where was I *what* night?

. . . Oh, *that* night.

Where to start? Why yes, magistrate, I suppose the beginning would be a good place. How wise you are. My sainted father once said, "Son, always endeavor to . . . "

The beginning . . . of course . . . the beginning.

It . . . it begins with . . . with a star! There I was, in the hills south of Bethlehem, fiercely alert, patrolling the perimeter around my flock, ever vigilant, ever wary. There are still wolves in those hills, you know, and thieves too. Once, single-handedly, with just my staff, I fought off a ravenous pack of . . .

The star. Well, perhaps I *was* lying on my back at that particular moment. An old war wound, you see, with the Edomites, would you care to see it? No, I suppose not.

Then I saw it!

When you spend most of your life outdoors, you study the heavens a lot. I can find the Pleiades and the band of Orion in a heartbeat. But on this night, I was studying Arcturus when suddenly I noticed a new star near Mazzaroth.

Forgive me magistrate, but this may not seem like much to you city-dwellers, but to shepherds, this is an event of singular importance.

(Pause.) Yes, magistrate, I'm aware that the royal astrologer saw nothing unusual. But may I suggest there was no reason for him to be studying the stars that night. It was, after all, a brisk evening with cool, raw winds coming off the Great Sea. If I may continue …

Yes, yes, the other shepherds noticed it as well, my lord, and came running toward me for, if I may say so, I'm somewhat noted among the shepherds for my—*ahem*—wisdom.

And as we stood marveling at the star, something even more miraculous occurred, something I'm hesitant to repeat even now. No, magistrate, I'm not hiding anything. It's just . . . it's just . . . how do you describe an angel? Light exploded around us, light that reached to heaven itself, light so intense that every blade of grass had a sharp black shadow. And in the middle of that light, surrounded by music, was . . . an angel.

That's right—an angel. The other shepherds threw themselves on the ground and trembled. I got down as best I could, for my knee gives me trouble on cold nights. We all cried in fear.

Suddenly, the angel spoke and it was like low bells ringing. What did the angel say? Magistrate, I'll never forget those words: "Fear not, for behold! I bring you good tidings of great joy, which shall be to all people! For unto you is born this day in the city of David a Savior, which is Christ the Lord. And this shall be a sign to you: Ye shall find the babe wrapped in swaddling clothes, lying in a manger."

166

And as I peeked between my fingers, the air around the angel was filled with thousands of more angels, all spiraling downward from heaven, all singing, "Glory to God in the highest and on earth peace to men and women of good will."

(Pause. The shepherd is looking upward, enraptured; listening to music only he can hear.)

Magistrate . . . forgive me . . . I seem to have something in my eye. My lord, I wish you could have been there. Scarcely an hour goes by when I do not ponder what I "saw and heard"!

What did we do next?

What choice did we have? We conferred a moment, and then darted down the dark hills toward Bethlehem! If it hadn't been for the light of that star, I would have broken a leg for sure. But it cast just enough light that . . .

Oh no, magistrate, I do not deny that I ran shouting through the streets of Bethlehem on the night of the 25th of Tammuz. We all did. The streets were clogged with visitors, sleeping in doorways, huddling around rude fires, all complying with our great beneficent Caesar's mandated census.

Um, yes magistrate. I suppose I did sing. And I most certainly did dance. I'm told I still possess a certain cat-like grace for a man of my age and . . . yes, yes, I did shout. But don't you see? I had no choice in the matter. The long-awaited Messiah! Here! In the City of David! In my lifetime! Praise Yahweh that I lived to see that day!

Well, yes, it is true we peeked in a few houses and tents, but we were looking for the Messiah! I'm truly sorry if we frightened the travelers.

Then we found them, in a rude barn near the old inn on the outskirts of town, not far from Rachel's tomb. I know this sounds crazy, but it seemed as if that star shone atop the inn!

What did we find? You mean you don't know? I thought *everyone* knew by now. Why, we found just what the angel had said we'd find. A family. A newborn baby. A manger. Born that very night, it was.

If I remember a'right, the man's name was Joseph; she was called Mary. And for the second time that night, I heard the angels sing around me. Out of the

The Court Testimony of Othniel the Shepherd

corner of my eye, I saw quick glimpses of them, doing cartwheels of joy in the air, celebrating the birth of the King!

Oh, he looked like any other baby, I suppose. We don't see many babies up in the hills. Lots of lambs, of course, but not many babies. We told Mary all that we'd seen up in the hills. She smiled a lot, but it was a sad smile. Even when we told what the big angel had said, she only nodded gravely and pondered the words. She seemed a little tired after that, so we left. And that's all.

Well, it is true that we kept singing and praising God and stopping people on the streets to tell them what we'd seen. Wouldn't you? No, no: I guess not.

And yes, yes it is true that we stopped by the house of the royal astrologer. We shouted that he needed to come out and look at the new star, but all he did was send for the night watchmen to arrest us.

No, I guess it never occurred to any of us that we were disturbing the peace. We *couldn't* be silent, magistrate. This was the greatest event in the history of humanity and you expect us to go back quietly to our flocks?

Oh—that's *exactly* what you expected us to do. I see.

(Suddenly emboldened.) With all due respect magistrate, if that's disturbing the peace, then so be it! I noticed when the caravan of rich astrologers came from the East a couple of years later, staying up all night singing those strange Babylonian songs, the night watchmen left *them* well enough alone. But let a few poor and raggedy shepherds . . .

(Recoils, as if from a blow.) Yes magistrate, no magistrate. I'm not implying that at all. Forgive me. Forgive a foolish old man. I meant no disrespect. It's just . . . it's just . . .

No magistrate, I'm not calling the royal astrologer a liar. *I saw the star*, we all did. The wise men from the East saw it too. That's how they got here.

Why didn't you see it? Why didn't either of you see it?

I don't know, my lord. Perhaps you had to *want* to see it. Perhaps the message the star brought was something that you had to be taught to see.

Magistrate, I know you are an educated man. I'm just a poor, uneducated shepherd. The lowest of the low. All I have are a few sheep and the stories my father, God rest his soul, told me. But in those stories, he told me time and time again

168

of how a branch out of David, a new Messiah, would someday come. And he said it would be here—in little Bethlehem! Can you believe it?!

But the people of Bethlehem, safe and warm in their little homes, sitting around their cozy little fires, couldn't be roused from their important business to see a star or a baby or even the King of the Universe.

My lord, when I lie out at night, listening to my sheep murmur in the dark, sometimes I think I still see that star. It's burning still. May I suggest that you didn't *want* to see the star? That the royal astrologer didn't *want* to see the star? Or that the people of Bethlehem didn't want to see it either? Why? *Because it wasn't convenient.* It would have interrupted their safe little routine. It would have required some effort on their part. It would have required . . . faith.

But that star burns whether we see it or not. And even if it disappears completely, it will continue burning in my heart because I believe. I *believe,* my lord.

(Pause.) Thank you magistrate. You are very generous. No, I promise on my father's grave that I will stay out of trouble in the future. I learned very quickly that night that no one wants to hear the good news if it isn't convenient.

What's that? No, sire. I've told no one else.

(Pause.) Well, that's not *exactly* true. I told a young physician-in-training named Luke, but I doubt if anything much will come of it.

Meanwhile, sir, you have my promise that you'll never see Othniel, son of Jephunneh in your courts again. No more running through the streets of Bethlehem, shouting about messiahs or angels or stars.

(Pause.) But then, my lord, this is an easy promise to make. That night, I saw an event that happens only once in eternity.

(With a wry smile.) There will, after all, never be a need for me to announce it again.

Good night, magistrate. A thousand blessings on your house for your mercy. Good night.

Seventeen

THE PERSONAL
TESTIMONY OF SIMEON
➡ (LUKE 2:25-35)

Just outside the temple in Jerusalem . . .

Good morning, my dear friends, good morning. Thank you for waiting for me. It gets harder and harder to rouse these old bones each morning, but who's complaining? I see some new friends in our group; this is good. Welcome, welcome. There is plenty of room in our niche in the temple walls for everyone who will learn.

I am so glad to see all of you, for I have something wonderful to tell you!

But first, a bit of background ...

Oh, stop your complaining! We have guests in our midst! They may not know our sacred laws. Now hush. Thank you.

As I was saying, I have been teaching here in the outer courtyard for many, many years—too many years. My young students say that I am part of the *remnant.* They say it with a touch of derision, but it is true. I am one of a small band of Jews who still earnestly seek the consolation of Israel—a Messiah.

Long years ago, an angel, perhaps it was an angel, it seemed bigger somehow, revealed to me in a dream that I shall not die until I have seen the Lord's Christ—the long-awaited Messiah. And so, every day, I have come to the temple, each day hoping and praying that THIS will be the day.

And when that day comes, I will die fulfilled and content.

No, no. You are too kind. In God's truth, I am ready to go. I have lived a full life. It is time to join Father Abraham. I was saying to my good friend Anna just the other day ...

Oh, my wonderful news, of course.

Yesterday, after class, as I walking inside the temple to pray, I saw a young family. Yes, yes, I know hundreds of young families come to the temple daily on the fortieth day after a new baby's birth for the ceremony of purification.

This particular family had just sacrificed two young turtle-doves; it was obvious that they could not afford a lamb. But amid the jostling throng—I saw them—an older man, a beautiful young girl, and her new baby. I had to go to them. No, I can't tell you why.

I must say, the mother was remarkably calm to allow a wild-eyed stranger to take her newborn into my old and shaky hands.

And at that moment, I KNEW! THIS was the baby! THIS was the consolation of Israel!

What did I do? Well, I was so astounded; I mumbled a blessing. I babbled. I sang a psalm.

What's that? You want to hear it?

Funny, I remember it word for word, although it just sprang from my mouth, unbidden. I don't even know how I know it:

Lord, now lettest thou thy servant depart in peace,
according to thy word:
For mine eyes have seen thy salvation,
which thou hast prepared before the face of all people;
A light to lighten the Gentiles,
and the glory of thy people Israel. (Luke 2:29-32, KJV)

This is the strangest part—it didn't feel like a song. It felt like prophecy. It felt like I was seeing this little babe's entire future—Perhaps *our* future.

Imagine my astonishment! Salvation for the Gentiles? Impossible! Even the mother, who had seemed pretty unflappable to that point, was amazed.

But I was not through yet. More words, more prophecy tumbled out. But these words were for the mother and baby alone:

172

Behold, this child is set for the fall and rising again of many in Israel; and for a sign which shall be spoken against; (Yea, a sword shall pierce through thy own soul also,) that the thoughts of many hearts may be revealed. (Luke 2:34-35, KJV)

I cringed when I said those words. I saw great sadness in the young mother's eyes. SHE KNOWS, I thought to myself, SHE KNOWS.

This child, this mother—they will see precious little peace in their lifetimes.

I mumbled my apologies and, in a daze, turned to walk away. What had I done?

But suddenly, the little babe, who had been lying so quietly, cried a little cry. I turned, and he was smiling at me. So I took his tiny hand in my own and kissed it.

My friends, I have seen the Messiah!

It was as if my whole life, my whole being, has been poised for this moment. I felt a peace like none I have ever felt before, nor do I expect to feel it again in this lifetime.

(Pause)

Eh?

Sorry. I . . . I must have been remembering. I am indeed sorry to keep you waiting.

What shall I do next, you ask? What else CAN I do?

My job is done. Class is dismissed—for all time. In the days that remain to me, in the hours that remain to me, I will tell all who will listen:

THE MESSIAH HAS COME!

All flesh is mortal, and the flesh assumed by the Word was no exception in mortal terms. So the birth of the Creator in human flesh and human time was an event as shattering and terrible as the eschaton. If I accept this birth I must accept God's love, and this is pain as well as joy because God's love, as I am coming to understand it, is not like man's love.

. . . My heart lifts at that first great cry which brought creation into being; Christ the second person of the Trinity making all those galaxies burning with incredible brightness, those brilliant flaming suns which themselves are not the light which made them: I rejoice. It's the Word, the Light coming to us as Jesus of Nazareth, which confounds my imagination. (Madeleine L'Engle, *The Irrational Season* [New York: The Seabury Press, 1983], 18–19)

Eighteen

THE LIFE OF JESUS
➤ (MATTHEW, MARK, LUKE, *AND* JOHN)

> Rome was a flea market of borrowed gods and conquered peoples, a bargain basement on two floors, earth and heaven, a mass of filth convoluted in a triple knot as in an intestinal obstruction. Dacians, Herulians, Scythians, Sarmatians, Hyperboreans, heavy wheels without spokes, eyes sunk in fat . . . double chins, illiterate emperors, fish fed on the flesh of learned slaves. There were more people in the world than there have ever been since, all crammed into the passages of the Coliseum, and all wretched.
> And then, into this tasteless heap of gold and marble, He came, light and clothed in an aura, emphatically human, deliberately provincial, Galilean, and at that moment gods and nations ceased to be and man came into being—man the carpenter, man the plowman, man the shepherd with his flock of sheep at sunset, man who does not sound in the least proud, man thankfully celebrated in all the cradle songs of mothers and in all the picture galleries of the world.
> (Boris Pasternak, *Doctor Zhivago* [New York: Pantheon Books, Inc., 1958], 40)

The four so-called Gospels (meaning "good news")—Matthew, Mark, Luke, and John—are forever intertwined. Most of us can't recall which event happened where. Were the shepherds mentioned in Matthew or Luke? Is there an account of the temptation in the wilderness in John? And where the heck is the rest of Mark? We read snippets and patches in church and never get a sense of the whole of the story. (The great actor Alec McCowen regularly performed the entire book of Mark as a one-man show. Hearing it straight through, most listeners realized— maybe for the first time—*it's a story*!)

The four accounts have been lumped together interchangeably almost since the beginning. Which is a shame because, taken on their own, they're four entirely different and pretty nifty stories, each worth a separate study, each illuminating a different facet of the life and teaching of Jesus Christ of Nazareth.

The church has traditionally used the Gospels mostly for teaching doctrine and theology, although in recent years there has been a lot of attention placed on the study of the gospels to help tease out the *historical Jesus*. The story contained in each gospel hasn't really attracted much attention. But to ignore the story is to miss something altogether wonderful in and of itself.

And since this book isn't about history *or* doctrine, here is all the history you're going to get. If we take the current most accepted dates assigned by religious scholars, we're looking at:

3–1 BCE   Birth of Jesus

30 CE   End of Jesus' earthly ministry

40–60 CE   Paul writes the bulk of his letters

70 CE   Jewish revolt ends in destruction of the temple and dispersal of Christians

70 CE   Date assigned for the writing of the book of Mark

85–90 CE   Books of Matthew and Luke written, perhaps using Mark as a basis

90–100 CE   Book of John written

Got all that? (Good, 'cause there's a quiz at the end of the chapter.)

Each Gospel stands alone. Each one tells a story. *Together* they tell a story. If you're looking for perfect harmony among them, forget it. Each writer has a distinctive voice and even more distinctive agenda. When it was assembling what we call the New Testament a thousand years ago or so, the church didn't have to have absolute agreement among the different accounts. The Four Gospels were accepted as inspired truth almost from the beginning because the Christian faith—again, almost from the beginning—*has accepted a splendid diversity among those who believe.*

The advantage of rereading the Gospels as story is that it allows each author to flesh out his account, to allow the story to "breathe" *without changing the unchanging basic truths.* Story is the one approach—not doctrine, not history, not theology—that allows us the gift of speculating on the person of Jesus Christ; to imagine for a moment, "What was Jesus really like?"

Think about it. The most important person in human history, the center point of all time—we still divide all historical events chronologically on either side of the birth of Christ (BCE for Before Common Era and CE for Common Era), and we don't know if he ever laughed or not. We don't know what he looked like.

The main agenda of the gospels is summed up in John 20:30-31 (the *italics* are mine): "Now Jesus did many other signs in the presence of his disciples, which are not written in this book. *But* these *are written so that you may come to believe that Jesus is the Messiah, the Son of God, and that through believing you may have life in his name.*"

Is any one of the Gospels more *right* than the others? Of course not. Each has an important story to tell. To take a single verse out of context, study it, and pronounce great doctrinal truths from it is *not* how these Gospels were meant to be read. They were written to be heard. For many, many centuries, long passages were read aloud to a mostly illiterate popular audience.

And remember—all four Gospel writers take pains to indicate that they're not interested in just writing some dry historical chronology (how could they when great chunks of Jesus' life are never mentioned?). They're much too creative for that. With our finite brains, we're able to see a few of the themes that are introduced. But, as Jeremy Begbie writes in his lovely books on the connections between Christianity and music, the great composers incorporate the smaller themes with a greater theme that won't resolve until the very end. That great over-arching theme was there all along; we just didn't have the overview of the complete composition to hear it. (See Jeremy S. Begbie, *Theology, Music and Time* [Cambridge: Cambridge University Press, 2000], chap. 4.)

So, let's look at this Great Story. The best way is to read each one in one sitting, with some time to reflect on what you've read. All are equally true. All are equally valid variations on the same theme.

But until you get around to doing that, maybe this overview of the Jesus narrative—told using the Hero's Journey model—may help you get a handle on the most extraordinary life of all time.

ACT I

Ordinary World (Luke 2:41-52)

Matthew and Luke contain the infancy narratives—the stories of the virgin birth, flight to Egypt, angels, shepherds, wise men, and stars— what songwriter Michael Been describes as "a scene beyond dreams." But Mark and John open with John the Baptist proclaiming Jesus' ministry. Our best guess is that Jesus would be about thirty years old at the time. Other than the tantalizingly brief incident at the temple in Jerusalem, we don't know anything about Jesus' first thirty years. The Ordinary World for Jesus was a dusty backwater town in an obscure corner of the vast Roman Empire. He was probably a skilled carpenter—most sons studied their dad's trade back then. Perhaps he worked on one of the many Roman forts that dominated the countryside.

When Jesus is about age twelve his family goes to Jerusalem for the Passover, but when they head for home, he's nowhere to be found. They return to Jerusalem and finally find him conversing with the teachers at the temple. Flabbergasted, his mom says: " 'Child, why have you treated us like this? Look, your father and I have been searching for you in great anxiety.' He said to them, 'Why were you searching for me? Did you not know that I must be in my Father's house?'" (Luke 2:48-49).

Besides the fact that this is the last mention of Joseph, it is an intriguing exchange for a lot of reasons. Why include this incident and not one of hundreds, perhaps thousands, of others from Jesus' boyhood? What does the author of this book want us to understand from it?

The fact that Jesus is hanging with the teachers at age twelve, on apparently even footing, tells us he's one pretty smart young fellow. At first glance, though, his response to Mary's understandably distraught question seems flippant, almost arrogant. We know, however, from all later dialogues with Jesus, that one thing he is *not* is arrogant. So we're left to assume that his response "Did you not know that I must be in my Father's house?" implies that Jesus has given his parents plenty of prior indications that he's focused on a higher calling.

If you're a storyteller, then, the primary dramatic question is this: "At what point in his life does Jesus know what's ahead?" Does he, at age twelve, know he'll be tortured and hung on a Roman cross to die, only to be resurrected in three days? It's not a particularly important question

178

from a theological standpoint, but it's a compelling question from a *story* standpoint. Motivation, after all, makes a character in a story come to life.

And that's it. Other than to say that he was obedient and got smarter (and taller) after that, the Gospels are silent on his life until he turns thirty. Then *boom!* The adventure begins. At some point, *something* calls him to leave the familiar, to leave the safe, for the unknown.

Call to Adventure (Luke 3:21-22)

If we're looking for a Call to Adventure, then let's move to the baptismal sequence in Luke 3:21-22, where, not only does John the Baptist baptize him, but the Holy Spirit descends on Jesus "like a dove." Then, a voice from heaven says, "You are my Son, the Beloved; with you I am well pleased." No mention of the virgin birth and Bethlehem narratives. Jesus just *is*. Jesus has apparently been a pretty good fellow to this point (or the *Voice* wouldn't have been "well pleased"), but again we don't get any details.

Refusal of the Call (John 2:1-11)

The other gospels go from here to the Temptation in the desert. Not the book of John. He takes Jesus to the so-called Wedding in Cana, which is *not* mentioned in the other three, but which is specifically said to be the third day following his *call* in John. It's a Jewish wedding like any other wedding but—horror of horrors!—they're running out of wine. Everybody's panicked. Mary (who is never identified as such, but is always called "the mother of Jesus") correctly identifies the problem but doesn't ask

Jesus directly for help. She knows he'll take care of things. How does she know? Has he already accomplished miracles known only to her? The fact that she orders the help to "Do whatever he tells you" (2:5) implies that she knows *something*.

Once again, Jesus' response to his mother sounds somewhat harsh to our ears, 2,000 years later: "Woman, what concern is that to you and to me? My hour has not yet come" (2:4).

I may be reading too much into Jesus' response here, but there seems to be a real reluctance in his voice. Is this Jesus' Point of No Return? Like Julius Caesar at the Rubicon River, once Jesus crosses this pivotal threshold, there is no turning back. The question remains the same: *Does he know what lies ahead at this point?* With the miracle, forces will be unleashed that can't be recalled, a *genie* that can't be forced back into a bottle. Once the ministry is initiated, Jesus knows it will build its own momentum until it becomes unstoppable. But does he know now *how* it will end? This is our Reluctant Hero. But Jesus is only reluctant a moment, he immediately changes the water into wine and saves the wedding.

180

One interesting side-note here: John plainly says the miracle in Cana is the beginning of miracles, "the first of his signs" (2:11), which directly refutes numerous stories in the apocryphal books about Jesus as a boy and adolescent—including one particularly goofy yarn where Jesus, miffed at some noisy birds—zaps 'em and turns 'em into clay!

The book of John diverges at this point from the accounts found in Matthew, Mark, and Luke—the "Synoptic" gospels. They go to the Temptation in the desert, although Mark's account is rudimentary at best. If I were telling this story, I would insert the Temptation in the desert just before the miracle at the wedding in Cana—the soul-searching *then* the miracle that formally initiates the ministry. John doesn't include the temptation stories at all. Why? Perhaps the real temptation takes place at the wedding in Cana.

Crossing the First Threshold (Matthew 4:1-11)

Of the three desert stories, Matthew's account is the most intriguing. Satan tries three different temptations to lure a gaunt and hungry Jesus into a misstep. Jesus, apparently, easily brushes them all aside. I like Matthew's account because Matthew seems to have his *own* Crossing the First Threshold in the verses that follow, 4:12-17. After the Temptation, Jesus hears that John the Baptist has been arrested by the king, and leaves his home in Nazareth and moves to Capernaum by the sea. Verse 17 is emphatic: "From that time Jesus began to proclaim,

YOU IDIOT! THAT'S THE HEAD OF JOHN THE METHODIST!

©2002 ROGER JUDD

'Repent, for the kingdom of heaven has come near.'" It's as if the arrest of John is the catalyst for Jesus' ministry.

From that time—the gauntlet has been passed from John to Jesus. *From that time*—Jesus is on a path that leads inexorably to a wooden cross on a wind-swept hill just outside the gates of Jerusalem.

181

With the Crossing of the First Threshold, our Act I is complete. Now we turn to the longest and hardest act.

ACT II

Tests, Allies, and Enemies

Particularly in John, it is easy to see the increased intensity of Jesus' mission and miracles, from the relatively low-key wedding in Cana through the dramatic raising of Lazarus, foreshadowing the greatest miracle of all—Jesus' own conquest of Death.

Likewise, the forces arrayed against Jesus grow as his fame grows, from a handful of Sadducees and Pharisees to *lots* of Sadducees, Pharisees, Priests, Scribes, Herodians—and just about anybody who feels their place in the religious status quo is threatened by this quiet man from Nazareth.

And always on the periphery, watching, waiting, are the Romans—creators of one of history's greatest

It's important to pause a moment and realize, 2,000 years later, just how small Jesus' world really was. The lands that he traversed in his lifetime are about the same distance as it is from Dallas to Waco, Texas—maybe 100 miles. Mike Yaconelli reminds us just how small Jesus' ministry was during his lifetime. Except for a few crowds (the feeding of the 5,000), which Jesus generally tried to avoid, he just couldn't physically reach all that many people in just over three years: "He hung out with a few guys, healed a leper or two and a couple of lame folk and a blind guy, made some wine, helped out three or four women, raised one person from the dead, calmed down a crazy person or two, caused a scene in the temple, and then disappeared" (*Messy Spirituality* [Grand Rapids: Zondervan, 2002], 109).

About all he did was change the course of history! He could have reached a lot more people had he concentrated on the big population centers. But Jesus never made it to Rome (the center of the known western world) and avoided Jerusalem whenever possible. Instead, Jesus preferred to work one on one or in small groups. A study of a particularly flashy crusade by a well-known televangelist a few years ago found that hundreds of people *made a commitment* at the end of the televangelist's emotional plea on the final night. But when researchers followed up, only a tiny fraction was still involved in religion (much less a local church) a year later and fewer still just five years after the fact.

182

dynasties and mightiest armies. Palestine is a small but troublesome province in an empire that spans the known globe. The Romans are an occupation army; a posting to Palestine is the equivalent of a Soviet soldier being sent to serve in Siberia during the hey-day of the U.S.S.R. The Romans have seen prophets come and go. They're content, for now, to let this one preach—at least until they're convinced that he poses a threat to the Roman-mandated peace, the *Pax Romana*.

On Jesus' side throughout the ensuing three and a half years, we find a motley band of disciples, a larger group of fair-weather followers, a few close friends—Mary, Martha, Lazarus, Mary Magdalene—a few pious men and women in the Jewish hierarchy, a handful of zealots who think Jesus is their ticket to overthrow Rome, and a few friends who don't turn out to be friends at all. It hardly seems like a fair fight.

But they never knew what hit 'em.

Cleansing of the Temple (John 2:13-22)

OK, back to the story. If we're following the book of John, we next

come to the cleansing of the temple in Jerusalem, one of the most famous incidents in the four gospels. Jesus, enraged that moneychangers stealing from hapless pilgrims are corrupting his Father's house, drives everybody and their dog (and sheep and goat and calf) out of the temple. Matthew, Mark, and Luke hold this story to the end of their narratives.

From a storytelling standpoint, is the cleansing told better now or later? In the Synoptics, it takes place the final week in Jerusalem, in the days before the crucifixion. It raises the stakes so much that the enemies of Jesus are forced to take action. It's a deliberate, high profile act that compels an equally ferocious response. But John chooses to start off with it. Why?

Perhaps John places it here to function as the prophetic inauguration of Jesus' ministry, to signal to the reader, "Hey! Hang on to your hat! You're about to read an in-your-face narrative about a guy who does what is right *at all costs*. Dismiss him if you like, but you're not going to be able to ignore him."

The incident at the temple doubtless galvanized the entire city. Years later, guys would still be trying to impress girls by saying things like, "Oh yeah, I was there that day. It was cool. Tossed a few pigeons out myself. Jesus was *seriously* irate that day."

The Personality of Jesus (Matthew 23; Mark 3:1-6, 6:34-49; Luke 10)

The cleansing of the temple is also one of the few tantalizing hints we have as to Jesus' personality. For all of the songs and stories of "sweet Jesus, meek and mild" we're shown many instances of Jesus' anger: the cleansing of the temple, the time he zapped a barren fig tree, and a venomous denunciation of the scribes and Pharisees in Matthew 23. Jesus didn't paint all Pharisees with one broad brush; he had friends who were Pharisees and some were doing some pretty important work in reviving the Jewish faith. But one particular batch gets this, his mightiest curse:

> "Woe to you, scribes and Pharisees, hypocrites! For you are like whitewashed tombs, which on the outside look beautiful, but inside they are full of the bones of the dead and of all kinds of filth." (Matthew 23:27)

His eyes must have been burning laser beams through the unfortunate souls at the receiving end of *that* polemic. Jesus never tolerated powerful men and women who exploited helpless people.

But my favorite, perhaps the most human expression of Jesus' anger and hurt, is found in Mark 3:1-6. Jesus is in a synagogue with the scribes and Pharisees (who apparently didn't have day jobs) when a man with a withered hand comes up to him. His enemies taunt him, daring Jesus to break the rules regarding healing on the Sabbath. Jesus' eyes narrow dangerously: "Is it lawful to do good or to do harm on the Sabbath, to save life or to kill?" (3:4). The scribes and Pharisees search desperately for a witty comeback. Nothing. Silence.

184

He looked around at them with anger; he was grieved at their hardness of heart and said to the man, "Stretch out your hand." He stretched it out, and his hand was restored. The Pharisees went out and immediately conspired with the Herodians against him, how to destroy him. (Mark 3:5-6)

Jesus is both angered *and* grieved, not because he knows the bad guys will use this against him, but because they would rather keep their petty laws and undermine Jesus than see this poor guy get his hand back. Jesus grieves for the injured man *and* he grieves for the hearts of those who hate him.

Conversely, we have dozens and dozens of instances of Jesus' compassion. He heals people until He's so exhausted he can barely walk. Again, one of my favorite examples of Jesus' love and compassion is in Mark's urgent, headlong gospel. Following the death of John the Baptist, a large group of people follow Jesus and, just prior to the feeding of the 5,000, we have this lovely passage in Mark 6:34:

"Hey, we're the first HMO."

> As he went ashore, he saw a great crowd; and he had compassion for them, because they were like sheep without a shepherd; and he began to teach them many things.

Exhausted and frazzled, Jesus still can't bear to see hurting, needy people. Moments later, when the food is ordered up, Jesus orders the disciples to arrange the hungry people "on the green grass" (Mark 6:39). This writer is in such a hurry that he never tells us a single intimate detail of Jesus' life, and yet he pauses to mention that Jesus wanted the crowd arrayed on the soft grass.

185

How about joy or happiness? Do we have many instances where we know that Jesus was happy? Not many. The writers of the gospel rarely share this side of his personality with us. But Luke 10 pulls aside the curtain ever so slightly. At the end of chapter 9, Jesus has made it clear that—regardless of the consequences—He's now heading toward Jerusalem. Knowing his time is short, Jesus appoints seventy or so missionaries to travel throughout the country, spreading the good news, taking nothing but the clothes on their backs. In time, all seventy return safely, thrilled at what they've seen: "Lord, in your name even the demons submit to us!" (Luke 10:17).

Perhaps a little relieved that his motley band of followers *do* have the right stuff to continue his ministry, Jesus' response reveals a rare, if fleeting, moment of joy:

> At that same hour Jesus rejoiced in the Holy Spirit and said, "I thank you, Father, Lord of heaven and earth, because you have hidden these things from the wise and the intelligent and have revealed them to infants; yes, Father, for such was your gracious will." (Luke 10:21)

Beyond incidents like these, we know precious little of his personality. Jesus sometimes allows himself a heartbeat of righteous anger; most of the time he is merciful and loving. Everything else is speculation.

Teaching and Miracles

We could spend an entire book (as many authors have) just analyzing the parables of Jesus, so we'll cover some of the best-known parables in the next chapter. Instead, as part of our study of his story, let's look at the teachings and the miracles—exorcisms, feedings, and healings—of Jesus. Here are a few of the more notable examples.

- Teaching (John 13–17) -

The greatest sustained period of teaching from the Gospels is found in the 13th through 17th chapters of John—five complete chapters devoted to the lessons taught at a single meal—the Last Supper. What gets only a couple of paragraphs in Mark is expanded and developed at length in John. While the mood is doubtless somber and weighty, it is infused with a powerful sense of urgency—Jesus alone knows that this is the final message, the final sermon, and that these are the final hours. It is like

186

the comprehensive examinations for doctoral candidates. The Teacher can't leave until he is sure his charges understand—for all of their bumbling blindness to this point—that they truly understand what is to come and what their roles will be.

These are some of the most direct, unequivocal teachings Jesus ever shares with his disciples. Nothing like this exists elsewhere in the Bible. Throughout these five chapters, Jesus carefully repeats and restates many of his most basic themes over and over again until even the dullest among the disciples begins to get an inkling of what is at stake. There are few parables here and the plan of salvation is spelled out in just a few, carefully chosen images . . . so much to tell and so little time.

Naturally, volumes have been written on these chapters and they require—no, deserve—much care and study. Still, a few basic lessons are worth outlining here.

The so-called Farewell Meal and Discourse begins with the meal itself (see John 13:1-30). This is the last time Jesus will eat with his friends and followers before the crucifixion and resurrection. He talks of a perfect love and then, as if to illustrate that love, tries to wash the disciples' dusty feet. Peter is aghast and refuses, but Jesus gently reproves him. He knows that not all of his followers are *clean*—Judas will shortly betray him. As a final act of mercy, Jesus *allows* Judas to leave and meet with those who will kill him.

The rest of these chapters, except for a final prayer at the end of chapter 17, are composed of Jesus deliberately, urgently reinforcing his message to the remaining eleven disciples. This *discourse* is the source of many of the most famous, most memorable sayings of Jesus, including:

> I give you a new commandment, that you love one another. Just as I have loved you, you also should love one another. By this everyone will know that you are my disciples, if you have love for one another. (John 13:34-35)

> Do not let your hearts be troubled. Believe in God, believe also in me. In my Father's house there are many dwelling places. If it were not so, would I have told you that I go to prepare a place for you? And if I go and prepare a place for you, I will come again and will take you to myself, so that where I am, there you may be also. (14:1-3)

> Thomas said to him, "Lord, we do not know where you are going. How can we know the way?" Jesus said to him, "I am the way, and the truth, and the life. No one comes to the Father except through me." (14:5-6)

> I will do whatever you ask in my name, so that the Father may be glorified in the Son. If in my name you ask for anything, I will do it. If you love me, you will

keep my commandments. And I will ask the Father, and he will give you another Advocate to be with you forever. (14:13-16)

I have said these things to you while I am still with you. But the Advocate, the Holy Spirit, whom the Father will send in my name, will teach you everything, and remind you of all that I have said to you. Peace I leave with you; my peace I give to you. I do not give to you as the world gives. Do not let your hearts be troubled, and do not let them be afraid. (14:25-27)

This is my commandment, that you love one another as I have loved you. No one has greater love than this, to lay down one's life for one's friends. (15:12-13)

By the way, if you only had a couple of verses to understand the entire Bible, you could do worse than two short verses from the book of John:

For God so loved the world that he gave his only Son, so that everyone who believes in him may not perish but may have eternal life. (John 3:16)

And Jesus said to him, "I am the way, and the truth, and the life. No one comes to the Father except through me." (14:6)

One final note on the *discourse*—at one point during the conversation, the disciples commend Jesus for finally speaking "plainly" (16:29) and say that they finally understand everything he's telling them. Jesus' response? "I have said this to you, so that in me you may have peace. In the world you face persecution. But take courage; I have conquered the world" (16:33)!

And yet—with irony that says as much about us as it says about the disciples—in twenty-four hours, these same folks who say they finally *get it* will abandon Jesus or deny him, or both, at his hour of greatest need.

When Jesus was not telling parables or teaching, he was invariably helping people. All of his miracles, in one way or another, made life easier for those he touched, and provided valuable lessons for all who witnessed them.

– Casting Out Demons (Mark 5:1-20) –

Matthew, Mark, and Luke each tell the story of the *demoniac* that Jesus and the disciples encounter in the land of the Gentiles, although there are slight differences in the three accounts. For instance, Mark and Luke place it in the land of the *Gerasenes*, while Matthew puts it in the land of the *Gadarenes*. Matthew says there are two demoniacs; Mark and Luke say there is only one. But the story is essentially the same.

188

Immediately after Jesus stills the storm (see Mark 4:35-41), we pick up the account in Mark 5:1-20. Jesus and his band land in a different country where a particularly unfortunate individual confronts them. This guy lives in a cemetery and is so prone to hurting himself that the townsfolk often restrain him in chains. But his demon-fueled strength is such that he breaks the chains and roams the countryside day and night howling in pain. (There go the property values!) In addition to superhuman strength, the demons in him give the man extrasensory perception—he senses the little boat before it lands and runs to the shore to meet Jesus.

"What have you to do with me, Jesus, Son of the Most High God?" (5:7a), the unnamed man—and his demons—howl: "I adjure you by God, do not torment me" (5:7b).

Jesus, no slouch in the supernatural department himself, immediately understands the man's problem and shouts, "Come out of the man, you unclean spirit!" (5:8).

This is intriguing. Whenever Jesus is confronted with a demon, the demon immediately recognizes who Jesus is, even if the humans all around him do not. The demons obviously see something in the spirit world not visible to human eyes. They're trying to ward off an exorcism and Jesus is having none of it.

"What is your name?" (5:9a), Jesus asks coolly.

"My name is Legion; for we are many" (5:9b), they reply.

Wow—this is a *seriously* split personality. A Roman legion is about 6,000 soldiers and all 6,000 demons beg Jesus not to send them out of the neighborhood. They spot a herd of pigs feeding nearby under the care of a couple of swineherds. Swine were considered unclean animals and don't show up much in primarily Jewish lands, but they were a popular food source in the neighboring countries.

189

In desperation, the demons implore, "Send us into the swine; let us enter them" (5:12).

The demons think they're out-foxing Jesus. Once he leaves, they'll leave the pigs and look for human hosts. But Jesus is not about to let 6,000 demons roam the countryside. Or is the number really 48,000? Look at what Jesus says about exorcised spirits in Luke 11:24-26:

> When the unclean spirit has gone out of a person, it wanders through waterless regions looking for a resting place, but not finding any, it says, "I will return to my house from which I came." When it comes, it finds it swept and put in order. Then it goes and brings seven other spirits more evil than itself, and they enter and live there; and the last state of that person is worse than the first.

Yee-ow! Fortunately, Jesus knows what will happen. Two thousand pigs panic and thunder away in confusion, throwing themselves off a cliff to drown in the sea. Suddenly unemployed, the swineherds dash off, run to the nearby town, and blame Jesus. (Swine-less swineherds not being in great demand, normally.) When the townsfolk arrive, Jesus and the now-sane man are conversing normally. Frightened, the people ask Jesus to leave. He does, but not before the guy begs Jesus to be allowed to tag along. Jesus gently refuses and tells him to go home and tell his friends (not that he probably had a lot—a crazy man who lives in a cemetery and howls all night isn't exactly the life of the party) what has happened. The guy does and takes the message to the Decapolis, the ten mostly Greek cities north of the Sea of Galilee. The Bible says those who heard were "amazed" (Mark 5:20)—and as so often happened, Jesus' message is conveyed by a few to the many.

- A Healing Miracle (John 9) -

Which ones to choose? Jesus hated to see people in pain and never refused (that we know of) a healing opportunity. The great majority we don't know anything about—He simply healed as he went. Contrast that to the televangelists, who make a great show with lights and music *healing* a select few for the cameras (although none of the healings has ever been medically verified), while desperately needy people sit outside the coliseums, denied entrance or access. Among the most fascinating of Jesus' healings is one that involves a smart-mouthed, formerly blind man in John 9. This guy could have been a standup comedian had he been around, oh, say, 2,000 years later.

As usual, this starts with the Pharisees trying to trick or trap Jesus, only to have their little plan blow up in their faces in the end. Jesus and

190

the disciples are walking along when they pass a guy who had been blind since birth. We'll call him "Bill." Let's see how this reads in "screenplay" format:

SCENE I: A JERUSALEM STREET

PETER
Rabbi, who sinned? This man or his parents that he was born blind?

JESUS
(*Patiently*) Neither this man nor his parents sinned. He was born blind so that God's work might be revealed in him. We must work the works of him who sent me while it is day; night is coming when no one can work. As long as I am in the world, I am the light of the world.
(*Jesus spits on the ground, makes a mud-pie and gently daubs the mud on Bill's eyes.*)

JESUS
(*To Bill*) Go, wash in the pool of Siloam.
(*Bill stumbles off, does as Jesus says, and suddenly he can see! He dances around in joy, looking at everything. A small crowd gathers.*)

NEIGHBOR #1
Isn't this Bill—who used to sit and beg?

BILL
Hey, it's me.

NEIGHBOR #2
Yup, that's Bill. Used to be blind as a bat.

BILL
It's me!

NEIGHBOR #3
Can't be. Bill's blind. Dude looks a lot like Bill, though.

BILL
IT'S ME!

NEIGHBOR #3

If you're really Bill—and I'll admit the resemblance is uncanny—how can you see? The Bill I know is blind.

BILL

(*Exasperated*) The man called Jesus made mud, spread it on my eyes, and said to me, "Go to Siloam and wash." Then I went and washed and received my sight!

NEIGHBOR #3

Dang, I coulda *sworn* that you were Bill.

NEIGHBOR #2

Say—where is this Jesus anyhow?

BILL

I don't know—I was blind, remember? *Helloooooo.*

NEIGHBOR #3

I know, let's take him to the Pharisees. They can sort this out.

SCENE II: JERUSALEM STARBUCKS— THE PHARISEES' HANG-OUT

PHARISEE #1

(*Soothingly*) How did you regain your sight, Bill? From the beginning, please.

BILL

I've told you this already! A guy named Jesus put mud on my eyes. Says go wash in the pool. I got nothing else going on, this being a Sunday and all—and being that I'm blind, I'm not going to be watching any TV—so I do. Then I see. Simple, easy.

PHARISEE #2

This Jesus guy can't be on the God Squad 'cause today's Sunday and *good people don't do work on Sunday.*

PHARISEE #1

Um, but then if Jesus *is* a sinner, then how can he do miracles?

192

PHARISEE #2

OK, then *you* explain it, smart guy.

PHARISEE #1

(To Bill) What do *you* say about him? I mean, after all, it was *your* eyes he opened, right?

BILL

Listen: Any guy opens my eyes is a prophet in my book.

PHARISEE #2

Of course he'd say that. I don't believe for a second this guy was ever really blind. Let's get his parents!

(Pharisee #1 dashes off. A few minutes later, Peg and Chuck, Bill's parents, return, order a latte to calm their nerves, and sit at the Pharisee table.)

PHARISEE #2

OK—look at this guy. Is this your son? The one you claim was born blind? How come he's all of sudden got 20/20 vision here, people?

PEG

(Nervously) That's our boy, but I have no idea how come he can now see. Bill, honey, you never write, you never call . . . would it hurt you so much to keep your old mother informed about the big events in your life sometime?

BILL

Aw, ma.

PEG

(To Pharisee #2) Hey, he's a big boy. You ask him.

PHARISEE #2

Last chance, big mouth. We know this Jesus is a sinner and sinners can't heal people. Period. Also, it isn't exactly healthy to go around blabbing about this Jesus guy, if you know what I mean and I think you do.

BILL

Man, I don't know *anything* about Jesus except this: I was

193

once blind, now I see. Case closed. End of story. Badda-bing, badda-boom.

PHARISEE #1
Not so fast. Exactly how *did* he restore your sight?

BILL
I've told you jokers this story a dozen times already. Why do you want to hear it again? Is your satellite dish on the fritz? *(BEAT)* Hey, I've got it—*you* want to become his disciples! Cool!
(Pharisee #2 angrily jumps up and spills his espresso on Pharisee #1.)

PHARISEE #2
No, *you* are his disciple! We're disciples of Moses! Moses we know, but this Jesus could be from anywhere! He appears out of nowhere and restores your eyesight? For nothing? A likely story.

BILL
Whoa, chill dude. This is pretty amazing, when you think about it. God may not be listening to sinners, but he *does* listen to the folks who worship him and obey him—or so I'm told. So this has gotta be a first—someone's sight is restored and you're saying this Jesus guy has got to be from Satan? Man, if Jesus *wasn't* from God, *how could he do this?*

PHARISEE #1
You're a crummy little formerly blind guy and you're trying to teach us teachers? The nerve of some people. *Getouttahere.*
(The Pharisees gang up on Bill, Peg, and Chuck and roughly drive them out of the Starbucks.)
(After a few minutes, they run into Jesus and his posse. Jesus walks up to Bill and puts his arm around him.)

JESUS
Bill, do you believe in the Son of Man?

BILL
And who is he, sir? Tell me, so that I may believe in him.

194

JESUS
(Whispers) You have seen him, and the one speaking with you is he.

(Bill falls on his knees and grabs Jesus' tunic.)

BILL
Lord, I believe!

JESUS
(To disciples) I came into this world for judgment so that those who do not see may see, and those who do see may become blind.

(By now the Pharisees have come storming up, still looking for trouble.)

PHARISEE #2
Oh, now you're saying that we're blind!

JESUS
If you were blind, you would not have sin. But now that you say, "We see," your sin remains!

BILL
You tell 'em, Big Guy!

PEG
Oh, I think I left the lamb in the oven! Bill, why don't you invite your new friends over for dinner?

PETER
(To Pharisees) You guys are toast!

As with many of Jesus' healings, much is happening here. Jesus is defying a notion that some people have held since Job's day—and some modern Christians still hold today—that sick people are sick because of sin in their lives. In the process, an innocent man is healed and set free. The Pharisees' hypocrisy is confronted. The disciples receive a valuable lesson on the nature of sin. And today, discerning readers can glean a valuable theological insight on the nature of *sight*. When Jesus heals, he heals on multiple levels.

Transfiguration—or—The Turning Point

And so the quest continues—more foes, more barriers, more teaching, more parables, more healings. This work is particularly poignant when you stop and wonder: When does Jesus know EVERYTHING—*including the death on the cross*—that's ahead for him? And is he given the ability to see beyond the cross to the resurrection? Death is horrible, but if you know, beyond a shadow of a doubt, that you'll be resurrected after a couple of days, does that make it more bearable? Or does Jesus' vision of the future, at least at this stage of the journey, meet with a dark wall at the blackness beyond the grave?

It's certainly possible to read Matthew 10:38-39 and Matthew 11:25-27 and come away with the impression that *Jesus knew*. Even so, it isn't made overt in Matthew's gospel until chapter 16:13-23, when Jesus asks his *homies*, "Who do people say that I am?" They give various answers until eager-beaver Peter pipes up, "You are the Messiah, the Son of the Living God" (16:16). Bingo! But Matthew follows this exchange with these ominous words:

> From that time on, Jesus began to show his disciples that he must go to Jerusalem and undergo great suffering at the hands of the elders and chief priests and scribes, and be killed, and on the third day be raised. (Matthew 16:21)

This account is very similar to the one outlined in Mark 8:27-33. The transfiguration follows in both books. *Transfiguration* means, "to change the appearance of." But the root of the term is found in the Greek word *metamorphosis*—indicating not just an outward change, but an inward one as well. Something is different about Jesus, but we're never told quite what. Perhaps it is this knowledge of the future beyond the cross—perhaps not.

The version of the transfiguration in Mark 9:2-9 is the most fascinating, a Technicolor spectacular right out of the old Hollywood movies. After cameo appearances by Moses and Elijah, Jesus' clothes turn a dazzling white. Suddenly, a voice from heaven booms, "This is my Son, the Beloved; listen to him!" (9:7). Moses and Elijah are *taken up* into heaven and the obviously shaken little band comes back down the mountain. Jesus orders " them to tell no one about what they had seen, until after the Son of Man had risen from the dead" (9:9).

Eventually, they figure out what he was telling/showing them. (Um, guys, that's why the Voice in the Cloud said, "LISTEN TO HIM!") The appearance of Moses and Elijah may be a clue to the purpose of having the transfiguration happen at this point in the life of Christ. Jewish readers would immediately remember that Elijah was *taken up to heaven* by the LORD and that the LORD buried Moses in secret. Something incredible is planned for this Jesus of Nazareth in the days following their little foray up Mount Hermon, something that will only become clear *after* the crucifixion.

In the classic screenplay format, this is the midpoint of the story. Until now, the movie was apparently heading for one ending; now it has changed direction and is moving inexorably toward a different ending. Jesus most certainly knows now what's ahead for him and begins in earnest preparing the disciples to carry on his work. And yet, the irony of the event is inescapable. The chosen few who witness this life-changing event— seeing Jesus, Moses, and Elijah in all their glory—will all abandon Jesus just a few days hence.

There is a slightly different version of all of this in Luke 9, which is followed by the scene where Jesus heals the possessed boy. Only *then* does Jesus tell the disciples of his fate in Luke 9:43-45. John places Jesus' public acknowledgement of his fate *much* earlier in his narrative than the other three accounts. John 6:60-66 is Jesus' most explicit revelation to those around him and the responses include petty complaints, disbelief, outright rejection, a few halting confessions of faith, and even a prophecy of a horrific betrayal. The winnowing of those who waver has begun. Only the true of heart, the loyal, and the brave will go forward from this moment.

The Inciting Incident (John 11)

It's impossible for our finite minds to *rate* the miracles of Jesus. Is the feeding of the 5,000 with little more than a child's packet of fish 'n' chips a *bigger* miracle than calming a storm at sea? Healing everything from paralytics to lepers and casting out mouthy demons is nothing to sneeze at either. But raising someone from the dead; *now* you're getting into big-time miracles! We pick up our story—at least in John's epistle, anyway—with the last major public miracle and the one that apparently seals Jesus' fate with the authorities.

The story of Lazarus is told only in chapter 11 of the gospel of John, but from a storytelling standpoint it makes a powerful transition into Act III. It also gives us one of those intimate glimpses of Jesus' personality that modern day readers crave. Lazarus and his sisters, Mary and Martha, are among Jesus' very best friends. They don't appear to travel with him much but their home is always a welcome respite. Near the end of Jesus' earthly ministry (though nobody appears to know this but Jesus), he receives word that Lazarus is deathly ill. Surprisingly, though we're told that Jesus loves them all dearly, he's in no hurry to get to his friend's bedside. After a few days, Jesus does decide to go to Lazarus' home near Bethany, even though there are numerous threats against his life in Judea.

En route, Jesus tells the disciples, "Our friend Lazarus has fallen asleep, but I am going there to awaken him" (11:11). Naturally, the disciples are confused—their most common state of affairs, incidentally. Finally, Jesus tells them plainly, "Lazarus is dead. For your sake I am glad I was not there, so that you may believe. But let us go to him" (11:14-15). More confusion follows, but Thomas pipes up and says, "Let us also go, that we may die with him" (11:16). They may call him *doubting* Thomas later, but the guy certainly doesn't lack for guts.

As they near Bethany, a distraught Martha meets Jesus and his band. She gently berates Jesus for not being there when Lazarus needed him most. Jesus assures her that Lazarus will live again. She thinks he's talking about the resurrection at the end of time and goes home to Mary. Mary is devastated and, trailed by a posse of professional mourners all wailing loudly, approaches Jesus. She, too, is inconsolable and repeats Martha's rebuff—"You should have been here."

Now this is where it gets interesting. The NRSV translation reports: "When Jesus saw her weeping, and the Jews who came with her also weeping, he was greatly disturbed in spirit and deeply moved" (11:33).

198

While various commentators point out that "greatly disturbed" and "deeply moved" indicate Jesus' great compassion, the actual Greek verbs are generally associated with *serious agitation* and *indignation*. Jesus is in tears, both for the loss of Lazarus and the pain felt by Mary and Martha, but something else is happening here. Perhaps he knows that this miracle will be the final straw with the chief priests and Pharisees. The end is so close he can sense it. And what he sees coming is painful beyond words.

Now in tears himself, Jesus is taken to Lazarus's tomb, where he commands that the stone be rolled away. Ever-practical Martha protests, saying that after four days, the smell will be unbearable. Jesus answers her evenly, "Did I not tell you that if you believed, you would see the glory of God?" (11:40). He says a short prayer of thanksgiving, praising God for the miracle he's about to perform, then shouts, "Lazarus, come out!" (11:43).

Some commentators have noted that Jesus *has* to identify Lazarus specifically by name; otherwise,

because his power is so great, all of those interred in the cave would come stumbling into the sunlight! Out pops Lazarus, still bound in cloth and rags like an Egyptian mummy, probably with an *epic* headache. (Contrast that to the resurrection of Jesus a few days later—he leaves his burial clothes in the tomb.)

The resurrection is so spectacular that the onlookers scatter in all directions, including a few tattletales who run straight to the religious power brokers, including that year's chief priest, Caiaphas. "Resurrections simply will not do under my watch," Caiaphas says darkly as he snarls at the other priests: "You do not understand that

199

it is better for you to have one man die for the people than to have the whole nation destroyed" (11:50). And at that moment, they begin plotting Jesus' death in deadly earnest.

How vindictive and murderous are Caiaphas and his deadly cohorts? A few verses later, they put a plan in motion to kill the newly raised Lazarus as well. We simply can't have walking proof of a miracle strolling our streets! (Plotting to kill a recently dead man hardly seems fair at all. Dying twice in one week would be a very bad week for most of us.)

The die has been cast. Jesus will no longer avoid the religious authorities. He will beard the lion in his own den. He will go openly into Jerusalem a few days hence to celebrate his last earthly Passover.

Approach to the Inmost Cave
(Luke 13:31-35; Mark 11:1-11)

Jesus chooses to spend his final days in Jerusalem—the stronghold of the enemy and the power base of the religious elite opposed to him. Luke expertly builds tension with a brief conversation in 13:31-35. A few of the sympathetic Pharisees secretly warn Jesus to flee; Herod is out for his blood. Jesus' response is at first defiant, then heartbreakingly empathic:

> Go and tell that fox for me, "Listen, I am casting out demons and performing cures today and tomorrow, and on the third I finish my work. Yet today, tomorrow, and the next day I must be on my way, because it is impossible for a prophet to be killed outside of Jerusalem." Jerusalem, Jerusalem, the city that kills the prophets and stones those who are sent to it! How often have I desired to gather your children together as a hen gathers her brood under her wings, and you were not willing! See, your house is left to you. And I tell you, you will not see me until the times comes when you say, "Blessed is the one who comes in the name of the Lord." (Luke 13:32-35)

Jesus goes right into the belly of the beast, not furtively, sneaking around back alleys, but in broad daylight, riding a donkey.

Spontaneously, people gather to welcome him and his befuddled band, throwing their cloaks on the dusty ground and waving "leafy branches" (Mark 11:8). My guess is that this group is composed of the poorest of the poor, the disenfranchised, and the dispossessed. They are welcoming the One they instinctively know is their salvation. In a few hours, another crowd, an angry mob, will gather to call for Jesus' death. But I

Reluctant Prophets and Clueless Disciples

would be surprised if *any* of these who so joyfully herald his triumphal entry into the city are among those who call for his death just hours later.

IN RETROSPECT, ANDREW OFTEN WONDERED IF HE HADN'T MISSED SOME SUBTLE CLUES FROM JUDAS THAT NIGHT...

The Supreme Ordeal (Luke 23:32-43)

Mel Gibson devotes much of *The Passion of the Christ* to depicting—in infinite detail—the kangaroo court trial and graphic torture of Jesus, culminating with his crucifixion. All four Gospels recount these horrific events, each with a slightly different slant. They are among the most familiar scenes in all of literature. There is little to add here save for the reminder that Jesus had the power to end the pain at any time and wreak a horrible vengeance on those who harmed him. But he did not, believing his death on the cross was a necessary part of his Father's plan for the salvation of all humanity.

In Luke 23:32-43 there is a short scene that, once again, encapsulates Jesus' entire mission. Two criminals are being crucified with Jesus. One man is like an injured dog on the side of the road that—in his pain—snarls and snaps at anyone who comes close. He lashes out at Jesus. The other, truly repentant, cries, "Jesus, remember me when you come into your kingdom" (23:42). Through cracked and bleeding lips, Jesus replies, "Truly I tell you, today you will be with me in Paradise" (23:43).

It isn't fair, of course. Jesus was innocent and yet here he is dying a monstrous death. The second criminal, after a lifetime of evil, is saved in his final seconds on earth and will see Jesus today in Paradise. Why should *he* get to go to heaven when I've got to spend my whole life going to church, trying to do good, tithing, and reading the Bible just to go to heaven? It just isn't fair. Shouldn't he have to at least repent? Say he was sorry? Beg for forgiveness? Something?

Which of the two criminals are we? Are we guilty of asking for grace for ourselves and justice for everyone else? God's love may indeed be unfair—but if it is extended to you and me, as Mike Yaconelli reminds us in *Messy Spirituality* (p. 36), who are we to argue?

How do we describe the crucifixion in human terms? It was torture, pure and simple, designed to exact the optimum amount of pain for as long as possible. A movie, such as *The Passion of the Christ*, reveals, as no other medium can, the horrific, excruciating nature of Roman-styled crucifixions.

And then, he is gone.

Mark adds a fascinating footnote. At the moment of Jesus' death, just as he cries in anguish for the final time, the holy curtain in the Jewish temple—which protects the Holy of Holies and which none may see save the

chief priest and even then only once a year—instantaneously rips in two "from top to bottom" (Mark 15:38). This is a potent sea change in the life of believers everywhere. No longer will sacrifices be required. This is the last *atonement*. It is, as Jesus says, finished.

For the emotionally devastated Mary, the mother of Jesus (who alone was there at both the beginning and the end of Jesus' earthly ministry), and the ever-faithful Mary Magdalene, the aftermath of Jesus' death must have been equally unthinkable.

That pain is reflected 2,000 years later in Wim Wenders's extraordinary 1988 German-language (with subtitles) film, *Wings of Desire* (don't bother with the bad remake with Nicholas Cage and Meg Ryan, *City of Angels*). In *Wings of Desire,* angels in long, dark coats lovingly shadow us everywhere, watching us, loving us. But when a distraught human commits suicide, Wenders's close-up of the man's angel reveals such uncontrolled horror and anguish that the viewer has to look away.

That grief is, in microcosm, the grief that the heavenly hosts must have felt at the crucifixion of Jesus.

The King of the Universe is dead. Or is he?

Reluctant Prophets and Clueless Disciples

If you have a good art history book or know a good art Website (try http://www.mystudios.com/gallery/giotto/preamble.html), find a section on the artists who lived just on the cusp of the Renaissance, before painting assumed an almost photographic reality. Once there, you'll find the works of an Italian gentleman working in the early 1300s in Northern Italy. Giotto worked in the most demanding medium of all, fresco—using fast-drying plaster infused with paint. Now turn to Giotto's work in the Scrovegni Chapel in Padua, where he was commissioned to fill the panels of the chapel with the life of Christ, from the birth of Mary to the book of Revelation. In these touching scenes (along with the western front of the massive cathedral at Chartres), scholars find the beginnings of the Renaissance, dramatically breaking with a thousand years of art tradition.

Now once in the Scrovegni Chapel, follow the sequence until you find the scene where Mary cradles the bloody body of her boy in her arms, just moments after he's been removed from the cross. Her pain is palpable. But now look at the ten small angels who contort in abject grief in the sky above the scene. There is so much naked emotion in their horrified lamentations that it still has the power to startle modern viewers.

ACT III

Reward (Mark 16)

He isn't.

It's the Divine Comedy. Satan *thinks* he has won, but there is—to quote C. S. Lewis's *The Lion, the Witch and the Wardrobe*—a "deeper magic" (p. 153). Jesus defeats death. There's a touch of comic absurdity added when you consider that we've just had the most astounding miracle of all time and there is nobody here to see it except for a handful of Roman guards who are forever sworn to secrecy on pain of death! Imagine *their* surprise when that boulder starts to roll away on Easter morning . . .

Once again, the four Gospel accounts differ here, each providing a different color of thread to the tapestry. But instead of John being the oddball, it is Mark. Mark's version is remarkably shorter and requires a response from the listener.

After Jesus has been placed in the tomb, three women: Mary Magdalene—who is the only person mentioned in all four accounts—Mary the mother of James, and Salome, return the following morning. The giant stone has been rolled away.

Trembling, the three enter the tomb. It is empty but—as Dale Bruner said at a seminar I once attended—it is the most significant, most hopeful void/empty space in the history of the universe! Instead of Jesus' body, they find a young man (the book of Luke says two men; Matthew has an angel; in John it's two angels) dressed in white. The man speaks to the women kindly:

> Do not be alarmed; you are looking for Jesus of Nazareth, who was crucified. He has been raised; he is not here. Look, there is the place they laid him. But go, tell his disciples and Peter that he is going ahead of you to Galilee; there you will see him, just as he told you. (Mark 16:6-7)

There is a nice touch in these words: "But go, tell his disciples *and Peter* . . . " Remember, Peter had a *really* bad weekend. He talked the biggest and toughest—and had the biggest fall. And yet, Jesus has already forgiven Peter. He knows he's been wracked with guilt and shame. This is a special invitation—just for him.

These are pretty tough women. They've survived the horrors of the previous week but—like virtually everybody else in the Bible—when

204

they see an angel, they are terrified. And that's how Mark ends, with the three women fleeing from the scene. That's it. *Finito.*

Obviously, they told *somebody* or we wouldn't have had the New Testament. But the ending seems pretty abrupt to modern readers. Over the next couple of centuries, different people tried adding different endings, none of which quite work for a variety of reasons.

From a storytelling standpoint, it doesn't work either. The Risen Christ is not shown—there is a resurrection but it is only implied. We still need The Road Back and the Return with the Elixir. It seems so . . . unsatisfying . . . to end this epic journey with three women shrieking in fear! But there is honesty about this account that, at the same time, is very appealing. It makes the reader confront the story. Do you or don't you believe in the life, death, and miraculous resurrection of one Jesus of Nazareth? Mark seems to be saying, "Take it or leave it. This is what I saw. Draw your own conclusions."

Resurrection (John 20–21)

To flesh out this story, turn to the book of John. If Mark is, as some believe, the oral history of Jesus as told (mostly) by Peter, then John is the memories of John as told to a group of his followers, perhaps as he nears death on the Isle of Patmos. It is these followers who call John "the beloved disciple." But as Dale Bruner also pointed out (at the same seminar mentioned above), Matthew, Luke, and John all contain hints of a fascinating, if sometimes unintentionally funny, subplot—the unspoken competition between Peter and John. Let's follow the story as John tells it in chapters 20 and 21.

Just before dawn on the morning after the crucifixion, Mary Magdalene returns alone to the tomb to complete the burial preparations that had been hastily begun on Jesus' battered body. Once in the cemetery, she sees that the massive stone has been rolled away. She dashes back to where the disciples hide and breathlessly shouts, "They have taken the Lord out of the tomb, and we do not know where they have laid him" (20:2).

Off at a dead run go Simon Peter and the Disciple Whom Jesus Loved—apparently John. The book of John carefully points out that John *beat* Peter to the empty tomb. John stands at the opening, peering inside. Peter brushes past him, like a bull in a china shop, and enters the tomb. They see the burial clothes, but no Jesus. John 20:8 says, "the other disciple" saw the empty tomb and "believed"—thus becoming the first person in history to believe in the resurrection.

Still confused—and perhaps a bit frightened—the two return to their safe house, leaving a *bawling* Mary standing outside. Dead or alive, she determines to stay near Jesus. Finally she composes herself enough to poke her head in as well. Only now there are two angels sitting there! "They said to her, 'Woman, why are you weeping?' She said to them, 'They have taken away my Lord, and I do not know where they have laid him'" (20:13). When they do not answer, she turns to leave. At that instant, materializing behind her, as through a transporter beam in *Star Trek*, is Jesus.

Mary doesn't recognize him at first. In fact, hardly anybody recognizes Jesus by sight after the resurrection—it's almost always by the sound of his voice. Why? In Mary's case, it may be because it is still dark or because she's still weeping or because Jesus has been changed physically by his ordeal or because she just doesn't expect to see him. (I wonder how many times that happens to us on a daily basis? How many times we miss Jesus because we're not expecting to see him somewhere in our lives?)

Jesus then slightly rephrases the very first question he asked the disciples of John the Baptist, way back in John 1:38, "What are you looking for?" This time, Jesus asks Mary, "Woman, why are you weeping? Whom are you looking for?" (John 20:15). Mary thinks he's the gardener and pleads with him, "Sir, if you have carried him away, tell me where you have laid him, and I will take him away" (20:15).

This time Jesus calls her name, "Mary!" (20:16).

And in that instant, she knows. She *knows* that voice—like sheep know their shepherd's voice. And in that instant, *she knows who he is and what has just happened*. She cries, "Rabbouni!" (Dear Teacher, 20:16) and throws herself onto him. Jesus gently disentangles himself and asks her not to cling to him. We can't continue to hold onto the Jesus of the past, as Bruner reminds us (more wisdom from that same seminar). Then Jesus says, "But go to my brothers and say to them, 'I am ascending to my Father and your Father, to my God and your God'" (20:17).

Jesus has clearly forgiven the disciples for abandoning him and ordains the faithful Mary Magdalene as the first minister of the gospel. She runs back to the safe house and shouts, "I have seen the Lord" (20:18)!

The disciples (sans Thomas and the now-expired Judas—we'll talk more about them in a later chapter) are still cowering in their hideout, uncertain and confused. They don't do anything. It's interesting to note

206

that, on the other hand, both the Jewish hierarchy and the Romans believed *immediately* in the resurrection—which is why they acted so quickly to suppress the news. Of all of the people who heard about the resurrection, the most skeptical were, apparently, that goofy band of disciples. Regardless, as before, Jesus simply appears in their midst, through locked doors and barred windows. "Peace be with you" (20:21). No recriminations, no admonishments, just unconditional love and acceptance. Imagine the mob scene! Like Mary, they can't embrace him—but they doubtless pepper him from all sides with a thousand confused questions. Jesus shows them his scarred hands and side, blesses them, and disappears once again.

Some time later, Thomas—known for his sensible, scientific nature—returns and the others excitedly tell him what has happened. Thomas wants to believe, but fears that the others are delusional, or are the victims of mass hysteria. He says, "Unless I see the mark of the nails in his hands, and put my finger in the mark . . . in his side, I will not believe" (20:25).

A week later, Jesus does return, appearing in their midst, despite the locked doors and windows. Graciously, he allows Thomas to touch his wounds. Shamefaced, Thomas shouts—for the first time—Jesus' true title: "My Lord and my God!" (20:28). Jesus asks, "Have you believed because you have seen me? Blessed are those who have not seen and yet have come to believe" (20:29). (By the way, that's *us*, people.)

The Road Back (John 21:1-14)

In the days that followed the resurrection—Matthew, Luke, and John report—Jesus made many strange, seemingly unrelated appearances throughout Israel. It was an exciting, frenzied time. Jesus' appearances almost seem random; two men here, a thousand people there, a handful of disciples somewhere else. It is almost as if he is tying up hundreds of loose ends, dealing with untold and uncounted needs that were never recorded. This is the Road Back.

But there is one last adventure, one last miracle; one last teaching for his harried followers and it is found in the 21st and final chapter of the book of John. Amid all of the excitement, the remaining disciples at last return to the Sea of Galilee—even apostles have to eat!—and their fishing. Led by Peter (and including good ol' Nathanael, whom we haven't seen since John 1), seven disciples push out for some night fishing. By

207

dawn of the following morning, they have caught nada, zilch, nothing. In the early morning mist, a lone figure stands on the shore.

"How are you doing?" he calls.

"We got a big fat nothing," Peter responds sourly. "Thanks for askin'."

"I've got an idea," the stranger says. "Throw your nets starboard—I'll bet you find something there."

"Yeah, yeah, everybody's an expert." But there is something about the stranger's voice and Peter reluctantly follows his advice.

Suddenly, the little craft lists dangerously to starboard. Their nets are bursting with fish! So many fish they're afraid the net will split and their boat will founder.

John peers through the fog at the stranger. He looks awfully familiar. "It is the Lord!" he shouts.

Peter drops his end of the net, grabs a cloak, and—like Forrest Gump jumping off the shrimp boat to see Lieutenant Dan—impulsively jumps in (no trying to walk on the water this time) and swims frantically to shore. The other six maneuver their craft toward shore as well, straining to drag the bloated nets.

On shore, Jesus has prepared a charcoal fire. It was at a shared meal, of course, in the hours before his trial and crucifixion, that Jesus last ate with his friends. "Come and have breakfast," he says. And they talk and talk, of old times and old friends and old adventures, sharing in communion on an unnamed beach—for the very last time. Jesus ascends, awaiting his glorious return. Peter, John, and the others fan out across the world to spread the good news they have seen and heard.

Return with the Elixir

This, then, is the Return with the Elixir, the potion that will cure the plague, the Holy Grail that will heal the wounded land, the riddle that will unlock the treasure chest—it is nothing less than the secret to eternal life! It is the gift Jesus brought back from the grave to redeem all humanity.

This is the Hero's Journey.

This is our journey as well.

Nineteen

THE PARABLES OF JESUS

It is often said the Church is a crutch. Of course it's a crutch. What makes you think you don't limp? (William Sloane Coffin, *Credo* [Louisville: Westminster John Knox Press, 2004], 137)

Some observers claim that the Bible is 51 percent story, 29 percent poetry, and only 20 percent didactic— direct instructional explanation, laws, and/or theology. And the best storyteller in the Bible is Jesus. Most of Jesus' stories—called parables—are very short. His teachings are usually longer. Every parable is a story. It's a story that tells WHO, WHAT, WHERE, HOW, and WHEN. It's usually up to the listener to supply the WHY.

Sometimes the parables only provide Act I (the beginning) and Act II (the middle). It is up to the reader to provide Act III (the end). As Karl Barth says, "Jesus is not the answer—he is the question"; *how* we respond to the parables, just as how we respond to Jesus, is entirely up to us.

"However much we want to read them like Morse code," Barbara Brown Taylor writes, "they behave more like dreams or poems instead, delivering their meanings in images that talk more to our hearts than to our heads" (*The Seeds of Heaven* [Louisville: Westminster John Knox Press, 2004], 33).

There are actually different kinds of parables in the New Testament. Some are mini-short stories, complete with a *moral-to-the-story* ending. Others are little more than vivid snapshots or traditional proverbs. Luke even calls Jesus' apparently straightforward story—about where people should or shouldn't sit at a banquet table (see Luke 14:7-10)—a parable, although it reads more like an illustration.

Mark says that Jesus used parables as sort of an *insider language*— something only those on the inner circle of this new religion were supposed to understand (see Mark 4:10-12). But Matthew maintains that most people *could* have understood Jesus' parables—had they really wanted to. Neither explanation is very satisfying today. Many modern scholars believe that parables weren't designed to explicitly teach, instruct, or answer—they were created to force the reader/listener to ask still more questions and examine his or her own belief systems. This seems to make sense when you remember that Jesus himself often answered questions with still another question. Besides, some (like the parable of the Pharisee and the Tax Collector in Luke 18) obviously have no one correct answer.

Still, why didn't Jesus just give his listeners more direct, unambiguous teaching and theology? Why talk in riddles?

For one thing, the parables helped sift out the audience. Folks who were only there for the showy miracles and the *surface* entertainment soon drifted away. "Man, I've got things to do down at the market—who wants to listen to another parable about a goofy mustard seed?!" But those who wanted to hear *the rest of the story*, those who wanted to delve deeper into the multiple meanings of the parables, stuck around. Besides, clever, compact stories are a lot easier to remember than hours of theology or a chronology of dates. We all remember good stories.

That's the beauty of the parables of Jesus. They are told in such a way that they have offered insight and wisdom to readers since Jesus' day. Each of us brings our own interpretation to the story, depending on what we need at that particular time. In that sense, the parables are not just timeless; they're *beyond* time. That means there are precious few absolutely right or absolutely wrong interpretations. (Well, I guess the ones where the Good Samaritan is a space alien and where the Prodigal Son is Elvis *might* be stretching it a little . . .)

Lumping all of those definitions together, there are about thirty-eight parables, primarily in Matthew, Mark, and Luke. (The largest collection—of twelve—are designed to help readers understand the kingdom of heaven.) When Jesus tells a story in the book of John, the author calls it a *paroimia*—which translates variously as "figure" or "cryptic saying"—not parable.

The one thing these stories all have in common is this: virtually all of Jesus' parables are about activities and concepts the average person living in first-century Palestine would readily understand—farming, worship, real estate, nature, landlords, vineyards, family relationships, even cooking and cleaning. People hearing these little tales would let their guard down. *"Hmm, this guy isn't preaching or hollering at us. He's a storyteller."* Sometimes his listeners would walk away, and the Worm of Truth hidden at the core of the story would slowly begin to gnaw away at them. But other times, the Truth would be like a bucket of cold Gatorade on their heads. *"Hey! This is about me! This is what the kingdom of heaven will be like!"*

210

Because the parables of Jesus are so simple, they're still accessible to highly urbanized readers 2,000 years later—even those who have never been on a farm or seen a lamb except when it's served with roasted potatoes and a little mint jelly.

Jesus tells parables in a variety of styles for a variety of purposes. But interestingly, the people in Jesus' parables are rarely what you'd consider religious; and when they *are* religious people, they're not necessarily very good people. Instead, these are real people, concerned with day-to-day issues: a flickering lamp, a wandering lamb, or a tiny, almost invisible seed.

But be forewarned: The parables may be simple . . . but they're not simplistic. You think they mean one thing for fifty years and suddenly—without warning—a familiar parable reveals a whole new level of meaning. It can be quite startling, believe me! That's the power of these little tales. There is more than just a *point* to each story. On a bigger scale, they can influence us. They make us see things differently. They can even . . . sometimes . . . change us.

Stories make sense of chaos. Stories can also trigger a connection between the listener and the events recounted in the story. Sure, when Jesus told the parable of the Good Samaritan, he wanted the lawyer, who asked the question that prompted the parable, to understand what a "neighbor" is. But he also had something more in mind—not just for the lawyer, but for everybody listening then *and now*.

Finally, many of Jesus' stories have a surprise ending. He expertly builds suspense and creates tension in his parables. We've heard so many of them so many times that we know the endings. But for the listeners of Jesus' day, these parables had a shock ending. It's probably impossible to get back to a place where we can really hear any parable for the first time, as Jim Carrey's character tries to do in the movie *Eternal Sunshine of the Spotless Mind*.

That's part of the process of retelling the parables in a slightly different way or trying to look at them from a different angle. The goal is to open our minds to these stories. If we'll just do that, Jesus can turn the expected ending into something quite different—forcing us, once again, to reevaluate our core beliefs or feelings.

Regardless of WHY Jesus told them, the parables have been preserved for 2,000 years. Obviously, God has something of value in them for us today. Story is a gift. It lets an outsider in—sometimes physically—back to a day when *all* stories were told around warming campfires. The stories/parables of Jesus are a gift to all who hear them for all time.

There is no way to study all thirty-eight stories. Instead, let's cherry-pick some of the best-known parables in the New Testament and see what these particular stories have to tell us, shall we?

Workers in the Vineyard
(Matthew 20:1-16)

Here's a parable that drives capitalists and Free Market economists crazy! There is radical love at work here, radical inclusiveness, radical forgiveness. It goes against everything we've come to expect in our consumer-driven economy. It feels so wrong and yet . . . and yet . . . in some distant corner of our brains it rings true, like something we once believed a long, long time ago, something we believed before we became adults, all grown-up, wise, and cynical.

This parable begins with a question at the end of Matthew 19. Against all of the prevailing wisdom of the age, Jesus has just told a rich young man that he can't get into heaven until he gives up his love of possessions and loves God more instead. Peter immediately pops up and crows, "Well, we've given up everything to follow you, Jesus—what will *our* reward be in heaven?" Jesus replies that there will be glory and rich thrones aplenty for the Twelve, "but many who are first will be last, and the last will be first" (19:30).

Now it's time for the disciples to scratch their heads. *Now* what is he saying?

It's parable time!

They didn't have newspapers in Jesus' day, but if they did, perhaps the story in *The Jerusalem Post* would have looked something like the next two pages . . .

212

Vineyard Row Involves National Labor Relations Review Board

Critics Cite Unfair Practices, Payments

By Dan "Beersheba" Rather

CAPERNAUM—Scores of migrant workers picketed outside the vineyard of noted Israeli winemaker Robert bar-Gallo Thursday, alleging violations of labor-relations law. A representative of the striking workers said that a top lawyer from the United Farm Workers of Israel was being rushed in by chariot to represent them.

"Bar-Gallo has set a dangerous, dangerous precedent," Caesar bar-Chavez, the strikers' spokesman, told reporters Thursday. "This is some kind of Communist, socialist plot. It's positively un-Israeli."

According to eyewitness accounts, bar-Gallo's problems began early Thursday morning

when he came into Capernaum before dawn to hire workers for the grape harvest. Capernaum, which is economically depressed, has numerous gathering points for unemployed workers. Bar-Gallo's representatives negotiated a standard wage for the day's work, thought to be about one *denarius*.

"About 9 a.m., I saw storm clouds gathering over the Mediterranean and worried we might lose the harvest," bar-Gallo said, "so I sent my foreman back into town to hire additional workers at the same rate."

Bar-Chavez confirmed bar-Gallo's account and reported that representatives from bar-

213

Gallo returned to Capernaum at noon and yet again at 3 p.m. for additional workers, also for the alleged wage of one *denarius*.

"By 5 p.m., big fat clouds were blocking out the sun," bar-Gallo said, "and I had to get the crop in. I rushed back into town and hired a few more grape-pickers on the spot."

It is at this point that the two accounts diverge dramatically. The crux of the complaint centers on bar-Gallo's decision to pay all of the workers at dusk.

"My biggest mistake was when I decided to pay the guys I'd hired last first," bar-Gallo said. "I paid them a *denarius* each. That's when the riot began."

"Absolutely!" said bar-Chavez angrily. "When it comes time to pay the rest of us, we all get a single stinkin' *denarius*, too—including the guys who'd been hired before dawn. Our men had been broiling in the sun, picking grapes all day . . . and yet these Johnny-come-latelies make the same amount for a single hour's work? When we seen that, we were expecting six, seven *denarii*, maybe eight. This kind of blatant union-bustin' ain't gonna happen on my watch, pal!"

In an unexpected development, bar-Gallo boldly walked through the picket line until he was inches from bar-Chavez, who was leading rousing chants of, "Boycott bar-Gallo! Boycott bar-Gallo!"

"Friend," bar-Gallo said quietly to bar-Chavez, "I did you no wrong. You and your men agreed to work for the usual daily wage. You were happy to get it. I alone chose to pay the last few guys the same thing I paid you. Are you going to get stingy because I am generous? Please, take your wages and go."

Bar-Chavez then stomped off in disgust and the chanting began again.

Federal marshals patrolled the area through the evening. Only minor incidents between the striking workers and security guards were reported.

Mediation between bar-Gallo Industries and the United Farm Workers will begin Monday morning in an undisclosed location in Jerusalem.

214

Oh my. What are we to learn from this story? If you're in a Business 101 class, you're probably thinking, "This just isn't fair."

But this parable isn't about Wal-Mart; it's about the kingdom of heaven. It's about a place where God's love envelops all. We're talking about heaven—where *none* are worthy but—by grace—some will enter anyway. "All have sinned and fall short of the glory of God," the apostle Paul says in Romans 3:23. It's not about paying a minimum wage; *it's about the love that surpasses all understanding.*

And just to make sure everyone gets it, Jesus adds this little coda at the end: "So the last will be first, and the first will be last" (Matthew 20:16).

Isn't that good news? No, that's *great* news!

But a lot of people *still* don't get it. In fact, immediately following the telling of this tale, James and John's mom comes up and asks Jesus if her *babies* can sit on thrones at Jesus' right and left hands when they all get to heaven. Jesus shakes his head sadly. In a few days, his throne is going to be made, not of gold and ivory, but of rough-hewn wood, stained by the blood pouring from his hands, feet, and side (See Matthew 20:20-23).

The problem—as it will be with several of the parables to come—is that we automatically identify with the wrong person in the parable. We think we're the workers who worked all day and got gypped at the end. But—for the most part—we're the workers who came in at the very end, worked only a little, and got a most pleasant surprise.

When the time comes to tally our triumphs and failures in the Lamb's Book of Life at the end of our lives, I don't want to be compared to Mother Teresa, the Rev. Billy Graham, C. S. Lewis, my saintly Grandmother Allie, or the apostle Paul. I expect I will squeak in by the skin of my teeth. I don't deserve to be with them and with the millions of martyred saints, bold soul-winners, and larger-than-life Christians who have preached and died spreading the good news since the dawn of time.

But I'll gratefully take whatever grace is tossed my way.

God loves us indiscriminately. God is supremely, unfathomably generous. God is good.

Fair? No.

Good? Yes.

The Parable of the Talents
(Matthew 25:14-30)

This parable is particularly poignant. This is the last parable Jesus tells in the book of Matthew—it leads immediately into the Last Supper and the terrible final hours of Jesus' life on earth. The author of Matthew apparently thought it important enough to place it in this crucial location.

It is also an uncommonly difficult parable, much like the parable of the Workers in the Vineyard because—on the surface—it implies reward for the undeserving (the whole *rich get richer* syndrome). Not so. This is the third of three consecutive parables that deal with, not the dangers of accumulated of wealth (or even prudent investments in stocks and bonds), but instead serve as a warning to be ready for Christ's return. And one way we can be ready is by wisely using the gifts we've been given for the kingdom of God. Being *saved* is great—but it is not an excuse to get lazy or to boast in your salvation!

The language here is one of those rare confluences when an ancient word (originally spoken by Jesus in Aramaic, but reported in the best available surviving manuscripts in Greek) and the modern English word actually coincide to make the meaning deeper and richer. "Talent" here is rendered from the Greek word *talanton*, a unit of money from the time of Jesus, or about 6000 *drachmas*. It was a lot of money. Today, of course, "talent" is another way of saying *gift*, as in, "She has a talent for piano."

This parable begins with a journey. A rich businessman is about to leave on a business trip. He calls for his three slaves (let's call them Moe, Larry, and Curly). He leaves five talents to Moe, two talents to Larry, and one talent to Curly, then he heads for the trade show at the Hebron Hilton.

While he's gone, Moe dashes over to the Jerusalem Stock Market and parlays a wise investment in pork bellies into five more talents. Larry loans his talents, at 100% interest, to a guy who has to pay off the Beersheba Mafia or find himself wearing cement sandals at the bottom of the Jordan. The guy gratefully repays Larry the two talents, plus two talents interest. But Curly panics. He digs a hole out by the master's jacuzzi and buries his talent.

Tanned and refreshed, the master eventually returns, calls for his slaves, and asks them to give an accounting of their activities while he was in Hebron. Here's how it might have gone . . .

216

MOE

Master, you handed over to me five talents. See, I have made five more talents.

MASTER

Great work! I trusted you—you produced! You're now the head slave. Come sleep inside—instead of in the gutter.

LARRY

Master, you trusted me with two talents. See, I have made two more talents.

MASTER

Good work! I trusted you; you produced. You're now my pool boy. Come sleep in the gutter—instead of in the sewer.

CURLY

Um, master, you've gotta believe me here, man. I know that you are a shrewd, hard-nosed businessman, making money from insider trading tips and some Enron-style accounting; and I *sure* didn't want to get on your bad side and take the fall when the federal regulators come calling! So I did the prudent thing and buried my talent. See? Here it is. Uh, don't mind the dirt.

MASTER

(*Veins pop dangerously on his forehead*) You wicked and lazy slave! You *knew* that I made a little on the side, did you? At least you should have gone down to the credit union and placed your talent in an interest-bearing account! But no! All you've got to show for your time—and my money—is a single stinkin' talent that smells like chlorine!

CURLY

Well, when you put it that way . . . But if you'll just give me a minute to explain . . .

MASTER

Silence! You're outta here, Bub. Guards, take his timecard, cancel his medical insurance, and pitch him outside the gate. You're history!

The key line in all of this is Matthew 25:29: "For to all those who have, more will be given, and they will have an abundance; but from those who have nothing, even what they have will be taken away."

Now *that's* an uncomfortable thought! If this wasn't a parable—and if the rest of Matthew didn't indicate decidedly to the contrary—you might think this meant that there'd be rich and poor people in heaven; and that the rich would have first shot at the Pearly Gates!

But once again, Jesus isn't interested in money. He's interested in people. The parable appears to be doing double duty (or triple duty . . . or even more!). First, Jesus is telling his listeners to be ready for his return. In that regard, Jesus might be seen as the Master and his disciples are the slaves. The message is: "Do the kingdom's work with the best of your ability until I return for you."

There is a second message here though, one that can be summarized, "To those to whom much is given, much is expected." In short, those who have been given much—money, fame, talents, looks, health—*can* get to heaven, but more will be expected of them along the way. The late, wealthy, industrialist Andrew Carnegie once said, "The man who dies . . . rich, dies disgraced" ("The Gospel of Wealth," *North American Review*, June 1889). Since you can't take it with you, dying with lots of toys when people are starving all around you does *not* earn you heavenly brownie points.

It's not that the rich can't get into heaven; it's just *harder* for them to make it.

C. S. Lewis puts it another way in *Mere Christianity*:

> The fact that you are giving money to a charity does not mean that you need not try to find out whether that charity is a fraud or not. The fact that what you are thinking about is God . . . does not mean that you can be content with the same babyish ideas that you had when you were a five-year-old. It is, of course, quite true that God will not love you any the less, or have less use for you, if you happen to have been born with a very second-rate brain. He has room for people with very little senses, but he wants every one to use what sense they have. (New York: Macmillan Publishing Company, 1952, 75)

With that in mind, when you consider the talents and resources most of us in America have (compared to much of the rest of the world), we need to emulate Slave #1 (Moe in our version)—doing everything we can for Jesus. But instead, most of us barely scrape by, doing as little as we can, frittering away our talents on ephemeral things, burying our gifts and money out by the cabana. It's a choice.

Fortunately, God gives us our gifts/talents for a reason. When we use them for God's glory, we feel good. This is what we're *called* to do. This is

Reluctant Prophets and Clueless Disciples

what we unconsciously, or consciously, *want* to do. A great artist *has* to paint; that's when she's happiest. A great writer *has* to write; that's when he's happiest. A great basketball player *has* to play; a great dancer *has* to dance.

In the Academy Award–winning movie *Chariots of Fire*, a young Scotsman is called to be a preacher of the Gospel. But he also has a great gift for running. He's so good, he can go to the Olympics. When his sister urges him to give up running and instead go straight into the mission field, this is his response:

"Ah, but darlin', *I can run*. And when I run, *I feel God's pleasure*."

When we use our talents for the kingdom, whatever those talents may be, big or small, we feel God's pleasure. It's as the master says in Matthew 25:21: "Well done, good and trustworthy slave . . . enter into the joy of your master."

The Parable of the Good Samaritan (Luke 10:25-37)

This is one of the richest, most challenging, most lyrical of all of the parables of Jesus. It follows hard on the heels of the return of the first missionaries—the seventy disciples sent out by Jesus in Luke 10. As we discovered in the chapter on the life of Jesus, it is one of the few times we see Jesus express unfettered joy. But his happiness is tempered by a pointed question from a legal expert: " 'Teacher,' " he said, 'what must I do to inherit eternal life?' " (10:25). The text says that the lawyer's question is a "test." If it is, Jesus deftly transforms it into a *teaching moment* on the importance of not just hearing but *doing* the Word of God.

Jesus pauses a moment and answers the man with—you guessed it!—another question, "What is written in the law? What do you read there?" (10:26).

The lawyer quotes from the Scriptures: "You shall love the Lord your God with all your heart, and with all your soul, and with all your strength, and with all your mind; and your neighbor as yourself" (10:27).

Jesus is impressed. "You have given the right answer; do this, and you will live" (10:28).

But the lawyer wants more. He asks, "And who is my neighbor?" (10:29).

The stage is set, but there is one more bit of information that is necessary to give this parable its full power. In Jesus' day, the term *Good*

Samaritan was an oxymoron. The Jews hated the Samaritans, perhaps more than they hated the Romans. They believed that the Samaritans were some kind of debased mongrel race who had twisted the Holy Torah. The Samaritans remained behind during the Babylonian exile, and some Jews believed they had defiled or even stolen holy property and ground. Most Jews, when walking from Jerusalem north to the cities around the Sea of Galilee (or vice versa), went miles and miles out of their way to avoid contaminating themselves on Samaritan soil. In fact, Jews at this time had a saying, "The Jew who accepts help from a Samaritan delays the coming of the kingdom." And the feelings of hatred were mutual.

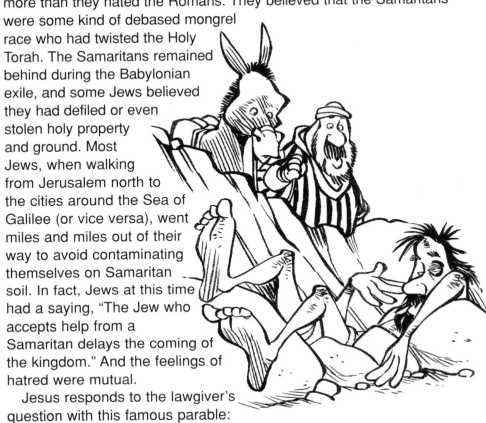

Jesus responds to the lawgiver's question with this famous parable:

> A man was going down from Jerusalem to Jericho, and fell into the hands of robbers, who stripped him, beat him, and went away, leaving him half dead. Now by chance a priest was going down that road; and when he saw him, he passed by on the other side. So likewise a Levite, when he came to the place and saw him, passed by on the other side. But a Samaritan while traveling came near him; and when he saw him, he was moved with pity. He went to him and bandaged his wounds, having poured oil and wine on them. Then he put him on his own animal, brought him to an inn, and took care of him. The next day he took out two denarii, gave them to the innkeeper, and said, "Take care of him, and when I come back, I will repay you whatever more you spend." Which of these three, do you think, was a neighbor to the man who fell into the hands of the robbers? (Luke 10:30-36)

The entire listening audience gasps in horror. This is an *unthinkable* story. The hapless lawyer is sweating bullets. Finally, he blurts out an answer to Jesus' final question, "The one who showed him mercy" (10:37). More gasps.

220

Jesus smiles his inscrutable smile. "Go and do likewise" (10:37), he says.

It is impossible to overstate the impact of this parable on Jesus' audience, including his disciples, who are probably speechless themselves.

To get a feeling for the power of this scenario, set it in modern-day America. Imagine the traveler to be a man who hates gays and lesbians. Suddenly, he's beaten by drug addicts on a busy city street, and left for dead. A priest steps over his bleeding body. A Baptist preacher walks around him and looks away. Then a young gay man stops. He carries the bleeding man to a hospital, gives the triage nurse his credit card, and says he'll be back in a couple of days to check on him and pay the balance of the account.

Or imagine the injured traveler to be a Jewish businessman in modern Jerusalem and that the *Good Samaritan* is a member of the PLO—the Palestine Liberation Organization.

Or imagine a member of the Ku Klux Klan who is tended to by an African American *gangsta* rapper.

Or imagine an American soldier who is nursed to health by a member of al Qaeda.

You get the picture.

Imagine *any* of those people, waking up and discovering that a representative of the group they hate most in the entire world has saved their life—at great personal expense—and they are now indebted to that person. Imagine how conflicted and torn they must be. Most Jews of Jesus' day would have died rather than accept (even unwittingly) help and succor from a despised Samaritan. The hatred was that real. Imagine their horror.

That's how horrifying the image was to some of Jesus' listeners. And that, of course, was what Jesus wanted. *Who is your neighbor?* Jesus makes the answer to the lawyer's question unmistakably clear. *Every man or woman on the planet is your neighbor.* To blindly hate anyone for religious, cultural, ethnic, or gender-related reasons is simply not of God. No exceptions.

> Time [is] a companion that goes with us on a journey and teaches us to cherish every moment, because it'll never come again. What we leave behind is not as important as how we've lived. (Captain Jean-Luc Picard, Commander, Federation Starship Enterprise; from the movie *Star Trek: Generations*)

Chapters 14 through 16 of Luke contain, in rapid-fire fashion, some of Jesus' greatest, most famous parables: the parable of the Great Dinner, the parable of the Lost Sheep, the parable of the Lost Coin, the parable of the Prodigal and his Brother, the parable of the Dishonest Manager, and the parable of Lazarus and the Rich Man. They are delivered while Jesus is under heavy attack from the Pharisees and scribes. And all are related in some way to twin themes: the joy and inclusiveness of heaven and the supreme value of every individual. They are some of the most comforting of all of the words of Jesus. But beware! Even these soothing parables sometimes have a hidden bite for unsuspecting readers!

The Parable of the Great Dinner (Luke 14:15-24)

The beginning verses of Luke's 14th chapter provide something unique in the Bible—a healing, followed by a teaching, followed by a parable— all amplifying the same concept!

The Healing (Luke 14:1-6)

During one particular Sabbath in the middle of his earthly ministry, Jesus and his disciples are walking to the home of a wealthy Pharisee, who will be their host for dinner. Around them are numerous other Pharisees and lawyers, each watching Jesus like a hawk, hoping for the slightest slip-up. Just before they reach their destination, a man with dropsy blocks their way. *Dropsy* is something we'd call "generalized edema" today—the body retains too much fluid. It's easily treatable now but back in Jesus' day, not only was it painful, but those who suffered from it were constantly thirsty and no amount of water would slake their thirst—which only made matters worse. Dropsy was often used as a metaphor for greed. No matter how much *stuff* a greedy person accumulated, it was never enough. The poor man begs Jesus for healing. Jesus looks casually at the faces of those in the entourage around him. "So—is it lawful to heal people on the Sabbath, or not?"

There wasn't much that *was* lawful on the Sabbath in those days and none of these bozos were going to heal anybody any time soon. So they scuff their feet, examine their nails, stare at the blue Palestinian sky . . . and say nothing. Jesus sighs at their cold hearts and heals the man.

222

The Teaching (Luke 14:7-14)

When he arrives at the rich Pharisee's house, Jesus notices how the invitees scramble to be near the rich man—and the best food and wine. He turns to those present and teaches them a couple of valuable lessons:

1. Don't grab the best seat without being invited. Someone a lot more prestigious than you could also be invited and you'd have to take the long walk to the end of the table by the kitchen, enduring the razzing of your buds.
2. When you have a banquet, don't always invite your friends and family. Invite the poor and impaired. Those are the kinds of banquets that God rewards.

The Parable (Luke 14:15-24)

One of the dinner guests, hearing Jesus' words, raises his goblet and offers a toast: "Hey! Here's to anyone who'll be feasting in heaven come judgment day." Jesus smiles and offers the following parable (updated *just* a little):

A rich man throws an elaborate banquet for a hundred or so of his closest friends and business partners. He pulls out the Waterford crystal, flies in Emeril Lagassee to cook, pays Justin Timberlake to perform, and contracts with Ben and Jerry to handcraft the ice cream for dessert on the premises. He has invitations printed up and hand-delivered months in advance.

But the night he has chosen for his banquet isn't particularly convenient for most people. There's a new episode of "The O.C." on TV and the local university is playing for the conference basketball championship. One guy just bought a condo in Florida. Another guy, who just bought a new Audi, is dying to try it out. Still another couple is honeymooning in Paris. Worse than that, a lot of people didn't even RSVP. They just don't show up. What's another lavish banquet when you're rich?

Just before dinner, one of the servants inches into the bedroom where the rich man is getting ready and tells him the bad news. "You've been *dissed*, master. Stiffed. No one showed up. Not even your lazy brother-in-law Larry who owes you all that money." The rich man is hopping mad. He sends Emeril and Justin home and calls all the servants together.

"Head out into the streets and alleyways and bring me everybody you can find—the poor, the crippled, the blind."

The servants hotfoot it out into the night. But not many people are on the streets during "The O.C." and when they come back, there are still empty seats.

The rich man roars, "Go into the nursing homes and half-way houses and rehab centers. Make people come. I will not waste this wonderful meal. MY HOUSE WILL BE FILLED! MY FOOD WILL BE EATEN! And none of those ungrateful flunkies I originally invited will ever taste a single canapé!"

The Replay

Wow! Taken together, this is an amazing few minutes in the life of Jesus. Let's go back to the miracle. Jesus isn't concerned whether it is the Sabbath or Tuesday or St. Patrick's Day—this man will be healed. As for the dinner itself, Jesus is eating with one of those who have persecuted him the most. In our modern society, you can tell a lot about someone by whom he or she chooses to dine with on a regular basis. As in the healing on the Sabbath business, Jesus doesn't care about protocol and how something looks, or even how something has always been done; he's

Reluctant Prophets and Clueless Disciples

going to do the right thing—regardless. Social climbing, trying to impress the social elite, is not something Jesus is interested in.

Which brings us to the parable itself. As with most parables, there are lots of interpretations, but the one that jumps out at me is that this is an allusion to the Heavenly Banquet that will come. We all have images of what we think heaven will be like. We all have expectations of whom we think we'll see there. But, as usual, Jesus turns our expectations upside down. He implies that if we expect to see the heavenly halls dominated almost exclusively by rich, white, politically savvy, evangelical Christians . . .

Who knows who'll be in heaven? Jesus may be supplying a hint here. Look back at the description of the people invited (or coerced) the second and third time around. The banquet must have come perilously close to a riot—homeless people, people with mental and physical disabilities, people dying of AIDS, filthy, smelly people, drunkards, drug addicts, people from other religions, society's rejects, criminals, troublemakers—*people vastly different than those the rich man had originally invited.* What a zoo!

And—if we're lucky—you and me. I don't know about you, but after all I've done, I'm hoping I just get to sweep up after the Heavenly Banquet, after all of the good people have gone to bed.

If we identify with the rich people out doing business deals instead of the obedient outcasts in this parable, I think we miss the point. If we begin to think we're somehow good enough, that we've somehow earned our way into heaven, that we're somehow entitled to be there, then we're making some very, very dangerous assumptions. The Good Book makes it clear over and over again—NONE are worthy. ALL have fallen short. NO ONE has the right to judge another.

One of the hallmarks of the kingdom of heaven is that it will be full of surprises. And one of the many surprises will be—WHO is going to be there?

Remember: It isn't what you do or don't do. It's Who you know.

The Parable of the Prodigal and His Brother (Luke 15:11-32)

There is nothing like returning to a place that remains unchanged to find the ways in which you yourself have altered (Nelson Mandela, *Long Walk to Freedom* [Boston: Little, Brown and Company, 1994], 73)

This famous parable has been told and re-told, made into plays and poems and songs, and painted by the great masters. It works on so many levels, we can only hint at some of the possibilities here (in a somewhat updated version). And like the parable of the Banquet, the central message is about heaven.

This is the story of a wealthy rancher and his two sons. In time, the younger son chafes under the early mornings and constant hard work of the farm. Eventually, he's so unhappy, he approaches his father.

"Father, give me the share of the property that will belong to me."

In many cultures, this is a terrible insult to the father. Still, he sadly splits the inheritance, although it will create a financial hardship for the family. The father knows this will end badly, but also knows he must let his sons make their own choices, no matter how disastrous. As the older brother grimly watches, the younger brother gathers his belongings and—whistling a happy tune—catches the first bus to Las Vegas. In Vegas, he blows his entire inheritance on the World Series of Poker, fast cars, faster women, slow horses, and booze.

But nothing lasts forever—including an inheritance. Meanwhile, the country is racked by a great depression. Eventually, the son has nothing. And when he runs out of unemployment benefits, he begins looking for a job. Nothing. In desperation, he becomes a migrant worker, working for less than minimum wage, living in substandard housing, eating the slops of pigs.

Sitting in the pigsty, the younger son finally has a coherent thought.

"Dang. My father's hired hands have enough food—and I'm sitting here half-starved with a bunch of pigs . . . and I don't even like pork! Man, I've got to get home somehow. I've got no other choice. I'll say, 'Dad, I have sinned big-time against you and heaven. I am no longer worthy to be your son. Please give me a job and just treat me as one of your hired hands.'"

The younger son hitches a ride back to the ranch. A kindly trucker lets him off at the front gate and he begins the long, humiliating hike to the house.

226

The father is mending the well. He's never fully recovered from the loss of his younger son, throwing himself into the ceaseless work of the farm. And each day, at dusk, he stares down the road, hoping beyond hope that his son will return; he never does. But on this day—since they don't get many visitors that far out in the country—the father notices the lone figure in the heat-shimmering distance. *"Could it be? It is! It's my long lost son!"* The father dashes down the dusty road and throws his arms around his boy.

Through great, heaving sobs, the boy—who probably reeks pretty good by now—begs for forgiveness and asks for a job. Any job.

"Here, here, we'll have none of that," the father says. He can hardly contain his joy. He calls to one of the hired hands. "Quick—bring out a clean suit and tie, and the Rolex watch and Italian leather shoes for my son! Then kill that fat little calf that's been hanging around the shed. We're going to have a Texas-sized barbecue and barn dance. And if people ask, tell them, 'My son, who we gave up for dead, has been found!' Let the party begin!"

Now out in the back forty, the older brother sits atop a 125-horsepower John Deere Series 6015 tractor with Turbocharged 6.8-L Power Tech Engine and Dual Temperature Cooling—where he's been since dawn—plowing up the stubble in the

The Prodigal Son Returns

heat. Over the roar of the engine, he suddenly hears fiddle music. He stands up in the tractor and sees a country band playing and a calf roasting on a spit and people dancing! He hollers to one of the hired hands.

"Hey! What the heck's going on?"

"Your missing brother has come home, sir. So your dad is throwing a big party. Come and join us!"

But the older brother sits back in the seat of the tractor like he's been shot. *"My kid brother is back? The one who nearly bankrupted us demanding his inheritance early? The one who squandered it all on wine, women, and tickets to Cirque de Soleil in Vegas? They're throwing him a party while I'm killing myself out here. No way! That's just not fair, man. That's just not right."*

So he goes back to work, grimly sweating in the choking dust under the midday sun until his father notices his absence and runs out to the back forty.

"Son! Your brother's back safe and sound! Come join the fiesta!"

"No way, man," the brother says angrily, fighting back tears. "You're just going to forgive him, aren't you? Just like that. You know he'll do it all over in a few years when he tires of living out here in the sticks.

"Father, all these years, I've worked like a slave for you. I've never grumbled, never complained. And when I wanted to have a birthday party, you wouldn't even give us so much as a goat to grill. We had to order take-out Chinese food! But when your precious baby boy comes strolling back—and I always knew you liked him best—after nearly destroying the family farm, nothing's too good for him. You can just take your fiesta and . . ."

By now, the tears are streaming down the older boy's face. The father climbs into the cab of the tractor and embraces him fiercely.

"Junior, I love you so much. Everything I have is yours. I cherish our time together more than you'll ever know. I'm so proud of you. But we *must* celebrate your brother's return. I . . . I thought we'd lost him forever. When you have children of your own, you'll understand. Trust me here. Now come on back—that cute little Maria Sanchez has been looking for you."

(Or something like that.)

It's not fair, of course. The older brother is right: *It's just not fair.* But this parable isn't about fairness. The thief on the cross next to Jesus didn't deserve to be in heaven with Jesus in fifteen minutes. And, as we'll see in the parable of the Vineyard, Jesus isn't particularly concerned about illustrating fairness. He's interested in showing the joy in heaven when another lost soul finds him. It's not about fairness. It's about joy and grace and eternal life.

But there's more. It's easy to see that the loving father represents God. But who are you? Are you the prodigal son? Or are you the miffed older

Reluctant Prophets and Clueless Disciples

brother? We tend to identify with the prodigal, but I suspect that, more often than not, we're more like the self-righteous older brother. That's what's great about the parables. We're *all* of the characters in *all* of the stories at one time or another.

It's interesting how Jesus doesn't tie up all of the narrative loose ends. He doesn't say whether or not the older brother grudgingly—or other-wise—joins the barbecue and woos the dark-eyed Maria. Like many of the parables, the story is open-ended, forcing the reader to examine his or her own response.

Think how different the story would have been had Jesus told it from a different point of view. Would the emphasis be different told from the older brother's POV? Would he appear a more sympathetic character? And what about the mom? She's never even mentioned. The parable of the Prodigal and His Brother would have a *radically* different emotional impact if told by the missing mother.

Regardless, one thing always emerges from this parable—that God's love for us is relentless and persistent, that God's forgiveness is bound-less and limitless, and that God's grace to a bunch of self-centered, undeserving little bipeds on a backwater planet on the edge of the galaxy is beyond comprehension.

It's not fair—thank goodness!

> Well, father said, "See my son coming home to me
> Coming home to me"
> Father ran and fell down on his knees
> Said, "Sing and praise, Lord have mercy on me"
> Oh poor boy stood there, hung his head and cried
> Hung his head and cried
> Poor boy stood and hung his head and cried
> Said, "Father, will you look on me as a child?"
> (Reverend Robert Wilkins, "The Prodigal Son" [copyright 1965, renewed.
> Wynwood Music Co., Inc.]. Used by permission.)

The Parable of Lazarus and the Rich Man (Luke 16:19–31)

This is an interesting parable for several reasons. First, Lazarus is the only person actually named in one of Jesus' parables. Second, Lazarus is also the name of one of Jesus' best friends, the one whom Jesus raises from the dead in the book of John (11:1-44), leading some

commentators to specu-
late on a connection
between the two pas-
sages. The parable is
preceded by still more
attacks from the
Pharisees and scribes
(didn't any of these
guys have a hobby?),
this time over the con-
nection with faith and
wealth. In their view,
someone's riches were
proof-positive that God
loved and favored the
person—a sentiment
echoed by most tele-
vangelists today!

Jesus, of course, will
have none of it. So he
tells a tale of a fabu-
lously rich man—oh,
let's randomly call him
Donald—who lives high
on the hog in a gated community. Each day, his limo drives past a desperately poor man named Lazarus who begs outside his gate, his emaci-
ated body covered with open sores. If this were set in modern times, perhaps Jesus would say that Lazarus has AIDS. Donald isn't necessarily a
bad man. He doesn't hate or torment Lazarus; he just ignores him. (After
all, the opposite of love isn't hate. The opposite of love is indifference.)
Donald is indifferent. He's got his. And he never makes eye contact with
Lazarus when en route to yet another lavish banquet.

In time, both Lazarus and Donald die. When Lazarus meets St. Peter
at the Pearly Gates, he's sent to heaven, where he gets to hang with
Abraham for all eternity. But when Donald faces St. Pete, Pete shouts,
"You're fired!" and sends him straight to hell.

In this parable, heaven and hell bump up against each other, kind of
like Minneapolis and St. Paul. They're so close that Donald can see
Lazarus and Abraham, and he cries out, "Father Abraham, have mercy
on me, and send Lazarus to dip the tip of his finger in water and cool my

230

tongue, for I am in agony in these flames" (16:24). Notice that Donald is still assuming a superior position: "*Send* Lazarus"—like he's another servant—"to take care of me."

But Abraham sadly shakes his head:

> Child, remember that during your lifetime you received your good things, and Lazarus in like manner evil things; but now he is comforted here, and you are in agony. Besides all this, between you and us a great chasm has been fixed, so that those who might want to pass from here to you cannot do so, and no one can cross from there to us. (Luke 16:25-26)

Donald's response, on the surface, is surprisingly generous. Instead of cursing his fate or whining to Abraham about how unfair everything is, he thinks of his surviving family: "Then, father, I beg you to send [Lazarus] to my father's house—for I have five brothers—that he may warn them, so that they will not also come into this place of torment" (16:27-28). But Donald still doesn't get it. First, he's ordering Lazarus around again like an errand boy. Second, he's only concerned with his immediate blood kin. That others will die without this message doesn't concern him. (That 8,000 people around the world die every day of AIDS was not his problem when he was alive, either.)

This final exchange between the two is a chilling word for us today. Abraham replies,

> "They have Moses and the prophets; they should listen to them." [The rich man] said, "No, father Abraham; but if someone goes to them from the dead, they will repent." [Father Abraham] said to him, "If they do not listen to Moses and the prophets, neither will they be convinced even if someone rises from the dead." (16:29-31)

Pow! If we *really* believe in the resurrected Christ, shouldn't we at least act like it?

The story of Lazarus and Donald isn't about being rich or poor. After all, in America today, most of us are rich! By the rest of the world's standards, we're fabulously rich. Most of us live in safe, climate-controlled houses or apartments, surrounded by nice things, eat three square meals a day, attend first-rate schools, and drive around in SUV-comfort. We are both Donald *and* the Rich Young Ruler (see that story in Luke 18:18-30). But even so, this parable isn't about riches, it's about what we value most in our lives. "For where your treasure is, there your heart will be also" (Matthew 6:21).

The so-called Word-Faith Movement (also known as the Name It–Claim It or Blab It–Grab It Movement) preached by the televangelists is a dangerous, seductive heresy. It's heresy to believe we somehow *deserve* our riches. It's heresy to claim that God will bestow unlimited blessings on you but only *after* you give money to a certain slick-haired televangelist. So why does God allow these televangelists to prosper? Perhaps as a vivid reminder that heresy still lives in our own hearts, the heresy of believing that we somehow deserve or are worthy of, not just our earthly riches, but of *automatic* entrance into heaven someday because of how good we are! The Bible tells us repeatedly that *no one* deserves all of this. What we have, and the promise of what's to come, *are bestowed by grace and grace alone.*

There was a bestseller a few years ago titled *Why Do Bad Things Happen to Good People?* It could just as easily have been titled *Why Do Good Things Happen to Good People?* The real question is, "Who is good?"

This parable contains some powerful words and images. But as the Rev. Raymond Bailey once said in a sermon, these parables in Luke were delivered in the final days before Jesus was crucified. There is urgency about them—so much to tell his disciples, so little time.

Like most parables, this one doesn't follow the Hero's Journey format. Neither Donald nor Lazarus is changed. But Jesus isn't telling this story for them, He's telling it for you and me.

Am *I* different? Are *you* different?

That's the Third Act.

It is ironic to think of the number of people in this country who pray for the poor and needy on Sunday and spend the rest of the week complaining that the government is doing something about them. (William Sloane Coffin, *Credo* [Louisville: Westminster John Knox Press, 2004], 52)

The Parable of the Pharisee and the Tax Collector (Luke 18:9-14)

This is another in the group of final parables, told by Jesus just moments before the shocking scene where he reveals to the Twelve that He's going to Jerusalem to die and—even more amazing—rise again! From a strictly story-oriented POV, these parables must be pretty important for Jesus to tell them close to the end of his life.

The parable of the Pharisee and the Tax Collector has a little twist. Jesus tells the disciples what it means—the punch line!—right off the bat. (It's kind of like telling a friend about the movie *Fight Club* and prefacing

232

your story by revealing the surprise ending. That's a good way to make *former* friends.)

Once again, context is important. This parable follows hard on the heels of the very short parable of the Widow and the Unjust Judge (see Luke 18:1-8). In that parable, a desperately poor widow keeps pestering a powerful and immoral judge until he—just to get rid of her—grants her request. Jesus also tells what this one is about: "[the] need to pray always and not to lose heart" (18:1). At the end, Jesus asks, "Don't you think God is more likely to grant justice to those who love and follow him and cry continually for mercy than to those who do evil?" Even the densest disciple has to agree, "Yup, that seems pretty likely to me, Lord. You certainly nailed that one."

Taken together, these parables reinforce two very serious points:

1. God likes folks who believe and who act on their beliefs.
2. God isn't exactly wild about the folks who are so self-consumed that they do what they like to do, regardless of the consequences to others.

If that's not clear enough, Jesus goes ahead and spells it out:

> He . . . told this parable to some who trusted in themselves that they were righteous and regarded others with contempt. (Luke 18:9)

That verse introduces the second parable, in which a Pharisee—one of those people in Israel who are most concerned about (some would say consumed with) keeping the letter of the law—stands on a busy street corner, raises his hands and eyes to heaven, and prays loudly. Substitute "preacher" or "priest" for "Pharisee" and see what you think:

"God, I thank you that I am not like other people: thieves, rogues, adulterers, or even like this tax collector. I fast twice a week; I give a tenth of all my income" (18:11-12).

OK, now substitute "pimp" or "drug-addict" for "tax collector" and see what you think.

"But the tax collector, standing far off, would not even look up to heaven, but was beating his breast and saying, 'God, be merciful to me, a sinner!'" (18:13).

Jesus' inescapable eyes suddenly lock on the eyes of the self-righteous people to whom he addressed the parable:

"I tell you, this man went down to his home justified rather than the other; for all who exalt themselves will be humbled, but all who humble themselves will be exalted" (18:14).

233

Funny thing is, the Pharisee was probably telling the truth. He probably *did* do all of those things. Heck, he didn't even take credit for himself; he gives God credit for the fact that he isn't like that low-life scum down the road.

But as pastor and blogger Gordon Atkinson made clear in a sermon (February 6, 2005), this isn't a parable about prayer. It's a para-ble about *spiritual pride*. It's like the guy who prays, "Lord, I'm proud of how humble you've helped me become."

Once again, we probably identify with the wrong guy. Jesus means for us to see ourselves in the proud Pharisee. Spiritual pride is a big no-no. Jesus spends a lot of time praising those who are "poor in spirit" and says things like, "theirs is the kingdom of heaven" (Matthew 5:3).

Isn't that backwards? Shouldn't he be holding up paragons of Christianity as examples? Shouldn't he be instructing us to read the books and watch the TV programs of the great, towering spiritual giants of our day? Instead, as Mike Yaconelli points out in *Messy Spirituality* (p. 37), Jesus always seems to prefer the broken in spirit, the confused, and the tenderhearted.

So, what's so bad about spiritual pride?

For one thing, when we're proud of how we're doing and think we're always doing the right thing, pride generally comes from comparing our-

234

selves with someone else. Whether we're talking about Christian individuals or Christian institutions, we (being human) have a tendency to judge. We judge the faith of others; we judge their motives; we even judge what's inside their hearts.

There are a couple of problems with that.

One, we don't know their hearts!

Two, we don't know what Jesus expects of them!

The end result is that Jesus says, "Fine. Go ahead and judge other people. Judge your head off. Just expect some judgment of your own down the road, Boudreaux."

As we've noted earlier, the times that Jesus gets the most hacked off is at people who sit in judgment on others. (Note to self: Probably not a good idea to get the Son of the Most High Omnipotent Living God, Creator of All Things hacked off at you.)

In other words, as the old blues song (which has been recorded by everybody from Eric Clapton to Creedence Clearwater Revival) goes:

> Before you accuse me, take a look at yourself.
> (Ellas McDaniel, better known as Bo Diddley, "Take a Look at Yourself")

Twenty

CLUELESS DISCIPLES

You gotta love those fussin', fightin', feudin', heroic, clueless, foolish twelve disciples. Throughout the Four Gospels, they serve as a collective Everyman—asking the questions we'd ask if we'd sat at the feet of the Savior. From a storytelling standpoint, we long to know more about each of these characters, but the accounts give only tantalizing glimpses of personalities and motivations.

Lots of people followed Jesus at different times—the actual numbers and relative passion of the crowds were constantly in flux. Besides the many who showed up exclusively for the miracles and healings, there was apparently a large, ever-changing group that followed him for days, weeks, sometimes months. Some of these followers left after the particularly difficult teachings of John 6, where Jesus' words, "Those who eat my flesh and drink my blood have eternal life, and I will raise them up on the last day; for my flesh is true food and my blood is true drink" (6:54-55), were just too much for some. Others, like Mary Magdalene, were with him for the long haul.

Jesus handpicked the core group over a period of time and included women as well as men:

> Soon afterwards he went on through cities and villages, proclaiming and bringing the good news of the kingdom of God. The twelve were with him, as well as some women who had been cured of evil spirits and infirmities: Mary, called Magdalene, from whom seven demons had gone out, and Joanna, the wife of Herod's steward Chuza, and Susanna, and many others, who provided for them out of their resources. (Luke 8:1-3)

Of this amorphous, fluid group, the gospels identify twelve disciples in particular (several never actually speak—or at least the gospels don't record their words if they do).

1. Simon (better known as Peter)
2. Andrew
3. James (a son of Zebedee)
4. John (another son of Zebedee)
5. Philip
6. Bartholomew (also known as Nathanael)
7. Thomas
8. Matthew (or Levi)
9. James, the son of Alphaeus (or James the Lesser—now there's an ego-boosting nickname!)
10. Thaddeus (sometimes identified as Judas, the son of James)
11. Simon the Zealot (or Simon the Cananean)
12. Judas Iscariot

Of this twelve, Jesus' closest friends and confidants are Peter, James, and John. John and Peter behave like squabbling siblings, vying for position and favor throughout the four accounts, right up until Jesus' last minutes on earth.

Most of the Twelve were Galilean fishermen, although Matthew was apparently a tax collector and Judas may have been from the southern city of Keriot. The connection between Simon the Zealot and the group known as the Zealots mentioned by Josephus is interesting. The Zealots were a rag-tag band

TWO OF THE DISCIPLES HAVE A POWER STRUGGLE...

"Oh yeah! Well who died, rose again, ascended into heaven and left you boss?!"

238

of guerilla fighters who briefly retook Jerusalem from the Romans around 67–68 CE. But since we have no other information on Simon, it could just as easily refer to his enthusiasm for the good news. Some of the other guys are such ciphers, we're not sure what their real names are—is it really Thaddeus or Judas son of James; is it Bartholomew or Nathanael?

We do have juicy snippets on a few of the Twelve—Andrew, Thomas, and Judas—Peter, of course, is worth his own chapter.

Andrew

Andrew is the consummate team player. He doesn't say much, but when you need him—he's there. He's dutifully mentioned in the various lists of the Twelve in the Synoptic Gospels (Matthew, Mark, and Luke), but doesn't get his moment to shine until the Gospel of John. We do know a few things about him. He's the brother of the impetuous, larger-than-life Simon Peter and, most of the time, he's content to follow Peter's lead. They're both fishermen on the deceptively calm Sea of Galilee, tossing their nets and—hopefully—dragging in scores of silvery fish. It's backbreaking, heartbreaking work, dangerous and fickle. But apparently, they've done well enough to own a home together in Capernaum, across from the synagogue (see Mark 1:29). They live there with Peter's long-suffering (and unnamed) wife and Peter's mother-in-law. The Synoptics say that Peter and Andrew were fishing when they were discovered and summoned by Jesus to become his followers. They dropped their nets and followed without question.

John 1:35-51

But in the first chapter of John we hear another account. Here, Andrew and another (unnamed) disciple are said to have become followers of John the Baptist during one of the Baptizer's crusades along the River Jordan. John is preaching (between snacks of low-carb locusts and honey) when Jesus strolls up to listen, as he has done on several occasions. John stops and points to the Man from Nazareth: "Look, here is the Lamb of God!" (1:36). All eyes shoot in Jesus' direction, who nods and gives a little embarrassed wave as he walks away.

Andrew and his friend (perhaps Philip) immediately, instinctively, take off after Jesus. After a few minutes, Jesus turns to them and says, "What are you looking for, guys?"

239

One of the two answers, "Um, where are you staying, rabbi?"

Jesus, who rarely has a roof over his head, smiles enigmatically and says, "Come and see" (1:39).

Andrew and the other man spend a mesmerizing day listening to Jesus teach about the kingdom of God. About 4 p.m., Andrew dashes off in search of his brother, then still called Simon. When he finds him, he grabs his brother's burly arm and shouts, "We have found him! We have found the Messiah!" He drags Simon along to meet Jesus, who welcomes him warmly. Jesus says, "You are Simon son of John. You are to be called Cephas (which is translated Peter)" (1:42); or in English, *Rock*.

The next day, Jesus goes to Bethsaida (which John says is the home of Andrew and Peter), finds Philip and Nathanael, and calls them too. Together, Jesus and the first four disciples head for Jesus' first date with destiny—the Wedding in Cana.

John 6:1-13

Andrew's next big moment occurs at the feeding of the 5,000. His buddy Philip is apparently in charge of the catering because Jesus pulls him aside and asks, "Where are we to buy bread for these people to eat?" (6:5).

Philip throws up his hands in desperation. "[Lord,] six months' wages would not buy enough bread for each of them to get a little" (6:7)!

Meanwhile, Andrew has been scouring the crowd. He finds a small boy with a picnic basket, happily munching away. (When Mom says, "Why

240

don't you take a snack along, dear? You might get hungry later," listen to her. Moms somehow instinctively *know* these things.) *"It's not much—but it is something. Jesus will figure something out,"* Andrew thinks. He reports back to Jesus: "There is a boy here who has five barley loaves and two fish. But what are they among so many people?" (6:9).

That's when Jesus gives him one of those infuriatingly enigmatic smiles of his and proceeds to multiply the loaves and fishes.

John 12:20-26

Andrew's last solo appearance comes in the final days, just after the triumphant entry into Jerusalem, and just before the climactic Passover dinner. While Jesus and the gang are dodging the religious authorities in Jerusalem, a group of Greeks track them down. They tell Andrew and Philip that they want to see the Big Guy in person. Just a minute, Andrew says—you can't be too careful with all of the religious nut-jobs out there. (This is exactly what the Pharisees have feared—the word is getting out about this Jesus.) Andrew and Philip walk around the corner and tell Jesus he has guests, prompting one of Jesus' most memorable responses:

> Very truly, I tell you, unless a grain of wheat falls into the earth and dies, it remains just a single grain; but if it does, it bears much fruit. Those who love their life lose it, and those who hate their life in this world will keep it for eternal life. Whoever serves me must follow me, and where I am, there will my servant be also. Whoever serves me, the Father will honor. (John 12:24-26)

That's the final mention of Andrew separately, though he is doubtless present at all of the resurrection events. When he is mentioned, it is usually in connection with his brother Simon Peter, along with John and James. But even in these fleeting glimpses, Andrew is shown as a decisive, resourceful person, one quite willing to serve as a witness to what he has seen; and a pretty good guy to have on your team.

Thomas

There's a little more on Thomas—who is forever saddled with that whole *doubting* tag. But Thomas is an intriguing fellow beyond that single incident. He's brave and inquisitive too. And there are worse things than being pragmatic . . .

241

John 11:1-16

In the Synoptic gospels Thomas, like Andrew, is only mentioned in the lists of the Twelve. But John, who identifies Thomas as a twin in 11:16, reports that Thomas suddenly takes center stage on several occasions near the end of Jesus' earthly mission. The first occasion is the death of Lazarus. Jesus and his followers have been forced out of Jerusalem by an increasingly violent persecution by the religious leaders. They've found a quiet corner of Ephraim, near the trackless wilderness of Judea—a good fallback position should the authorities come looking for them. While there, they hear that Jesus' beloved friend Lazarus is critically ill. Jesus waits for a couple of days, and then finally decides to risk a foray back into the village of Bethany, virtually in the shadow of Jerusalem's walls.

The disciples are horrified: "Jesus, the Jews were just now trying to stone you; are you going there again?" Following Jesus is one thing; certain death is quite another!

But Jesus won't be deterred. "Lazarus is dead. For your sake I am glad I was not there, so that you may believe. But let us go to him" (11:14).

The others still hold back—but not Thomas. He doesn't know what Jesus is talking about any more than the other disciples do, but he's come to love the Man so much over the past three and a half years that he'll follow him even unto death. Thomas says fiercely, "Let us also go, that we may die with him" (11:16). Brave? You bet.

And off they go.

John 14:1-7

The second appearance follows the Last Supper in what is often called the Farewell Discourse, the long, detailed, incredibly rich teaching that makes up a good chunk of John.

Jesus has told them about Peter's impending betrayal and says that where He's going shortly, they won't be able to follow:

> Do not let your hearts be troubled. Believe in God, believe also in me. In my Father's house there are many dwelling places. If it were not so, would I have told you that I go to prepare a place for you? And if I go and prepare a place for you, I will come again and will take you to myself, so that where I am, there you may be also. (John 14:1-3)

242

Fortunately, we have Thomas there to ask the question we would have asked at the time. Thomas doesn't know Jesus is talking about his hideous death and resurrection. So he blurts out, "Lord, we do not know where you are going. How can we know the way?" (14:5).

Jesus' response is the great central message of the book of John:

> I am the way, and the truth, and the life. No one comes to the Father except through me. If you know me, you will know my Father also. From now on, you do know him and have seen him. (14:6-7)

John 20:19-29

Thomas's most famous scene follows the crucifixion and resurrection. He's not there when Jesus appears to the disciples in the locked room. When he returns from his errand, they excitedly babble about what they've seen. Now no one wanted Jesus to rise from the dead more than Thomas, but perhaps this is mass hysteria or some kind of group hallu-cination. So he's skepti-

cal—who wouldn't be? Maybe they've even seen a ghost!

"[Sorry guys,]" he says, "unless I see the mark of the nails in his hands, and put my finger in the mark of the nails and my hand in his side, I will not believe" (20:25). It seems that Thomas was there during the crucifixion and saw every soul-numbing blow. The others berate him for his lack of belief—conveniently forgetting that they didn't believe Mary Magdalene initially, either!

A week passes and the disciples still mill around aimlessly, still avoid the authorities behind barred doors, still feverishly discuss what they've seen. Thomas sits in a corner, pragmatically pondering what to do next. Then, in an instant, Jesus is there, amidst them, touching and soothing their frantic hearts. He sees Thomas, sitting alone, and walks to him. Thomas stumbles to his feet as Jesus addresses him: "Put your finger here and see my hands. Reach out your hand and put it in my side. Do not doubt but believe" (20:27).

Thomas sinks to his knees and delivers the most potent confession, in the entire book of John, of who Jesus really is: "My Lord and my God!" (20:28).

Jesus gently raises him back up and whispers: "Have you believed because you have seen me? Blessed are those who have not seen and yet have come to believe" (20:29).

The neat thing here is that this story isn't really about Jesus berating Thomas for his disbelief; it's about the crazy, limitless, unbelievable grace of God that is available to everybody—including Thomas, Andrew, Peter, and the rest of the world!

We have one last fleeting mention of our friend Thomas in John's final chapter. Seven of the disciples have returned to the Sea of Galilee, where they've resumed fishing, waiting for further instructions from Jesus. Of the seven, Peter is mentioned first, then—for the first and only time in the Gospels—Thomas is mentioned second. Why? Perhaps it is to honor honest doubt.

After all, as the old saying goes, "To believe greatly, it is necessary to have doubted greatly."

Judas Iscariot

The Bible is full of great villains: Pharaoh, Herod, and—the most infamous—Judas Iscariot. (That's not counting Satan, the *uber*-villain, since he's in a whole separate category of Bad.) Of the earthly biblical baddies, only Judas's name has become synonymous with betrayal and deceit. The name Benedict Arnold is synonymous with betrayal in the United States; the name Vidkun Quisling (the Norwegian turncoat who helped the Nazis) carries the same sense of disgust in Europe—

244

but only the name Judas evokes near-universal revulsion. After all, the man betrayed the Son of God, the only perfect human to ever walk this crazy, mixed-up world of ours. What could be more appalling and less forgivable?

But the strange thing is, the more you read about Judas Iscariot, the less you're sure *why* he did what he did and if—somehow, some way—he thought he was doing the *right* thing! It's a complicated narrative, one made more confusing by several competing versions of the events and their inevitable aftermath.

If you'll look back at the list of the twelve disciples, you'll notice that Judas is always listed last and is the only one who is identified with a place name. The most plausible explanation for *Iscariot* is "Ish" (man) "Kerioth" (a town in far southern Judea). It seems that he's the only non-Galilean; a loner and something of a misfit in the tightly knit disciples, many of whom are related by blood or profession. And, in each of the four lists of disciples in the Gospels, he's called "traitor" or "betrayer."

And yet, Jesus (who, being able to read minds, has a slight advantage over most personnel directors) specifically chose Judas, not just to be one of the Twelve, but to be the treasurer for their little band! Why not Matthew the tax collector, for instance, unless Judas was pretty good at his job?

John 12:1-7

Part of the problem is that, until we get to the passion stories, there is hardly anything written on or about Judas. He doesn't become a presence until the final chapters of Matthew, Mark, or Luke. His only real non-betrayal scene is in John 12 when Jesus and the disciples are at the house of Mary, Martha, and the recently raised Lazarus, just six days before the Passover in Jerusalem. While Martha bustles around the kitchen, Mary slips into the den and pours extravagantly expensive perfume over Jesus' dusty, blistered feet, wiping it away with her long black hair. Judas, the treasurer, not surprisingly, pipes up: "Hey! Why was this perfume not sold for three hundred *denarii* and the money given to the poor?" John adds an editorial comment here, saying Judas only said that because he'd been dipping in the community chest all along, not because he really cared about the poor. Jesus, of course, comes to Mary's defense:

245

Leave her alone. She bought it so that she might keep it for the day of my burial. You always have the poor with you, but you do not always have me. (John 12:7-8)

John 13:15-27

From here, John differs markedly from the Synoptics once again. All four Gospels place Judas's treachery at the Last Supper, but only John specifically places it at the climactic foot washing, which makes the infidelity more shocking:

> "For I have set you an example, that you also should do as I have done to you. Very truly, I tell you, servants are not greater than their master, nor are messengers greater than the one who sent them. If you know these things, you are blessed if you do them. I am not speaking of all of you; I know whom I have chosen. But it is to fulfill the scripture, 'The one who ate my bread has lifted his heel against me.' I tell you this now, before it occurs, so that when it does occur, you may believe that I am he. Very truly, I tell you, whoever receives one whom I send receives me; and whoever receives me receives him who sent me."

> After saying this Jesus was troubled in spirit, and declared, "Very truly, I tell you, one of you will betray me." The disciples looked at one another, uncertain of whom he was speaking. One of his disciples—the one whom Jesus loved—was reclining next to him; Simon Peter therefore motioned to him to ask Jesus of whom he was speaking. So while reclining next to Jesus, he asked him, "Lord, who is it?" Jesus answered, "It is the one to whom I give this piece of bread when I have dipped it in the dish." So when he had dipped the piece of bread, he gave it to Judas son of Simon Iscariot. After he received the piece of bread, Satan entered into him. Jesus said to him. "Do quickly what you are going to do." (John 13:15-27)

Pretty straightforward, right? Judas is a monster, scurrying off into the night like a cockroach to set in motion the death of the Savior. But why? What was in it for Judas? And what about Matthew 26:25 where, when Jesus tells the Twelve that one of them is going to betray him, each disciple says, "Surely not me, Lord" until it's Judas's turn. Judas says, "Surely not I, Rabbi?" Jesus replies, "You have said so." Taken at face value, this would almost imply that Judas really didn't know—until that moment at the Last Supper.

Or perhaps you subscribe to the theory offered in the Webber/Rice musical *Jesus Christ Superstar*. In this version, Judas is a helpless pawn. He doesn't want to betray Jesus; he can't help himself because he's *destined* to betray Jesus. He's the cosmic fall guy. This, of course, doesn't fit with what we know about Jesus Christ in the New Testament.

246

This Jesus *chose* to be the Sacrificial Lamb, to die for people like you, me, *and* Judas. From a dramatic standpoint, it's not a very plausible motive (although it does give Judas some of the best songs in the hit musical!).

One *why* theory springs from another plausible interpretation of Judas's last name, Iscariot, as an Aramaic translation of the Latin word *Sicarius*—which means, "dagger-man." This, according to this line of thought, identifies Judas with the Zealots, who sought, by violent means, to overthrow the Roman occupation. Judas's actions weren't really a betrayal as much as an attempt to force Jesus' hand and hurry the liberation of Israel. Judas had certainly seen all of the great miracles; he certainly knew of the prophecies of a messiah who would conquer kingdoms on a white horse. Besides, all of Jerusalem was already hailing him—now was the time to strike! In this theory, Judas's otherwise inexplicable—and overwhelming—grief at Jesus' subsequent torture and crucifixion makes more sense. They are the result of a plan gone horribly, horribly wrong.

But that flies in the face of the three (mostly) complementary accounts in the Synoptics that all have Judas approaching the high priests and promising to identify Jesus at a time and a place away from the increasingly restless crowds. In return, they offer him thirty pieces of silver—or the amount a Jewish slave could claim if his master drew blood during a beating.

Still, even the *blood money* idea is problematic, especially when you consider this powerful passage in Matthew:

> When Judas, his betrayer, saw that Jesus was condemned, he repented and brought back the thirty pieces of silver to the chief priests and elders. He said, "I have sinned by betraying innocent blood." But they said, "What is that to us? See to it yourself." (Matthew 27:3-4)

We'll never know whether Judas threw the silver back at their smug faces angrily or remorsefully. Either way, does *this* sound like someone in it for the money?

John 18:1-10

Even the manner of Jesus' betrayal has two somewhat conflicting accounts. In Matthew, Mark, and Luke, Judas leads the temple police into the Garden at Gethsemane, betrays Jesus with the legendary kiss, and Jesus is then seized. But John, again, presents a different picture entirely.

247

In this account, while Judas leads the armed police to Gethsemane, Jesus steps forward voluntarily and asks:

"This looks like a search party. Who's the subject?"

"Jesus, once of Nazareth, sometimes called the Christ," comes the reply.

"That's me."

Immediately, the priests, Pharisees, soldiers—and Judas—step back and fall to the ground.

"Again, who is the subject of your search?" Jesus asks.

"Um, Jesus?" one Pharisee says, his voice betraying his uncertainty.

"That's me, friend. You've got me. Why don't you let these other people leave? They don't have anything to do with this."

Judas is a non-player in this drama and a passive observer as Peter rushes the police, slashing away with his sword.

Jesus quickly restores order; then they march him off to meet his fate, even as the remaining disciples scatter into the Judean night.

The Death of Judas

Finally, we come to the manner of Judas's death. The two main accounts offer significantly different approaches (once Judas actually

248

betrays Jesus, Mark, Luke, and John give no indication of Judas's ultimate fate):

- **Matthew 27:3-10:** After his ugly encounter with the chief priests, the
repentant Judas rushes to the edge of Jerusalem, where he hangs
himself. This places the priests in a bit of a quandary. They can't put
the *blood money* back into the temple treasury, so they use it instead
to buy a field where foreigners can be buried, thus fulfilling a prophecy alluded to in Zechariah and Jeremiah.
- **Acts 1:18-20:** As Peter retells the story, Judas uses the silver to buy a
field but accidentally falls; his belly splits open and he dies an agonizing death. After his death, the place becomes known as "The Field of
Blood" (1:19).

Which account is closer to what actually happened? Some commentators try to reconcile the two, speculate that Judas did, indeed, hang himself from a tall tree, but that the limb broke (or something) and that his
body split open upon impact.

From a storytelling standpoint, I like a happy ending. With Matthew's
story, at least there is Judas's, apparently, heartfelt repentance. Frederick
Buechner favors Matthew's story in light of a particularly touching tradition in the early church. They believed that Judas's suicide was prompted
by—of all things—*hope*, not by despair. He had genuinely repented; he
knew Jesus would forgive him. Why wait? Why spend the rest of his life
hating himself for what he'd done? (*Peculiar Treasures* [San Francisco:
Harper & Row, 1979], 83)

So if—as the early Christians believed—Jesus spent the three days
between the crucifixion and resurrection in Hell, saving the souls of the
damned, then what better place for Judas to meet Jesus and beg for forgiveness in person? It might be his last, best chance for salvation. And
so, that's Judas's last prayer as he leaps from the gnarled tree, the rope
firmly around his neck:

> In any case, it's a scene to conjure with. Once again they met in the shadows,
> the two old friends, both of them a little worse for wear after all that had hap-
> pened, only this time it was Jesus who was the one to give the kiss, and this
> time it wasn't the kiss of death that was given. (Frederick Buechner, *Peculiar
> Treasures*, 83)

The Fate of the Twelve

Considering that these are twelve of the most important figures in the history of the Christian faith (along with Jesus and Paul), we know very little about what happened to each of them.

Peter

After his many courageous missionary exploits—chronicled in the Acts of the Apostles—he is said to have been crucified in Rome by Nero. Perhaps still grieving over his betrayal of Christ, he asked to be crucified upside down.

John

The "beloved disciple" is said to be the lone disciple who died of old age. John (who may or may not have written both the book of John and the Revelation of John) died in his bed on the Isle of Patmos, where he had been exiled.

James

The brother of John (and one of the sons of Zebedee) is the only disciple besides Judas whose death is recorded in the Bible. He is stabbed to death at the order of Herod Agrippa in Acts 12:1-2.

Andrew

Some old sources say that the brother of Peter worked as a missionary in what is now Russia. He was crucified, they say, on an X-shaped cross at Patrae in Achaia, a Roman province.

Philip

Early Church writers claim that Philip preached the gospel in Phrygia before suffering martyrdom in Hierapolis.

Nathanael/Bartholomew

Some accounts say that he was martyred in what is now Albania.

Matthew/Levi

Matthew is said to have lived a long, productive life, embarking on several missionary journeys before dying in modern Ethiopia.

Thomas

Perhaps fueled with fire from his final encounter with Jesus, various ancient sources say that Thomas took the good news as far as India, where he was martyred.

James the son of Alphaeus

Different accounts say that he preached throughout what is now Syria, but was martyred in Jerusalem.

Thaddaeus

One early church historian writes that he was martyred while preaching in modern Turkey, although he is said to have been buried in Beirut, Lebanon.

Simon the Zealot

There is no consensus on Simon's life and ultimate fate. Different stories have him preaching in Egypt, Northern Africa, perhaps as far as the British Isles. The legends about his death are equally scattered and conflicting.

Judas

Dies, perhaps by his own hand, following his betrayal of Jesus.

251

Twenty-one

PETER

God bless Peter. We know more about him than virtually any other individual in the New Testament, except for Jesus and Paul. He's a story-teller's dream—a big, sympathetic action hero with obvious flaws and a heart of gold. When his life is recounted chronologically, from the Four Gospels through the book of Acts, it neatly fits the Hero's Journey format. His is an epic life, with dramatic highs and lows. Peter sees things few people in the history of the world are privileged to see. And through it all, his responses are those of the common man or woman. Peter is Everyman (and Everywoman).

The facts about Peter's life are scattered through several books. He was originally named Simon. He is the son of a certain John (perhaps Jonah); he has a brother named Andrew; they are fishermen, fishing the Sea of Galilee. They own a boat, perhaps in conjunction with Zebedee and his sons. The brothers, Peter's unnamed wife, and his unnamed mother-in-law live in Capernaum, not far from a synagogue.

He and Andrew are obviously pious, religious men—early followers of John the Baptist. It is with John that we first meet Peter and that Jesus first speaks to him: "'You are Simon son of John. You are to be called Cephas' (which is translated Peter)" (John 1:42). He's called *Peter* or *Simon Peter* from that moment forward. This new nickname means "Rock," although in the days ahead Peter will appear like any-thing but a rock. Perhaps it is a prophecy that Peter—quite unknow-ingly, at least for now—will someday fulfill. Jesus calls; Peter answers—and leaves the Ordinary World for an Extraordinary World where miracles are commonplace and the supernatural is only a breath away.

In the days that follow, Peter is a first-hand observer to the miraculous life and times of Jesus of Nazareth. He sees the miracle at the wedding in Cana (see John 2:1-12), his own mother-in-law cured (see Mark 1:29-31), and a host of other healings, teachings, and the odd exorcism.

Matthew 14:22-33

One story in particular captures Peter's careening emotional state (I've always suspected he suffered from mild ADD), and it is found only in the book of Matthew. After the feeding of the 5,000, an emotionally spent Jesus retires to rest and pray in solitude in the mountains, while the disciples take the boat out, probably to do a little fishing. Suddenly, a great storm blows up, howling from the west over the Gulf of Pigeons near the town of Magdala. The small boat is cruelly tossed all through the night and by dawn, appears close to capsizing.

Jesus—probably sensing their plight—walks across the choppy waves toward the disciples. They're more afraid of this spectral apparition than they are of drowning—"It's a ghost!" they cry. But Jesus calms them, "Take heart, it is I; do not be afraid" (14:27).

Up pops Peter. "Lord!" he shouts, "If it is you, command me to come to you on the water" (14:28).

"Come," Jesus replies, his voice cutting through the wind.

Peter throws himself overboard and begins to walk cautiously—on the water!—toward Jesus. If the disciples are astonished, then Peter is stupefied. *"I'm actually doing it!"*

A strong blast of wind staggers him—not having much experience walking on water, Peter probably doesn't have his *sea legs* yet—and with the first wave, his confidence washes away. Without his belief to sustain him, Peter sinks into the dark waters.

"Lord, save me!" (14:30), he cries.

Jesus, who by now is just feet away, reaches down and hauls him out of the water, then helps the wet and bedraggled Peter onboard. He asks gently, "You of little faith, why did you doubt?" (14:31).

Immediately, the wind ceases and the remaining eleven disciples fall to their knees. They cry, "Truly you are the Son of God" (14:33).

This is the prototypical Peter story—unbridled enthusiasm and belief, followed by failure. But it is important to remember that Peter alone dares to try. Only Peter gets out of the storm-tossed boat and tries to walk to Jesus.

In the cartoon's thought bubble: "I COULD'VE SWORN PETER WAS HERE JUST A MOMENT AGO..."

Caption below cartoon: JESUS WALKS ON THE WATER A LITTLE TOO FAR FROM THE BOAT.

Gradually, Peter becomes part of Jesus' most intimate circle, along with the sons of Zebedee, John and James. Peter's house in Capernaum becomes their headquarters whenever the disciples are in Galilee, and his boat is always at Jesus' disposal. And whenever the Twelve are listed, Peter's name is always mentioned first.

Mark 5:21-43

Because of this close relationship, Peter, John, and James are privy to miraculous things unseen by the other disciples. For instance, after the healing of the Gerasene demoniac, the disciples return to more familiar (read: Jewish) territory. Upon their arrival, Jairus, the leader of the local synagogue, a man of some means and prestige, throws himself at their feet, begging for Jesus to heal his daughter. Jesus agrees and walks through the town—healing a woman with a twelve-year hemorrhage along the way—until they reach Jairus's house. A group of mourners bars the way. "You're too late," they say bitterly, "the little girl is dead." Jesus takes only the closest three disciples into the house, where they are confronted by still more mourners. Jesus dismisses them as well, takes the bereaved parents in to the child, and whispers, *"Talitha cum,"* which means, "Little girl, get up!" (5:41). Immediately, her eyes fly open. She's alive! And since the Hebrews of this era didn't believe that ghosts or

255

Peter

spirits could eat human food, Jesus tells the family to bake up some brownies for her.

Matthew 16:13-23

Sometime later, after the healing of the blind man at Bethsaida, Jesus takes the disciples to the village of Caesarea Philippi, in the far north. Along the way, he asks them, "Who do people say that the Son of Man is?" (16:13). The disciples casually mention that they've heard that Jesus might be John the Baptist or one of the prophets or even Elijah. Jesus continues: "But who do you say that I am?" (16:15). Peter stops dead in his tracks and blurts out, "You are the Messiah, the Son of the Living God" (16:16), as if it is the most obvious answer in the world. Jesus' response is among the most telling in all of the Gospels:

> Blessed are you, Simon son of Jonah! For flesh and blood has not revealed this to you, but my Father in heaven. And I tell you, you are Peter, and on this rock I will build my church, and the gates of Hades will not prevail against it. I will give you the keys of the kingdom of heaven, and whatever you bind on earth will be bound in heaven, and whatever you loose on earth will be loosed in heaven. (Matthew 16:17-19)

Moments later, Jesus predicts his own gruesome death and resurrection in Jerusalem. Peter, probably empowered by Jesus' praise, pulls Jesus aside and berates him—"This will never happen, Lord God forbid it!"

But Jesus knows better and responds with some of the most scathing comments in the Gospels aimed at someone other than a Pharisee or Sadducee:

> Get behind me, Satan! You are a stumbling block to me; for you are setting your mind not on divine things but on human things. (Matthew 16:23)

Shaken, it must have been days before Peter mustered enough nerve to speak again.

Matthew 17:1-4

By way of contrast, compare that overpowering response to this little insight into Peter's personality at the transfiguration. After the mind-blowing

256

spectacle of seeing Elijah and Moses talking with Jesus on the mountain-top, James and John are struck mute with awe. Not Peter. He babbles excitedly:

Lord, it is good for us to be here; if you wish, I will make three dwellings here, one for you, one for Moses, and one for Elijah. (Matthew 17:4)

The account in Mark wryly notes that Peter's ramblings are due to the intense fear that swept over the three of them. Peter's impulsive, and probably a little inappropriate, response is all too human.

These incidents are a foreshadowing of the roller-coaster ride Peter's emotions will undergo during the passion of Jesus.

John 13:1-10

During the Last Supper, Peter repeatedly doesn't get it. After all he's seen, he still doesn't grasp what is happening. When Jesus tries to wash Peter's feet, Peter yanks them away. "You will never wash my feet" (13:8). But Jesus, who is making a crucial point here about the nature of leadership, rebukes him: "Unless I wash you, you have no share with me" (13:8). Wonderful, dense Peter retorts: "Lord, not my feet only but also my hands and my head!" (13:9). Jesus gently corrects him, "One who has bathed does not need to wash, except for the feet, but is entirely clean" (13:10).

John 13:31-38

After dinner, Jesus foretells his betrayal and sadly watches Judas scurry away into the night. What happens next is one of the saddest, most touching exchanges in all of Scripture. Jesus gives the remaining disciples the "new commandment . . . Just as I have loved you, you also should love one another" (13:34), then tells them that where he is going, they will not be able to follow.

Once again, it is Peter who pipes up. "Lord, why can I not follow you now? I will lay down my life for you" (13:37).

Jesus pauses the longest pause in history before answering his dear friend. "Will you lay down your life for me? Very truly, I tell you, before the cock crows, *you will have denied me three times*" (13:38, italics added).

How those words will come to haunt Peter, perhaps every waking moment for the rest of his life.

257

Mark 14:28-42

The wildly opposing sides of Peter's nature are exposed further on the Mount of Olives, just hours later. There, hidden in the Garden of Gethsemane, Jesus, for the last time, calls Peter, John, and James to sit with him as he prays in agony over his impending torture and death. When Peter nods off, Jesus awakens him and says, "Simon, are you asleep? Could you not keep awake one hour? Keep awake and pray that you may not come into the time of trial; the spirit indeed is willing, but the flesh is weak" (14:37-38).

Three times he implores them to stay awake with him as he bares his soul. Three times Peter, John, and James rouse themselves, only to fall asleep once again. In the moments before Judas leads the soldiers and priests into their midst, Jesus awakens the three a final time: "Are you still sleeping and taking your rest? Enough! The hour has come; the Son of Man is betrayed into the hands of sinners. Get up, let us be going. See, my betrayer is at hand" (14:41-42).

Luke 22:47-53

Peter, still groggy, whips into action. Even as the other disciples are scrambling furiously into the night, Peter grabs the closest sword and hacks at the mob surrounding Jesus. But Peter is a fisherman—not a swordsman—and all he can do is slice the ear off of one of the high priest's slaves. Jesus, who knows what's ahead, doesn't resist. Instead, he shouts at Peter, "No more of this!" (22:51). Luke notes that Jesus pauses long enough to restore the slave's ear before being dragged away.

Luke 22:54-62

But Peter's trials have only just begun. Unlike the remaining disciples, he trails behind the procession that escorts Jesus to his fate. Three times, Peter is asked if he knows Jesus. Three times Peter, his heavy Galilean accent instantly betraying him, denies any knowledge of Jesus.

And somewhere, in the last hour before dawn, a rooster crows the new day—its raucous voice cutting through the darkness. Just then, already battered and bruised, Jesus is led away from the high priest's house en route to the council. His eyes meet those of Peter. But there is not anger

258

or disgust in Jesus' eyes—only love. Peter stumbles away, weeping uncontrollably. It is just as Jesus had said it would be.

Hapless Peter disappears from the narrative for a time. Perhaps he follows all the way to Golgotha, hiding in the shadows, watching helplessly as Jesus is crucified. There is an intriguing hint that he may have been there in 1 Peter 5:1, where the author—presumably Peter—writes, "Now as an elder myself and a witness of the sufferings of Christ . . ."

If you're looking for a Big Gloom, this is it. Peter feels it more than any man or woman alive. It is a deeper, darker hole than he's ever experienced before, and the next three days are doubtless the worst of his life. Peter will never be the same. He is completely broken. His ego, his need for attention, and his sometimes-reckless behavior—all are gone now.

John 21:15–24

The resurrection account—and Peter's place in it—is covered more thoroughly in the chapter on the life of Jesus. So let us return to the book of John. The Gospels end in John 21 with this highly personal exchange between Peter and the resurrected Jesus, walking along the beach after breakfast. When they're far enough way that the others can't hear, Jesus turns to Peter,

> "Simon son of John, do you love me more than these?" He said to him, "Yes, Lord; you know that I love you." Jesus said to him, "Feed my lambs." A second time he said to him, "Simon, son of John, do you love me?" He said to him, "Yes, Lord; you know that I love you." Jesus said to him, "Tend my sheep." He

259

said to him the third time, "Simon, son of John, do you love me?" Peter felt hurt because he said to him the third time, "Do you love me?" And he said to him, "Lord, you know everything; you know that I love you." Jesus said to him, "Feed my sheep. Very truly, I tell you, when you were younger, you used to fasten your own belt and to go wherever you wished. But when you grow old, you will stretch out your hands, and someone else will fasten a belt around you and take you where you do not wish to go." (John 21:15-18)

Peter can only stand dumbfounded. By now, he's got to have made the connection between his three denials back in Jerusalem and Jesus repeating the question of Peter's fidelity (with slight variations) three times.

Jesus smiles, perhaps for the first time that day. "Follow me" (21:19).

This would be a great ending for the gospels, a *great commission* for all believers everywhere to take care of not just the spiritually hungry but the physically hungry as well. This, many believe, is the question Jesus will ask *all* of us someday. If we really do love him, then we'll be driven— no, we'll be *compelled*—to do just that! As for Peter, he's found redemption. Not only has Jesus forgiven him, he's entrusted him with his most important task—to share the good news.

But the account doesn't end there. Instead, we get one last glimpse of Peter's all too human nature, perhaps as a reminder that there is a lot of Peter in each of us.

Still at a loss for words, Peter glances up and down the beach. There, standing a few yards away, but obviously following Jesus and Peter the entire way, stands John. Peter yanks a thumb over his shoulder at John and asks, "Jesus, what about him?"

Reluctant Prophets and Clueless Disciples

Jesus can only shake his head. In the process of baring his greatest hope and fears to a mere, fallible mortal, Jesus has just given Peter an awesome responsibility—and all Peter can think about is his ongoing competition with John!

Jesus arches a single eyebrow and stares at Peter. "If it is my will that he remain until I come, what is that to you? Follow me!" (21:22).

And Peter did. And so did John.

Peter may be forgiven but he's still not perfect!

Sometime after that, Jesus returns to heaven, waiting for the proper time to return in all his glory, a time that no man or woman can know. The lone detailed account of Jesus' subsequent ascension into heaven is found in Luke, and segues neatly into the book of the Acts of the Apostles.

That means that John 21:24 is really a *P.S.*, perhaps written by John himself, perhaps written by his disciples: "This is the disciple who is testifying to these things and has written them, and we know that his testimony is true."

As for Peter, many scholars believe that it is his account that constitutes much of the book of Mark. Not surprisingly, Peter is shown in an unflattering light more often in Mark's account than in any of the other gospels.

Acts 1:12–26

Fortunately, we have the book of Acts to finish the story, especially Peter's story. Jesus' example of unconditional love and forgiveness, coupled with Peter's own natural leadership qualities, make Peter the logical choice to assume command of the suddenly rudderless disciples. Gone is the impetuous, sometimes self-serving Peter. The new broken-and-now-remade Peter is stronger, more commanding, and less full of himself. From a story standpoint, Acts is needed to complete the Hero's Journey. Peter has been given a priceless gift. Now he must prove worthy of it by continuing Christ's example and message. Not a day will pass that he doesn't remember Jesus' parting words—"Feed my sheep." And boy, does he!

The book of Acts is the sequel to the book of Luke and pretty much our sole source for information on the early church. After the ascension, the surviving disciples, men and women, convene again in Jerusalem—about one hundred twenty in all. Immediately, Peter takes charge and suggests that they replace Judas. Two men are named as having followed Jesus almost from the beginning. Although they're never actually mentioned in the Four Gospels, they are part of a large group of men and women who stuck with Jesus through thick and thin. The group prays and elects Matthias.

Acts 2

The Day of Pentecost—and the arrival of the Holy Spirit—is one of the pivotal events in the Bible. The roaring sound, the tongues of fire, and the excited babble of new voices, convince some onlookers that the followers of Jesus have been hitting the wineskins a little too hard. Once again it is Peter who takes a commanding role. Peter dismisses the charge, eloquently quotes Scripture, and explains the importance of Pentecost for all to hear. Peter will make four more speeches in the days ahead. His words—coupled with the arrival of the Holy Spirit—make such an impression that the first converts are saved on the spot.

Acts 3:1-26

In the heady atmosphere after Pentecost, Peter is part of the first post-Jesus miracle. When Peter and John encounter a lame man outside of the Beautiful Gate, Peter says, "I have no silver or gold, but what I have I give you; in the name of Jesus Christ of Nazareth, stand up and walk" (3:6). He then uses the miracle to preach to the gathering crowd.

Acts 4:1-22

When the temple authorities hear and see the crowd, they arrest the pair. And just as they did with Jesus, Annas, the high priest Caiaphas, and the other powerbrokers in the temple band together and call Peter and John to stand trial before them. This time, however, Peter doesn't run, despite a withering attack from the temple officials. *This is the new Peter.* This time, he speaks boldly, empowered by the Holy Spirit, confronting the corrupt authorities with the moral authority of his words:

> Rulers of the people and elders, if we are questioned today because of a good deed done to someone who was sick and are asked how this man has been healed, let it be known to all of you, and to all the people of Israel, that this man is standing before you in good health by the name of Jesus Christ of Nazareth, whom you crucified, whom God raised from the dead. This Jesus is

262

"the stone that was rejected by you, the builders;
    it has become the cornerstone."
There is salvation in no one else, for there is no other name under heaven given among mortals by which we must be saved. (Acts 4:8-12)

The boldness and righteous power of Peter and John intimidate the officials, who briefly confer. "What can they be charged with? What can we do about them?" The answer? *Nothing!*

So they call Peter and John back and strictly command them to speak no more about this Jesus.

"Not a chance," Peter and John say. They have no choice.

Flabbergasted, the officials set them free.

Acts 4:32—5:16

Under the leadership of Peter (who is, in turn, under the leadership of the Holy Spirit), the tiny body of believers flourishes. They share their belongings, take care of each other, preach fearlessly, and heal the sick and afflicted. In time, a belief arises that even Peter's shadow will heal you; and the sick and possessed are brought, by the hundreds, to Jerusalem.

Acts 5:17-42

Naturally, the men who killed Jesus will have none of this. They order the apostles imprisoned again but angels break their chains. They once again call in the ringleaders—Peter and John—and threaten them for daring to speak the name of Jesus. The answer from Peter and the apostles remains the same:

> We must obey God rather than any human authority. The God of our ancestors raised up Jesus, whom you had killed by hanging him on a tree. God exalted him at his right hand as Leader and Savior that he might give repentance to Israel and forgiveness of sins. And we are witnesses to these things, and so is the Holy Spirit whom God has given to those who obey him. (Acts 5:29-32)

The high priest and his cronies are infuriated—and out for blood. But a wise Pharisee, Gamaliel, prevails. "If they've got anything worthwhile to say," he notes, "God will support it. If not, they'll fail on their own. Better not take a chance and oppose God if this *is* the real thing." But Gamaliel cannot prevent the vengeful temple authorities from having Peter and

John brutally whipped. Even then, the pair continues to praise Jesus through cracked and bleeding lips.

And so it goes. With the new, more Christ-like Peter leading the way, the Jesus movement snowballs. Not even the murder of the saintly Stephen can slow the momentum (see Acts 6:8–7:60). Present at the stoning of Stephen is another man, an educated Jew with Roman citizenship, Saul. His name will loom large in the days ahead.

Acts 10:1-35

As for Peter, there are more miracles, more healings, more conversions and, in the end, one life-changing vision.

Chapter 10, in many ways, is the culmination of Peter's journey and marks a new direction for the band of believers who follow what has come to be called *The Way*. Peter falls into a trance where God informs him that the good news is for *all* people—not just Jews. This is a radical departure for many in the Way, but Peter's great message signals a sea change that transforms the movement:

> I truly understand that God shows no partiality, but in every nation anyone who fears him and does what is right is acceptable to him. (Acts 10:34-35)

Reluctant Prophets and Clueless Disciples

Peter gently but firmly convinces the others in the movement that it must be—for now and always—totally inclusive. Even as the persecutions heighten, now by the civil authorities as well as the Jewish officials, Peter doggedly spreads the word.

Acts 12:1-17

Finally, King Herod Agrippa I, grandson of Herod the Great, imprisons him. At the same time, he has James, the brother of John, murdered. But once again, an angel frees Peter.

Still, Peter's time has come. After his miraculous release, he defers authority to James, the brother of Jesus, and disappears from the story, even as James and Paul now become the focal points of the book.

Acts 15:1-21

Peter does return one last time, to testify at a council of apostles and elders in Jerusalem. The issue at hand is whether the new Gentile converts should be circumcised. The debate is apparently heated and at the most crucial moment, Peter slowly, painfully stands to address the believers:

> My brothers, you know that in the early days God made a choice among you, that I should be the one through whom the Gentles would hear the message of the good news and become believers. And God, who knows the human heart, testified to them by giving them the Holy Spirit, just as he did to us; and in cleansing their hearts by faith he has made no distinction between them and us. Now therefore why are you putting God to the test by placing on the neck of the disciples a yoke that neither our ancestors nor we have been able to bear? On the contrary, we believe that we will be saved through the grace of the Lord Jesus, just as they will. (Acts 15:7-11)

The book of Acts reports that total silence follows Peter's speech. Moments later, both Barnabas and Paul leap to their feet to tell of the signs and wonders God has done through them among the Gentiles.

At last, James speaks. The brother of Jesus probably smiled at Peter first, for this is *exactly* the kind of thing Jesus would have said. It's settled. The new believers will *not* be required to be circumcised (see Acts 15:12-21).

265

The Rest of Peter's Story

From here the record is silent. There are fleeting mentions of Peter's visits to Antioch (see Galatians 2:11-21), Corinth (see 1 Corinthians 1:12), and perhaps Rome (see Romans 15:20-22) in the days before Paul's arrival. Two of the oldest Christian historians, Eusebius and Origen, write that Peter was very old by this point. During Nero's hideous persecutions of 64 CE, Peter was crucified. An old tradition has Peter requesting that he be crucified upside down—because he is not worthy of being crucified like Jesus.

There are two books that bear Peter's name, 1 Peter and 2 Peter. First Peter, one of the loveliest books in the New Testament, may actually have been written by Peter, or at least dictated by Peter to someone (perhaps Silvanus) who writes and speaks a beautiful, elegant Greek. It seems to have been written in Rome during the final persecution, maybe even the persecution that took Peter's life.

Regardless of the details, it is a gentle, sweet-spirited benediction to a life well lived, by a man who has seen it all, who has been broken and humbled, and yet who—through the redeeming power of Jesus Christ—has lived to make a difference in this world and the next. Peter's final words on leadership are particularly poignant:

> Do not lord it over those in your charge, but be examples to the flock. And when the chief shepherd appears, you will win the crown of glory that never fades away. (1 Peter 5:3-4)

It is a crown that Peter wears, even now.

Reluctant Prophets and Clueless Disciples

Twenty-two

PAUL

If you can't preach like Peter
If you can't pray like Paul
Just tell the love of Jesus
And say, "He died for all."
(African American Spiritual, "There Is a Balm in Gilead")

In the end, there is no more controversial figure in the entire Bible than the apostle Paul—except, of course, for Jesus. Scholars and laypeople alike have spent countless hours arguing about just exactly what Paul said, is alleged to have said, and probably never said at all. How important is Paul? Of the twenty-seven books in the New Testament, it is believed that he either wrote or heavily influenced at least thirteen of them.

And of all of the stories we've read to this point, few reveal as dramatic and defining a Faith Journey as that of Paul of Tarsus.

For the most part, we'll leave his theology and teachings to academics, scholars, researchers, and preachers. His quest is quite amazing enough for one small book, thank you.

As with most of the major figures in the Bible, we know precious little about Paul. A couple of verses hint that he wasn't a first-century Mel Gibson or Jude Law (most notably 1 Corinthians 2:3 and 2 Corinthians 10:10). Plus, this intriguing description in the apocryphal *Acts of Paul and Thecla* from the second century has the ring of truth about it:

And he saw Paul coming, a man small in size, bald-headed, bandy-legged, of noble mien, with eyebrows meeting, rather hook-nosed, full of grace. Sometimes he seemed like a man, and sometimes he had the face of an angel. (*The Apocryphal New Testament* [New York: Oxford University Press, 1993], 364)

Other hints about Paul's life are sprinkled throughout the New Testament. He was related to the tribe of Benjamin. He lived in the thriving metropolis of Tarsus, the cosmopolitan gateway to the eastern Mediterranean, and while there, he became a citizen of Rome. Greek is, apparently, his first language and he appears to be aware of the dominant Greek philosophies. As a pious Jew, at a very early age he studied in Jerusalem under Gamaliel, one of the era's most famous rabbis. While not a particularly compelling speaker, he was an educated man. There are several suggestions that he was from a family of some prominence, if not means. And Paul himself tells us that he was a tentmaker by trade, a valuable skill, particularly in Palestine.

He was also zealous to the point of fanaticism about his faith. When we first meet him, he is using his zeal to persecute the small, struggling band of people following the risen Jesus—then called the Way.

Acts 7:58–8:3

Paul first appears as *Saul* at the very end of Acts 7. Stephen has been arguing in the synagogue of Freedman—emancipated Jews and their descendents—and some in the hall aren't happy. Alas, just as it is today when some people feel they are losing an argument, they start shouting down the person they're arguing with. When that doesn't work, the crowd drags Stephen outside of Jerusalem's walls and brutally stones him to death, even as he prays for their forgiveness. In their eagerness to murder Stephen, the men strip off their coats and give them to a young Jew named Saul for safekeeping. Chapter 8 begins with this chilling line: "And Saul approved of their killing him" (8:1).

Thus begins one of the earliest persecutions against the followers of Jesus in Jerusalem. But as always in God's providence, this evil is transformed into good. The persecution scatters many believers, who then take the good news throughout the region. Those who remain must contend with the implacable Saul who—empowered with near-absolute authority from the Jewish leaders—ravages "the church by entering house after house; dragging off both men and women" (8:3) and throwing them into prison.

Acts 9:1–19

But this is not enough to slake Saul's blood-thirst. He receives permission from the high priest to take his *pogrom* to Damascus. So he gathers

268

some followers and promptly marches north toward Damascus. But a curious thing happens along the way. No, a miraculous, astonishing thing happens along the way! Angry, self-righteous, proud, bullying Saul is blasted by a bolt of light from heaven that knocks him on his *keister*.

He lies there a moment, dazed and blinded. Suddenly, a voice fills his head.

"Saul, Saul, why do you persecute me?"

" . . . Who are you, Lord?"

" . . . I am Jesus, whom you are persecuting" (9:4-5).

Saul continues to lie there, digesting this information. It means, of course, that everything he's believed is wrong. In fact, everything he's done has been horribly wrong. It means, from this moment forward, his life will never be the same. The voice jolts him out of his stunned confusion.

"Get up and enter the city, and you will be told what to do" (9:6).

As for Saul's companions, they've neither seen nor heard any of this. They help him to his feet, only to discover that he's now blind. Together, they finish their journey to Damascus and take him to the home of a man named Judas. There, Saul broods on what he's heard, refusing food and drink for three days.

Meanwhile, a follower of Jesus named Ananias, also living in Damascus, receives a word from God:

269

Get up and go to the street called Straight, and at the house of Judas look for a man of Tarsus named Saul. At this moment he is praying, and he has seen in a vision a man named Ananias come in and lay his hands on him so that he might regain his sight. (Acts 9:11-12)

I love Ananais. He's a whole lot like me. He's so afraid of Saul that he gently reminds an Omniscient God (who, by very definition, knows everything and can see everything) about the facts of life:

"Um, Lord, this guy is bad news," he says, his voice shaking with fear. "Everybody knows it. It's common knowledge how he persecuted your followers back in Jerusalem. And I realize you've been kinda busy lately going to heaven and back and all, but you should probably know that the religious big wigs at the temple have given Saul the power to toss everybody in jail who even mentions your name! He's like a one-man Homeland Security department! Are you absolutely sure about this?"

But the Lord is adamant. "Go, for he is an instrument whom I have chosen to bring my name before Gentiles and kings and before the people of Israel; I myself will show him how much he must suffer for the sake of my name" (9:15-16).

Ananais musters his courage and heads for Judas's house, shaking his head in dismay the whole way. Once there, he takes a deep breath, walks in, and lays his hands atop Saul's head:

"Brother Saul, the Lord Jesus, who appeared to you on your way here, has sent me so that you may regain your sight and be filled with the Holy Spirit" (9:17).

Immediately, Saul bounds up. He can see!—both literally and spiritually. Saul is then baptized.

This whole *chosen* business disturbs some people. It's as if, in their minds, God chooses to save some people and not others, that there is no free will involved. The Acts passage echoes Luke 9:35 where, after the transfiguration, the Lord says, "This is my Son, my Chosen; listen to him!" But remember, in both cases, being *chosen* also means a lifetime of pain and suffering, of abuse and torment, culminating in a nasty and degrading death. Like Jesus, Saul's troubles have just begun.

Acts 9:20-31

Soon, Saul preaches the gospel of Jesus Christ on the streets of Damascus with the same fervor with which he once persecuted the followers of Jesus. Saul's own account of his conversion, in Galatians 1,

270

says that he went to Arabia for three years then returned to Damascus where his message attracts a large and devoted following. So large in fact, that the Jews of the city begin to plot to kill him, watching the gates, hoping to ambush him outside the city walls. However, his new friends in Damascus secretly lower him down in a basket through a window one night and he safely disappears into the dark.

Back in Jerusalem, Saul's appearance causes quite a commotion. The Christians avoid him at all costs until Barnabas mercifully (and coura-geously) takes him under his wing and vouches for his complete transfor-mation. Still, within two weeks, the Greek-speaking Jews turn on him and Saul is forced to flee again, this time back home in Tarsus by way of Caesarea.

Acts 13:1-3

While Saul lies low in Tarsus—his so-called Silent Period of nearly ten years—the narrative of Peter once again takes center stage in Acts. With the death of Herod, Saul and Barnabas finally return to Jerusalem, accompanied by a young man named John Mark. From there, they travel to Antioch, where a number of "prophets and teachers" (13:1) arrive and—at the urging of the Holy Spirit—Saul, Barnabas, and John Mark are commissioned for the mission field. Some scholars suggest this takes place about 46 CE.

First Missionary Journey

Welcome to
Seleucia

- (Acts 13:4-12) -

From this point on, Saul is called *Paul* (a common Greco-Roman name; Saul is the Hebrew equivalent). Their initial journey takes them to Seleucia, a port at the mouth of the Orontes River on Syria's

Mediterranean coast (Barnabas's home town), then across the Mediterranean to the island of Cyprus. Once on Cyprus, the Roman proconsul calls for them—he's interested in their intriguing message. But a local magician, angered by a couple of newcomers invading his turf, opposes them. Paul delivers a curse of his own and the man is struck blind. As for the proconsul, he immediately believes when he hears the good news.

Welcome to Antioch

– (Acts 13:13–52) –

From there, they eventually end up back in Antioch, but not before John Mark returns home—much to Paul's annoyance, as we'll see later. In Antioch, Paul and Barnabas preach in a local synagogue. Like Stephen's sermon a couple of chapters earlier, Paul's message includes a mini-history of the Jewish people and ends with a call for repentance. They are a smashing success and receive an invitation for a return engagement the following Sabbath. The second time, however, the local Jews have had enough and drive them from the city. Paul and Barnabas sadly shake the dust from their sandals and continue their journey.

Welcome to Iconium

– (Acts 14:1–7) –

Next stop is Iconium where the results are the same. Their message strikes a chord with the Gentiles but Paul and Barnabas are eventually driven from the city by the powerful Jewish leadership.

Welcome to Lystra and Derbe

- (Acts 14:8-28) -

They escape stoning and flee to the city of Lystra, still in the general area of what is now Syria. In Lystra, Paul heals a cripple and the people go absolutely nuts! They proclaim Barnabas *Zeus* and Paul *Hermes* and start offering sacrifices to them. Our heroes are mortified. They tear their clothes and plead with the crowds that they're just mortal men. But you know how hard it is to stop a party once it builds momentum.

In the midst of the revelry, fanatical Jews from Antioch and Iconium arrive and convince the partygoers that Paul and Barnabas are demons rather than gods. The fickle crowd stones Paul and, thinking him dead, toss him out the city gates. This event is followed by this curious little verse: "But when the disciples surrounded him, he got up and went into the city" (14:20). Was he raised from the dead? in a coma? Just what happened here? The next day, slightly the worse for wear, they limp out of party-mad Lystra and head to Derbe, about sixty miles east.

After some success in Derbe, our little band of disciples bravely return to Lystra, Iconium, and Antioch, supporting and ministering to the new converts in those cities. They then return to Jerusalem for an important meeting of representatives of this new faith.

Welcome to Jerusalem

- (Acts 15:1-41) -

At the Council at Jerusalem, Paul and Barnabas tell of their journey and strongly make the case that Gentile converts don't need to be circumcised or keep the Jewish dietary laws to be saved. Despite strong opposition, and bolstered by powerful testimony from Peter in his final

273

major appear-
ance in the
Bible (see the
chapter on
Peter), they win
the day. (It is
during this
period, some
believe, that
Paul wrote his
letter to the
Galatians, while
others believe
most of the letters
were written ten years
later.)

But the happy occasion can't
last for long. Paul wants to return to the cities from his first missionary journey and continue to support the new believers. Barnabas agrees—but
wants to give John Mark (who deserted them earlier) another chance. Paul
is unyielding. So the two old friends part ways. Barnabas, who was among
Paul's first supporters, takes John Mark to Cyprus. A man named Silas, who
is said to be a prophet, joins Paul and the pair head for Syria. As for
Barnabas, we will not hear from him again.

Second Missionary Journey

Welcome to
Derbe, Lystra, and
Troas

- (Acts 16:1-10) -

Paul and Silas return first to Derbe and Lystra, where they pick up
another new convert, Timothy, son of a Jewish mother (Eunice) and
Greek father. The more traditional converts, however, insist that Timothy

274

be circumcised. Paul and Silas reluctantly agree. (There is no mention of Timothy's feelings on the subject!) But strange things happen as they leave Derbe and Lystra. The Holy Spirit repeatedly stops them from preaching until they end up in Troas, not far from legendary Troy—in what is modern-day Turkey. In Troas, Paul has a vision. In it, a Greek man pleads with him to come save souls in Greece. The small party sets sail the next morning.

- (Acts 16:11-40) -

The narrative makes a significant shift here. This is the first of four *we* sections indicating that the author—perhaps Luke himself—was part of this missionary journey. Once our heroes reach Philippi, events begin to happen at a rapid clip. First, Paul's preaching converts a wealthy woman named Lydia. Second, they encounter a slave girl who is possessed by a spirit of some kind (it's never called a demon). Her owners have been exploiting her as an oracle or prophetess. She follows Paul, Silas, and Timothy for days shouting, "These men are slaves of the Most High God, who proclaim to you a way of salvation" (16:17)! Moved by the poor slave girl's plight, Paul finally turns to her and says to the spirit, "I order you in the name of Jesus Christ to come out of her" (16:18). Unfortunately, this means that the girl's owners have now lost their cash cow. They stir up a handy crowd, drag our trio before the magistrates, and claim that they're disturbing the peace and inciting a riot. The magistrates have Paul and Silas (no word on the fate of Timothy or Luke) stripped, beaten with rods, and thrown into Philippi's darkest, deepest prison.

- Paul and Silas in Prison (Acts 16:25-40) -

Secured in heavy chains, battered and bloody, Paul and Silas spend their evening in the dank cell singing hymns until about midnight. Suddenly, a mammoth earthquake rocks the prison. Not only are the prisoners' chains broken, the massive prison doors are cracked wide open. The

275

earthquake sends the sleeping jailer sprawling. He sees the open doors and grabs his knife to commit suicide—all of his prisoners have escaped! But Paul shouts at him, "Do not harm yourself, for we are all here" (16:28). The jailer rushes to them and begs for his salvation. They answer, "Believe on the Lord Jesus, and you will be saved, you and your household" (16:31). The jailer bravely takes them home and tends to their wounds, even as Paul and Silas preach to his sleepy family and slaves. That night, the jailer's entire household is baptized.

The next morning, the magistrates are having second thoughts—Roman authorities tend to frown on savage beatings of their citizens without trials. They send word to the jailer to free Paul and Silas. But Paul has had enough and rages at the poor policemen:

> They have beaten us in public, uncondemned, men who are Roman citizens, and have thrown us into prison; and now are they going to discharge us in secret? Certainly not! Let them come and take us out themselves. (Acts 16:37)

Thoroughly shaken, the magistrates all stream down to the jail, apologize profusely, and beg them to leave Philippi to avoid stirring up further trouble. (Why did Paul and Silas wait until after their illegal beating and imprisonment to declare their Roman citizenship? Good question.) They limp off to the home of Lydia, which has already become a meeting place for new converts.

Welcome to Thessalonica and Beroea

– (Acts 17:1–15) –

Their wounds healed, Paul and Silas travel to Thessalonica, where they stay at the home of another new convert, Jason. As before, Paul invites himself to the local synagogue and preaches for many weeks with much local success among the Jews and Greeks. But once again, the Jewish community eventually becomes outraged by his words about the resurrected Jesus. They storm Jason's house looking for Paul and, when they can't find him, drag Jason off to appear before the magistrates. And once again, Paul and Silas slip out under cover of darkness. They now head for Beroea, about fifty miles to the southwest of Thessalonica. The same pattern repeats itself in Beroea: excellent early success, followed by persecution by the pious Jews. Paul—the main focus of their ire—is smuggled to Athens, while Silas and Timothy briefly remain behind in Beroea.

Welcome to Athens

- (Acts 17:16-33) -

In Athens, Paul finds one of the great cities in all of history, a cosmopolitan wonder full of commerce and art, and overflowing with new ideas and radical belief systems. In addition to the full pantheon of Greco-Roman gods, there are learned men espousing radical Epicurean and Stoic philosophies.

Paul joins the great debates in the marketplace of ideas, forcefully arguing his cause, alluding to classical Greek philosophers like Epimenides and Aratus. Unlike Paul's earlier sermons, this one doesn't cause an immediate riot. Most learned Greeks initially listen with interest but eventually drift away in search of new thrills. Only a few become followers of the Way and Paul reluctantly leaves

Athens. His stay there is most notable for how he shapes the presentation of the Gospel, adapting his approach and citations to reach a much more educated (and jaded) audience than the fishermen and herdsmen of Galilee. It also shows, perhaps better than any other single passage, the sheer breadth of his learning.

– (Acts 18:1-17) –

From Athens, Paul travels to the bustling port city of Corinth, still thriving in modern-day Greece. He stays with the husband and wife team of Aquila and Priscilla, refugees from the purge of Christians from Rome by the Emperor Claudius. Paul joins their tentmaking business and eventually reunites with Timothy and Silas. Once he's established, Paul returns to preaching in the local synagogue—with predictable results. Frustrated by their heated opposition, he finally disavows responsibility for converting Jews and turns his attention to the Gentiles in Corinth. Despite rising opposition, Paul remains a year and a half, preaching fearlessly. At last, the Jews plead their case before the proconsul, who dismisses their complaints as inter-denominational squabbling, so they promptly beat up an unlucky official of the synagogue who happens to be standing nearby! (It's not good to be around bloodthirsty mobs, as a general rule of thumb.) Paul stays as long as he can in Corinth, building a strong and vital body of believers and—possibly—writing the Letter to the Thessalonians.

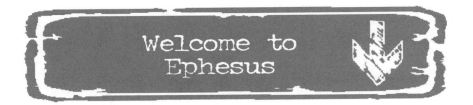

– (Acts 18:18–19:41) –

Eventually, Paul feels compelled to return home, so he leaves again, this time taking Aquila and Priscilla with him. They journey first to the

278

important port city of Ephesus (where he leaves them), then to Jerusalem (where he greets the church, including James, the brother of Jesus) and eventually goes back to many of the communities of believers in Syria.

Back in Ephesus, Aquila and Priscilla meet the eloquent, charismatic Apollos, who had known John the Baptist (and possibly Jesus) but hadn't yet received the Holy Spirit. Aquila and Priscilla patiently teach him the Way and he becomes a powerful apostle and is, eventually, sent to work with the believers in Corinth.

As for Paul, he returns to Ephesus where he gathers several followers of John the Baptist and baptizes them in the Holy Spirit:

> When Paul had laid his hands on them, the Holy Spirit came upon them, and they spoke in tongues and prophesied—altogether there were about twelve of them. (Acts 19:6-7)

Paul stays more than two years in Ephesus, attracting both Greek and Jewish converts, and establishing another enduring church. It is in Ephesus that Paul performs some of his most spectacular miracles. He is so full of the Holy Spirit that a handkerchief that has touched Paul will cure a sickness or cast out a demon. Paul has become something of a star in Ephesus. Soon every freelance Jewish exorcist is trying to emulate him, including the seven sons of the High Priest Sceva. They hold an ill-advised exorcism on some unfortunate soul, carefully following Paul's example, chanting: "I adjure you by the Jesus whom Paul proclaims" (19:13).

Boom! Suddenly, a black pall fills the room. From the mist comes an unearthly hiss, "Jesus I know, and Paul I know; but who are you?" (19:15). The demon-possessed man leaps up and begins attacking the seven brothers with supernatural strength. He beats them all bloody and tosses them naked out into the streets! (This sounds like an out-take from the movie *Constantine*.) Soon, word of the demonic attack is common knowledge in every book club and Internet café in Ephesus, and throngs of people—Greeks and Jew alike—come to know Jesus, even as former magicians toss their books in a communal bonfire. As for Sceva, he probably grounded his sons for a month.

Empowered by the spread of the Word in Ephesus, the Holy Spirit instructs Paul to return to Greece and Jerusalem before eventually heading to Rome. But before he can leave, the silversmiths of Ephesus begin plotting against him. The rise of the Way has definitely cut into their business—making silver shrines for the goddess Artemis (known as Diana to

279

the Romans). They incite a full-blown riot, and a number of Paul's followers are roughly treated. Fortunately, cooler heads in the city government
ultimately prevail but it is time, once again, for Paul to move on.

Third Missionary Journey

Welcome to
Corinth

- (Acts 20:1-6) -

He heads once again for Greece, where he takes a collection for
the struggling followers in Jerusalem, but before he can make it back
to Antioch, another plot against his life emerges. Paul returns instead
to Corinth with a sizeable entourage of both disciples and bodyguards. It
would appear that this takes place around 57 CE; it is during these three
months that many scholars believe that Paul writes his great gospel of
salvation, the Letter to the Romans, whom he hopes to see soon.

St. Paul's first draft.

280

Welcome to Troas

- (Acts 20:7-12) -

The *we* narrative returns here as the scene once again shifts to Troas, indicating that the author is along for the ride once again. In Troas, the followers of the Way join Paul for long discussions that last deep into the night. At one such conversation, a young man nods off and—in his sleep—falls three stories to his apparent death. But Paul rushes to the young man's side, picks him up, and carries him upstairs: "Do not be alarmed, for his life is in him" (20:10). The boy's friends are happy, if a little confused—but probably not as confused as the boy himself!

Welcome to Miletus

- (Acts 20:13-38) -

The following day, Paul and his friends begin an arduous voyage throughout the many islands of the Aegean Sea. They stop briefly in Miletus and Paul sends for the leaders of the church in Ephesus. Once they arrive, he delivers a very personal speech, reminding his listeners how he has tried to be faithful to his call, preaching repentance to Greek and Jew alike:

> And now, as a captive to the Spirit, I am on my way to Jerusalem, not knowing what will happen to me there, except that the Holy Spirit testifies to me in every city that imprisonment and persecutions are waiting for me. But I do not count my life of any value to myself, if only I may finish my course and the ministry that I received from the Lord Jesus, to testify to the good news of God's grace. (Acts 20:22-24)

281

Then he delivers the stunner:

> And now I know that none of you, among whom I have gone about proclaiming the kingdom, will ever see my face again. Therefore I declare to you this day that I am not responsible for the blood of any of you, for I did not shrink from declaring to you the whole purpose of God. (Acts 20:25-27)

I imagine the elders have begun murmuring among themselves: "What is he saying? Is Paul never coming back? Is he prophesying his death?" Paul silences them with a wave of his hand:

> Keep watch over yourselves and over all the flock, of which the Holy Spirit has made you overseers, to shepherd the church of God that he obtained with the blood of his own Son. I know that after I have gone, savage wolves will come in among you, not sparing the flock. Some even from your own group will come distorting the truth in order to entice the disciples to follow them. Therefore be alert, remembering that for three years I did not cease night or day to warn everyone with tears. (Acts 20:28-31)

Paul's listeners know that this is a prophecy. By now, Paul himself is in tears:

> And now I commend you to God and to the message of his grace, a message that is able to build you up and to give you the inheritance among all who are sanctified. I coveted no one's silver or gold or clothing. You know for yourselves that I worked with my own hands to support myself and my companions. In all this I have given you an example that by such work we must support the weak, remembering the words of the Lord Jesus, for he himself said, "It is more blessed to give than to receive." (Acts 20:32-35)

By now, all are in tears and they kneel in a communal embrace, kissing each other and weeping in the knowledge that this is the last time they will ever see their dear mentor.

Welcome to Caesarea

– (Acts 21:1-16) –

Paul's farewell tour continues, with several stops in the Mediterranean Sea. The disciples at Tyre say that the Holy Spirit has informed them that Paul is not to continue to Jerusalem. But Paul forges ahead, eventually ending up in Caesarea at the home of Philip. While there, a prophet

282

named Agabus appears, traveling across country from Judea. He grabs Paul's belt and binds his own hands and feet with it, saying:

> Thus says the Holy Spirit, "This is the way the Jews in Jerusalem will bind the man who owns this belt and will hand him over to the Gentiles." (Acts 21:11)

The prophecy sends ripples of unease through the faithful and they urge Paul to remain with them. But Paul will not be dissuaded:

> What are you doing, weeping and breaking my heart? For I am ready not only to be bound but even to die in Jerusalem for the name of the Lord Jesus. (Acts 21:13)

And with that, they left for Jerusalem.

Welcome to Jerusalem

– (Acts 21:17–23:11) –

The small party arrives in Jerusalem in time for the Passover, where the leaders of the church, James and the other elders, embrace them. Paul briefly recounts his adventures, emphasizing the success among the Gentiles, and a loving reunion follows. During the weeklong ceremonies, Paul lies low and quietly worships in the temple. But in the end, some of the Jews who had earlier opposed him in Asia see him and start still another riot. They are about to murder Paul on the spot when authorities arrive in the nick of time to rescue him. They fight through the bloodthirsty mob and hustle Paul to their barracks. At the last minute, Paul asks to speak to the crowd in Aramaic. The tribune, Lysias, reluctantly agrees.

Paul's impassioned message to the rioters retells the story of his persecution of the followers of Jesus, his dramatic conversion, and his work among the Gentiles. But before he can finish, they begin calling for his death again. Befuddled, the tribune Lysias orders Paul flogged—which serves as something of a lie-detector test in the first century. Just before the soldier raises his whip, Paul whispers to the Roman centurion who is standing nearby, "Is it legal for you to flog a Roman citizen who is uncondemned?" (22:25). The centurion says, "Nope, it is not all right" and storms in to see the tribune. Now it is the tribune's turn to be afraid. He

283

releases Paul and orders the high priests and council (or Sanhedrin) to examine him the following day.

The next morning, Paul begins by "looking intently at the council" (23:1). This is a hostile crowd and Paul quickly goes on the offensive, especially against the high priest Ananias. When he notices both Sadducees and Pharisees in attendance, he expertly exploits their long-simmering rivalry and pits the two political parties against each other. Once again, pandemonium erupts. Lysias orders his men to make a foray onto the council floor, snatch Paul, and retire with him once again to their fortified barracks. That night, the Lord whispers in Paul's ear:

> Keep up your courage! For just as you have testified for me in Jerusalem, so must you bear witness also in Rome. (Acts 23:11)

– A Glimpse of Family (Acts 23:12-24) –

The next passage reveals a rare glimpse into the private life of Paul of Tarsus, one of the few such glimpses we're allowed in the entire New Testament. While Paul sits in the barracks, a secret cabal of fanatics vows a terrible oath—they'll not eat again until they have slain the heretic Paul. They take their blood-oath to the chief priests and concoct a plan to murder him in cold blood on the council floor. By God's providence, Paul's nephew—his sister's son—somehow hears about this ambush. The nephew manages to get word to the centurion, who takes it seriously enough to pass it on to Lysias. He believes the earnest young man and summons a large detachment of soldiers who whisk Paul away to safety in Antipatris, a Roman garrison halfway between Jerusalem and Caesarea.

This is our lone mention of Paul's family. We know he never marries. All we have is this tantalizing tidbit about an unnamed sister. What's her name? What happens to her? Does Paul have other siblings? We probably will never know on this side of heaven.

Reluctant Prophets and Clueless Disciples

Welcome to Caesarea

– Paul's Trial before Felix (Acts 23:25–24:27) –

The tribune writes a long letter to Felix, the governor of the province, outlining the problem, including the death-threat. Once Paul is safely under Roman jurisdiction, he orders that Paul's accusers travel to Caesarea for a trial. Five days later, crafty old Ananias and a lawyer, Tertullus, state their case. Tertullus flamboyantly accuses Paul of being an outside agitator, head of a secret cult of Nazarenes, and of plotting to desecrate the temple. Tertullus's charges are ridiculously easy for Paul to refute—although he admits to being a follower of the Way. Felix, who has been apprised of the growth of the

Way, orders Paul kept in protective custody until the arrival of Lysias the tribune, who will bring corroborating testimony.

One night, days later, guards hustle Paul to an unexpected location—the home of Felix and his Jewish wife, Drusilla, the daughter of Herod Agrippa I. The couple claims that they want to hear Paul's strange new message. The three talk long into the night until, at last, Felix can handle it no more. He says, "Go away for the present . . . I will send for you" (24:25). Perhaps Felix really was interested in hearing the message of salvation at one point, but the text says he was actually hoping that Paul would bribe his way out of prison. Still, in the days to come, Felix repeatedly calls for Paul and they speak for hours on end. Paul is well treated in open detention, visited regularly by his friends, and able to write prolifically. But wanting to curry favor with the powerful Jewish hierarchy, Felix does not release Paul. After two years have passed, Felix himself is replaced as governor by Porcius Festus.

- Paul's Trial before Festus (Acts 25:1-12) -

As soon as Festus arrives, Paul's enemies petition him to have Paul transferred to Jerusalem to stand trial; they still plan to ambush him en route. But Festus smells a rat and tells the Jews to once again come to Caesarea. The usual charges and counter-charges are hurled. The priests still don't have a case against Paul, but urge Festus to send him to Jerusalem to stand trial. Festus turns to Paul and asks, "Do you wish to go up to Jerusalem to be tried there before me on these charges?" (25:9).

Paul knows he'll never reach Jerusalem alive and, if he does, the trial will be a deadly farce. As a Roman citizen, he plays his final ace in the hole:

> I am appealing to the emperor's tribunal; this is where I should be tried. I have done no wrong to the Jews, as you very well know. Now if I am in the wrong and have committed something for which I deserve to die, I am not trying to escape death; but if there is nothing to their charges against me, no one can turn me over to them. I appeal to the emperor. (Acts 25:10-11)

This is a serious—and unexpected—development. Festus has no other option. "You have appealed to the emperor; to the emperor you will go." (25:12).

- Paul's Trial before Agrippa and Bernice (Acts 25:13—26:32) -

But before arrangements can be made, King Herod Agrippa II and his wife Bernice (sister of Felix's wife Drusilla) arrive at Caesarea to formally welcome Festus to his new job. In exasperation, Festus tells Agrippa about this infuriating case that Felix dumped on him when he left. Agrippa and Bernice are also intrigued with Paul's testimony and ask to hear the old warrior for themselves.

For the fifth and final time in the book of Acts, Paul re-tells his dramatic life story. Midway through the speech, Festus bounds out of his chair.

286

"You are out of your mind, Paul! Too much learning is driving you insane!" (26:24). Paul shakes his head. "I am not out of my mind . . ." (26:25). Now he turns his attention to Agrippa, who has been listening intently.

"King Agrippa, you know what? I bet you're a believer. Am I right? Am I right? Admit it—you dig the prophets and the whole Old Testament vibe, right?"

"Hey? Who do you think you are, Billy Graham? Are you trying to convert me?" Agrippa says not unkindly.

Paul replies, "Your call, big guy. But I will say this: I'm putting in a word with the Lord for everyone gathered here tonight. Sure, I'd like you to believe the way I do. I wouldn't be here if I didn't. It's that important to me."

With that, Agrippa ends the audience. As he leaves with Bernice, she says, "Sweetie, I think we've got the wrong fellow here. He's as pure as the driven snow—and he certainly doesn't deserve another stint in the slammer." Agrippa can only nod his head sadly.

Festus comes running up after them, hoping for some kind of closure on this long-standing problem, but Agrippa can barely hide his contempt for Festus.

"Is this the kind of shoddy work you do? You've ruined my evening and Bernice's, and you're about to ruin the emperor's evening through your incompetence . . . because now Paul's going to see Caesar, and this could have been handled ever so easily here."

Festus cowers—Agrippa's meaning is clear: You have bungled this whole affair little man. This does not reflect well on you. The emperor will not be pleased.

It is time for Paul to make his last trip.

The Final Journey

Welcome to . . .
Somewhere on
the Mediterranean

- (Acts 27:1-38) -

Only desperate men sail the waters of the eastern Mediterranean from October through April when the weather is risky at best. For a final time, the author includes a *we* section as Paul and a small band of friends set sail for Rome. The captain hugs the shoreline of Asia Minor, but loses much time to unfavorable winds. Finally, anxious to take a valuable cargo (probably grain) from Egypt to Rome, the captain takes a dangerous gamble—he hopes to pass between the winter storms and somehow reach safe harbor in Crete. But as they say in the Air Force: "There are old captains and there are bold captains. But there are no old, bold captains." The small ship runs smack into a northeaster and soon veers hopelessly off-course. Day after day the wind and waves pound the ship until the crew starts tossing its expensive cargo overboard.

After nearly two weeks, adrift and half-starved, all seems lost and the sailors despair. Finally, Paul calls to the sailors and passengers:

> I urge you now to keep up your courage, for there will be no loss of life among you, but only of the ship. For last night there stood by me an angel of the God to whom I belong and whom I worship, and he said, "Do not be afraid, Paul; you must stand before the emperor; and indeed, God has granted safety to all those who are sailing with you." So keep up your courage, men, for I have faith in God that it will be exactly as I have been told. But we will have to run aground on some island. (Acts 27:22-26)

Welcome to Malta

- (Acts 27:39–28:10) -

And that's just what happens. The ship runs aground on Malta, far from their destination. The crew wants to kill the prisoners to keep them from escaping, but the centurion, hoping to spare Paul, forbids it. As the ship is breaking up on the reef, the last of the passengers and crew swim to safety.

The inhabitants of the island help the castaways build a life-saving fire to protect them from the cold rain. As they are gathering wood, a snake darts out of the underbrush and bites Paul. The natives think this proves that Paul is a murderer, but when he simply shakes off the snake and shows no ill effects, they begin to think he is a god.

The crew and passengers are taken to the estate of one of the most powerful men on Malta, a certain Publius, who houses and feeds the miserable survivors. Paul learns that Publius's father is dying of some disease, so he lays hands on the poor man and prays for him. Soon, he is as good as new and Publius can't do enough for his guests— especially Paul!

289

- (Acts 28:11-31) -

When the first ship from Italy arrives that spring, Publius provisions the survivors and gratefully sees them off. Paul's arrival in Italy has long been awaited by the Roman Christians, who gather from throughout the peninsula to greet him as he treks toward Rome. Still under very loose house arrest, Paul requests that the local Jewish leadership visit him at home. He delivers an impassioned series of evangelical sermons, and both Jews and Gentiles stream to his house to hear this strange new message. Some believe, but most do not. In response, Paul cites Isaiah:

> "Go to this people and say,
> You will indeed listen, but never understand,
>   and you will indeed look, but never perceive.
> For this people's heart has grown dull,
>   and their ears are hard of hearing,
>   and they have shut their eyes;
>   so that they might not look with their eyes,
>   and listen with their ears,
> and understand with their heart and turn—
>   and I would heal them."
> Let it be known to you then that this salvation of God has been sent to the Gentiles; they will listen. (Acts 28:26-28)

The text says that Paul lived in Rome two more years, preaching to all who would listen. The author does not know—or does not reveal—his fate.

Careful cross-reference of the various names and incidents mentioned both in Acts and other New Testament works seems to indicate that this is about 63 CE. It is possible Paul was released, visited Spain, re-visited the churches in Greece, and ultimately met martyrdom at the hands of the madman Nero about 67 CE.

Conflicting Nature: Thorn in the Flesh

The book of Acts is long on history and preaching, but short on intimate detail. To know Paul the man, therefore, modern readers must rely on hints and whispers gleaned from his letters.

2 Corinthians 10-13

One of the most illuminating insights comes in 2 Corinthians, apparently written late in Paul's life. There has been some kind of spat between Paul and the believers in Corinth. Some even snidely comment that, while Paul's letters are impressive, his physical appearance and speaking are not! The second chapter hints that someone in Corinth publicly insulted Paul the last time he was in town. Some researchers think that chapters 10–13 constitute the letter that Titus took to the Christians in Corinth after the first steps of reconciliation were taken.

Whatever the reason, we see a rare portrait of Paul on the defensive, worried about his reputation, justifying himself with a litany of the pain and suffering he has endured on behalf of the message of Jesus Christ:

> But whatever anyone dares to boast of—I am speaking as a fool—I also dare to boast of that. Are they Hebrews? So am I. Are they Israelites? So am I. Are they descendants of Abraham? So am I. Are they ministers of Christ? I am talking like a madman—I am a better one: with far greater labors, far more imprisonments, with countless floggings, and often near death. Five times I have received from the Jews the forty lashes minus one. Three times I was beaten with rods. Once I received a stoning. Three times I was shipwrecked; for a night and a day I was adrift at sea; on frequent journeys, in danger from rivers, danger from bandits, danger from my own people, danger from Gentiles, danger in the city, danger in the wilderness, danger at sea, danger from false brothers and sisters; in toil and hardship, through many a sleepless night, hungry and thirsty, often without food, cold and naked. And, besides other things, I am under daily pressure because of my anxiety for all the churches. (2 Corinthians 11:21-28)

This is an unbelievable laundry list of Paul's pain and torment. But there's more. Throughout Paul's life, he has been forced to endure some kind of unexplained "thorn in the flesh"—on top of everything else:

> Therefore, to keep me from being too elated, a thorn was given me in the flesh, a messenger of Satan to torment me, to keep me from being too elated. Three times I appealed to the Lord about this, that it would leave me, but he said to me, "My grace is sufficient for you, for power is made perfect in weakness." (2 Corinthians 12:7-9)

What in the world could it have been? Some kind of disability or chronic illness? It appears to have been something noticeable that may have interfered with his ability to witness, perhaps something disfiguring, something repulsive in his face. Some commentators see hints and allusions in various texts that it may have something to do with his eyes; that he suffered both from vision impairment and some kind of discharge. It could have been, for instance, glaucoma. Whatever it was, it was a heavy load to bear.

Romans 7

Another vivid glimpse into the mind of Paul comes in the book of Romans. Even Paul, who heard the Lord in a bolt of light, is sometimes wracked by depression:

> For we know that the law is spiritual; but I am of the flesh, sold into slavery under sin. I do not understand my own actions. For I do not do what I want, but I do the very thing I hate. Now if I do what I do not want, I agree that the law is good. But in fact it is no longer I that do it, but sin that dwells within me. For I know that nothing good dwells within me, that is, in my flesh. I can will what is right, but I cannot do it. For I do not do the good I want, but the evil I do not want is what I do. Now if I do what I do not want, it is no longer I that do it, but sin that dwells within me. (Romans 7:14-20)

Some of the letters to the churches may be harsh, but no one is harder on Paul than Paul himself!

2 Timothy 4

Still, there are plenty of other openings and closings where Paul tenderly salutes beloved comrades and dear friends. None is more intimate and revealing than the final words of 2 Timothy. There are some who dispute that this is actually a Pauline letter. If these actually are the words of Paul, it is certainly one of his last letters, perhaps written in the Roman prison while waiting for Nero's decision. It has a lovely elegiac tone, a winsome combination of poetry and practicality; the final thoughts of a scarred old warrior, marking time until he is with the Jesus he has followed so long:

> As for me, I am already being poured out as a libation, and the time of my departure has come. (2 Timothy 4:6)

As with 1 Timothy, this letter appears to be written to Timothy, Paul's boon companion on so many extraordinary journeys. And in this penultimate passage, the litany of names we've heard so often in the book of Acts comes with sharp little shocks of recognition:

> Do your best to come to me soon, for Demas, in love with this present world, has deserted me and gone to Thessalonica; Crescens has gone to Galatia, Titus to Dalmatia. Only Luke is with me. Get Mark and bring him with you, for he is useful in my ministry. I have sent Tychicus to Ephesus. When you come, bring the cloak that I left with Carpus at Troas, also the books, and above all the parchments. Alexander the coppersmith did me great harm; the Lord will

Reluctant Prophets and Clueless Disciples

pay him back for his deeds. You also must beware of him, for he strongly opposed our message.

At my first defense no one came to my support, but all deserted me. May it not be counted against them! But the Lord stood by me and gave me strength, so that through me the message might be fully proclaimed and all the Gentiles might hear it. So I was rescued from the lion's mouth. The Lord will rescue me from every evil attack and save me for his heavenly kingdom. To him be the glory forever and ever. Amen.

Greet Prisca and Aquila, and the household of Onesiphorus. Erastus remained in Corinth; Trophimus I left ill in Miletus. Do your best to come before winter. Eubulus sends greetings to you, as do Pudens and Linus and Claudia and all the brothers and sisters.

The Lord be with your spirit. Grace be with you. (2 Timothy 4:9-22)

Prisca (Priscilla) and Aquilla, Luke, and Mark we know. This may be the same Titus as in the Letter to Titus. Erastus may be the same Erastus who was the city treasurer of Corinth, mentioned in Romans 16:23 and again in Acts 19:22. Trophimus shows up in Acts 20:4 and—if he is an uncircumcised Gentile—his presence at the temple in Acts 21:27-29 may have been the catalyst to Paul's arrest. Tychicus is variously described as a beloved brother, faithful minister, and fellow servant in Acts 20:4, Colossians 4:7, and Titus 3:12—but we know nothing else about him, except that he served as a letter carrier and messenger for Paul (see Ephesians 6:21-22). This is the only reference to Carpus, Crescens, Eubulus, Claudia, Linus, Pudens, and the household of Onesiphorus (who may actually be dead!). Demas (thought to be short for Demetrius) was a Gentile co-worker who shared Paul's first imprisonment and sent greetings to Philemon's family in Philemon and to the Colossian community (see Colossians 4:14), but now—in the time of Paul's greatest need—abandons him. However, his harshest words are for the coppersmith Alexander, perhaps the same Alexander (who, with Hymenaeus) "turned over to Satan" in 1 Timothy 1:20.

This mixed-bag of greetings, blessings, and curses neatly summarizes the conflicting nature of Paul, twice a zealot, an elder statesman, a wounded veteran, a melancholy survivor, a serene servant in his final hours, awaiting his well-deserved crown in Heaven.

Perhaps the most telling parts of this final blessing are not the list of names, but the other references. If these really are Paul's last hours in a dank Roman prison, his mind turns first to his heavy winter cloak, tattered and stained from a lifetime of sacrifice. This is the cloak that kept him warm in winter, dry on storm-tossed ships, and comforted in black, rat-infested cells. Think of what the pockets in such a cloak must have contained: the correspondence of the new churches, notes on new believers, letters of complaint from Corinth, letters of praise from Ephesus, and so much more.

From there, Paul asks for his books—probably scrolls—the Torah perhaps, to comfort him while he awaits mad Nero's pleasure.

And last, but most urgently, Paul asks that his parchments be brought to him. Parchment was an expensive luxury, and the primary means of letter writing in those days. Paul's parchment letters would be read and re-read and handed, not just from church to church, but down through the generations—precious keepsakes from the New Testament's most courageous soldier. Even as Nero's minions march their way down to Paul's damp quarters, he was probably scribbling away in the half-light, answering questions from Troas, sending needed advice to Beroea, settling a dispute in Jerusalem.

Paul's Legacy

How do we remember Paul of Tarsus? For all of the controversies engendered by his teaching and theology, here is the ultimate model for the Hero's Journey:

> I have fought the good fight, I have finished the race, I have kept the faith. (2 Timothy 4:7)

It is all any of us can ask.

> Paul and Silas, bound in jail,
> Sing God's praise both night and day;
> And I hope dat trump might blow me home
> To de new Jerusalem.
> (African American Spiritual, "Blow Your Trumpet, Gabriel")

Twenty-three

JOURNEY'S END

> Begin at the beginning . . . and go on till you come to the end: then stop. (Lewis Carroll, *Alice's Adventures in Wonderland* [London: Penguin Books, 1998], 105)

You've reached the end of this book, but you certainly haven't reached the end of your Hero's Journey. In fact, you've only just begun.

Not sure if you're even on the road? Congratulations! According to Henri Nouwen, that's a sure sign you're on the right track:

> "He who thinks that he has finished *is* finished." How true. Those who think that they have arrived, have lost their way. Those who think they have reached their goal, have missed it. Those who think they are saints, are demons. (Henri Nouwen quoting Rabbi Menahem Mendl of Kotzk in *The Genesee Diary* [Garden City: Doublday & Company, Inc., 1976], 112)

Oddly enough, that quote reminds me of something similar that the great theologian and philosopher Mick Jagger once sang with the Stones:

> Just as every cop is a criminal
> And all the sinners saints
> (Mick Jagger/Keith Richard, "Sympathy for the Devil")

Your entire life to this point has been a complex, multi-faceted Faith Journey, whether you've realized it or not. You may still be in the Ordinary World. Or maybe you're on the cusp of facing your own Big Gloom. But everybody is somewhere along that road.

Hopefully, this little book has helped you—will help you—along the way. If you're a Christian, you know you can find guidance by returning again and again to the Bible, which can serve as something of a roadmap for you.

(If you're not a Christian and you're interested in the things we've talked about so far, there is a special note just for you at the very end of this chapter. It's a guide to still another journey that everyone has to take at one time or another. Look for the ★.)

The interesting thing about your Faith Journey is that it doesn't really have an earthly destination. As the Rev. Mike Masser is fond of saying in sermons and Bible studies, "We don't become Christians. We are always in the process of becoming Christians." We don't ever get perfect at it. That doesn't happen until we get to heaven.

This is not an easy journey. Let no one tell you otherwise. (It wouldn't be a quest if it were easy!) If it's the real thing, it's a long, hard road—just like the Hero's Journey. If you've read J. D. Salinger's wonderful *Franny and Zooey*, then you may remember this funny little bit of ironic dialogue:

> I don't want you to go away with the impression that there're any—you know—any incon*veniences* involved in the religious life. I mean, a lot of people don't take it up just because they think it's going to involve a certain amount of nasty application and perseverance—you know what I mean? . . . As soon as we get out of the chapel here, I hope you'll accept from me a little volume I've always admired . . . *God Is My Hobby*. (Boston: Little, Brown and Company, 1961, 115)

Still, there are some things you can do to make the trip less painful. First, this is a tough road to travel alone. You need to share this journey—where you've been, what you've done—with others. "I believe that the greatest gift we can offer to each other is the telling of and listening to our stories," writes Lynn W. Huber. Lynn thinks this "empowers" us on our journey (*Revelations on the Road* [Boulder: WovenWord Press, 2003], x). Someone may benefit greatly from the stories you tell, just as you may benefit from their experiences. "Sometimes," notes Jean Shinoda Bolen, "a person needs a story more than food to stay alive" (*Crossing to Avalon* [San Francisco: HarperCollins, 1994], 273).

Second, if you decide at a very early stage that you're going to do this, then go all out. Doing something only halfway actually makes it harder down the road. If you commit to really following Jesus, he'll be there each step of the way:

> Where will the call to discipleship lead those who follow it? What decisions and painful separations will it entail? We must take this question to him who alone knows the answer. Only Jesus Christ, who bids us follow him, knows where the path will lead. But we know that it will be a path full of mercy beyond measure. Discipleship is joy. (Dietrich Bonhoeffer, *Dietrich Bonhoeffer Works, Volume 4* [Minneapolis: Augsberg Fortress, 2001], 40)

Even the *faith* part of your journey will be a little rocky at times. In fact, trying to follow Jesus will make it even harder in some ways. Still, it's the best decision you can possibly make:

> Acceptance does not guarantee a sudden illumination which dispels all darkness forever. On the contrary, it means seeing life as a long journey in the wilderness, but a journey with an invisible Companion, toward a secure and promised fulfillment not for the individual believer alone, but for the community of man to whom salvation has been promised in Jesus Christ. (Thomas Merton, *Faith and Violence: Christian Teaching and Christian Practice* [Notre Dame, IN: University of Notre Dame, 1968], 63)

Will you falter and fail on your journey? Of course. Every hero fails, every hero falls: from Luke Skywalker to Frodo and Sam to Neo to the great heroes of our faith—Peter, Paul, Mary Magdalene, and the gang. We're human, after all.

One of the surprise hit pop songs of 2002 was from a gospel album by Donnie McClurkin. The song, written by Kyle Matthews, struck a chord with believers and non-believers alike:

> For a saint is just a sinner who fell down
> and got up
> (Kyle Matthews, "We Fall Down")

You're going to stumble regularly if you're on the Hero's Journey. That's how we learn. But here's the great thing: If you persevere, God will honor your journey! If we keep striving forward; if we keep seeking God's will for our lives, the striving itself is priceless and precious in ways we can never understand:

> My Lord God, I have no idea where I am going. I do not see the road ahead of me. I cannot know for certain where it will end. Nor do I really know myself, and the fact that I think I am following your will does not mean that I am actually doing so. But I believe that the desire to please you does in fact please you. And I hope I have that desire in all that I am doing. I hope that I will never do anything apart from that desire. And I know that if I do this you will lead me by the right road, though I may know nothing about it. Therefore, I will trust you always though I may seem to be lost and in the shadow of death. I will not fear, for you are ever with me, and you will never leave me to face my perils alone. (Thomas Merton, *Thoughts and Solitude* [New York: Straus and Cudahy, 1958], 83)

As for this book, we've come to the end of our journey together. I will leave you with the wonderful *walking song* from *The Lord of the Rings*. Bilbo wrote it but Frodo sings it as the four hobbits begin the greatest quest in the history of Middle-Earth:

> Now far ahead the Road has gone,
>   And I must follow, if I can.
> (J. R. R. Tolkien, *The Fellowship of the Ring* [New York: Ballantine Books, 1982], 102)

Happy trails, pilgrim, as you follow *your* road!

* <u>The Romans Road to Salvation</u>

Perhaps you've come to your own particular fork in the road. You've heard about this Jesus and you'd like to do something—but what? If you're feeling that call, there is one more journey for you to take. The apostle Paul wrote the great letter to the Romans, in part, just to answer the questions you're struggling with right this very moment. Somewhere along the way, someone noticed that Paul included a clear sequence of steps in his letter. They outline what you've got to do to accept Jesus into your heart. It's called "The Romans Road to Salvation." Perhaps this is the roadmap you've been looking for all of your life—and didn't know it until right this very minute.

1. Romans 3:23

" . . . All have sinned and fall short of the glory of God . . ."

2. Romans 5:8

"But God proves his love for us in that while we still were sinners Christ died for us."

3. Romans 6:23

"For the wages of sin is death, but the free gift of God is eternal life in Christ Jesus our Lord."

4. Romans 10:9-10

" . . . Because if you confess with your lips that Jesus is Lord and believe in your heart that God raised him from the dead, you will be saved. For one believes with the heart and so is justified, and one confesses with the mouth and so is saved."

5. Romans 10:13

"For, 'Everyone who calls on the name of the Lord shall be saved.' "

298

That's it. There is no other ritual, no other creed. If you believe, if you confess your sins, if you ask Jesus to become the Lord of your life, you're in! You will experience "the peace of God, which surpasses all understanding" (Philippians 4:7). If you invite Christ into your heart, he will come. But he does not come uninvited. The first step of this journey is up to you. If you take it, get ready to begin a great roller-coaster ride. You'll want to find a group of believers to help you along the way. And you'll want to read the Great Road Map—the Bible—that God left us for directions. But you're good to go on The Greatest Journey of All. Hang on tight!

> I know not where the road will lead I follow day by day,
> or where it ends: I only know I walk the King's Highway.
> I know not if the way is long, and no one else can say;
> but rough or smooth, up hill or down, I walk the King's Highway.
> (Evelyn Atwater Cummins, "I Know Not Where the Road Will Lead")

Amen!

For Further Study

Our hope is that—having read this book—you'll now want to read THE Book. But which one is THE Book? There are so many choices available now. Little can compare with the King James Version. As befitting a document translated around the time of Shakespeare, its words often soar to poetic heights rarely matched elsewhere in the English language. But— also like Shakespeare—it is often alien sounding and difficult for modern ears to follow. Of the many modern translations, The Jerusalem Bible is closest in spirit, lyrically, to the King James.

In the end, however, I chose to use the New Revised Standard Version because of the elegant simplicity of its diction and the genuine, rigorous scholarship behind its research. It has been my translation of choice both for Bible studies and for pleasure reading. I never fail to see something new each time I open its pages.

There are other modern translations, of course, and each has something wonderful about it. Don't be intimidated by the sheer number of choices—they're all good.

Below is a list of some of the other books and films that have meant a lot to me over the years. Some of the books are novels, some are nonfiction; some are instructional, some are inspirational. I've referenced most of them at least once in the text of this book. All touched me personally and I commend each and every one of them to you.

Additionally, I've scribbled notes at a lifetime of sermons, lectures, and interviews. Those who most inspired me are listed after the books. If you get a chance to hear any of these speakers/pastors/authors—do so!

Books

Jeremy Begbie – *Voicing Creation's Praise: Towards a Theology of the Arts*
Frederick Buechner – *Peculiar Treasures and Telling Secrets*
Joseph Campbell – *The Hero With a Thousand Faces*
John Gardner, John Maier and Richard A. Henshaw – *Gilgamesh: Translated from the Sin-legi-unninnai Version*
Madeleine L'Engle – *The Wrinkle in Time* quartet
C. S. Lewis – *The Chronicles of Narnia*
Joyce Carol Oates – *Faith of a Writer: Life, Craft, Art* and *First Person Singular: Writers and Their Craft*
Katherine Paterson – *Bridge to Terebithia* and *Jacob Have I Loved*
Ben Patterson – *He Has Made Me Glad: Enjoying God's Goodness with Reckless Abandon*
Barbara Brown Taylor – *The Seeds of Heaven: Sermons on the Gospel of Matthew*
J. R. R. Tolkien – *The Hobbit, The Lord of the Rings,* and *The Silmarrilion*
Chris Vogler – *The Writer's Journey: Mythic Structure for Storytellers and Screenwriters*
Mike Yaconelli – *Dangerous Wonder* and *Messy Spirituality*

Films

Sherman Alexie, *Smoke Signals*
Wim Wenders, *Wings of Desire*

Speakers/Pastors

The Rev. Raymond Bailey, pastor/author
Dr. Rosalie Beck, Baylor University
Dr. Jeremy Begbie, University of St. Andrews, Scotland
Dr. Dale Bruner, author
Dr. James Kennedy, Baylor University
The Rev. Mike Massar, pastor
Dr. Liz Ngan, Baylor University
Joyce Carol Oates, author
Katherine Paterson, author
The Rev. Ben Patterson, pastor/author
The Rev. David Peterson, pastor/author
Dr. William Robinson, President, Whitworth College
Dr. Lynn Tatum, Baylor University
The Rev. Barbara Brown Taylor, author/pastor